Inherently Unequal

INHERENTLY UNEQUAL

The Betrayal of Equal Rights by the Supreme Court, 1865–1903

LAWRENCE GOLDSTONE

WALKER & COMPANY

NEW YORK

Published by Walker Publishing Company, Inc., New York

All papers used by Walker & Company are natural, recyclable products made
from wood grown in well-managed forests. The manufacturing processes conform
to the environmental regulations of the country of origin.

LIBRARY OF CONGRESS CATALOGING-IN-PUBLICATION DATA

Goldstone, Lawrence, 1947–
Inherently unequal : the betrayal of equal rights by the Supreme Court, 1865–1903 /
Lawrence Goldstone.—1st U.S. ed.
p.   cm.
Includes bibliographical references and index.
ISBN: 978-0-8027-1792-4
1. African-American—Legal status, laws, etc.—History—19th century.   2. Race
discrimination—Law and legislation—United States—History—19th century.
3. United States. Supreme Court—History—19th century.   I. Title.
KF4757.G655 2010
342.7308'73—dc22
2010015538

Visit Walker & Company's Web site at www.walkerbooks.com

First U.S. edition 2011

1 3 5 7 9 10 8 6 4 2

Typeset by Westchester Book Group
Printed in the United States of America by Quad / Graphics, Fairfield,
Pennsylvania

Many lawyers complain that constitutional law is not law but politics.
Perhaps, however, all law is more politics than some may be willing to confess.
—Thomas Reed Powell

Every important principle which is developed by litigation is in fact and at
bottom the result of more or less definitely understood views of public policy.
—Oliver Wendell Holmes

How many times can a man turn his head and pretend that he just doesn't see?
—Bob Dylan

CONTENTS

CONTENTS

A Death in Georgia

On April, 11, 1899, twenty miles southwest of Atlanta, Georgia, just outside Palmetto in Coweta County, a laborer named Sam Hose approached his employer, a wealthy farmer named Alfred Cranford. Hose asked for his accrued wages and permission to visit his mother, Mary Wilkes. Mrs. Wilkes, who lived in a cabin on a farm forty miles to the south, was a near-invalid, forced to care for another son who was retarded. Sam Hose had that day received a letter informing him that she had taken a turn for the worse. Hose, who was about twenty-five years old, had taught himself to read and write, the better to provide support for his family.

Cranford refused either to pay his employee or allow him time off. Sam Hose made the mistake of talking back. Cranford, known for a hot temper, stalked off. He seethed all night at the unimaginable slight.

Sam Hose, of course, was black. Alfred Cranford was white.

The next day, Cranford walked out to where Sam Hose was chopping wood. Cranford drew a gun and announced that he intended to shoot his disrespectful field hand dead on the spot. As they both knew, such a crime would have drawn not the slightest recrimination from the local authorities. In the unlikely event Cranford did go to trial, his acquittal by an all-white jury was a certainty. Sam Hose was a small man, only five feet eight inches tall, weighing not more than 140 pounds. In fear for his life, he flung his ax, striking the white man in the head and killing him instantly. He then fled in terror.

For the previous three months, a series of suspicious fires had plagued Palmetto. Two businesses and a home had gone up in flames. County officials insisted Palmetto Negroes were responsible and, further, that the fires were part of a grand conspiracy. White leaders would be murdered and the entire town burned to the ground. Local citizens were frantic.[1]

In March, nine local black men had been arrested. All were later described by an outside investigator as "hard-working and intelligent." No evidence against any of them was ever produced, and each claimed to be able to easily prove his innocence. Palmetto had no jail, so the men were incarcerated in a local warehouse, to be guarded, at least in theory, by sheriff's deputies. The night of their arrest, before any formal proceedings could be initiated, a group of concerned citizens, 150 white men, visited the prisoners. With the guards either ignoring the mob or joining it, eight of the nine were shot. Four died, and the others were seriously wounded.

Although the fires ceased—actually, they had stopped weeks before the arrests—talk of insurrection by marauding Africans continued to spread panic throughout Palmetto. The day after the shootings, for example, an Atlanta newspaper reported, "All business has been suspended, the town is under military patrol, and every male inhabitant is armed to the teeth, in anticipation of an outbreak which is expected to-night."[2] Although no uprising ever took place, news, a month later, of Alfred Cranford lying dead outside his home with an ax in his head revived fears of an impending race war. Bloodhounds were set on Sam Hose's trail.

Sensational as the killing already was, rival newspapers in Atlanta, the *Journal* and the *Constitution*, decided that the story should be made even more lurid. Making no effort whatever to determine the actual facts of the case, they competed with each other for maximum embellishment and, one assumes, maximum sales. Sam Hose therefore became "a monster in human form." This "beast," the *Journal* reported to its readers, had burst in on the Cranford family during dinner, attacking the farmer from behind, cleaving his head in two. The *Constitution* took up the story from there. After brutally murdering the husband with the ax, Sam Hose then repeatedly raped Cranford's wife, Mattie, on the kitchen floor, "within arm's reach of where the brains were oozing out of her husband's head." What's more, this rampaging savage was afflicted with syphilis, which he intended to pass on to the pitiable widow. Not content with what he had done to the adults, Sam Hose then set upon either a Cranford infant, or two young Cranford children depending on which account one read. The infant was dashed to the ground. Or the young children were assaulted. The details of this final outrage were kept from the *Journal's* God-fearing readers, but the clear implication was that the assault was "unnatural."*

For ten days, Sam Hose was tracked by a posse said to number as many as three hundred men. During the hunt, on April 18, the *Constitution's* headline read CIRCLE OF VENGEANCE SLOWLY CLOSING ON FLEEING SAM HOSE. HUNDREDS OF ARMED MEN ARE BEATING THE COUNTRY FOR THE MURDERER OF ALFRED CRANFORD. HE CANNOT ESCAPE, THEY SAY DETECTIVE BEDFORD HAS FOUND THE MURDERER'S DISCARDED SHOES. ONE NEGRO CAPTURED SEVERAL TIMES. THE ENTIRE SECTION THROUGH WHICH HE IS SUPPOSED TO BE MAKING HIS ESCAPE IS UP IN ARMS, DETERMINED TO LYNCH HIM. The article went on to say, "When Hose is caught he will either be lynched and his body riddled with bullets or he will be burned at the stake." The newspaper added, "There have been whisperings of burning at the stake and of torturing the fellow low, and so great is the excitement, and so high the indignation, that this is among the possibilities."[3] Two days later, the *Constitution* added, "Several modes of death have been suggested for him, but it seems to be the universal opinion that he will be burned at the stake and probably tortured before burned." Clark Howell, the editor of the newspaper, offered a $500 reward, an amount matched by Georgia's new governor, Allen D. Candler. The town of Palmetto added $250 more.

On April 22, Sam Hose was finally apprehended at his mother's cabin. He was taken by train to Newnan, the Coweta County seat, which, unlike

---

* As in many criminal cases, the precise details remained hazy. After events had played out, the antilynching crusader Ida B. Wells-Barnett hired a Chicago private detective, one Louis P. Le Vin, to conduct a forensic investigation of the crime. Le Vin did a remarkably thorough job, even succeeding in obtaining an interview with Mattie Cranford. Mrs. Cranford confirmed the newspaper accounts of rape and would do so until her death in 1923. But although the family was wealthy and upper-class, neither she nor her children saw a doctor in the aftermath of the crime. Mattie Cranford went to stay with her father-in-law, speaking to no one, particularly not to law enforcement officials and newspaper reporters. The infant who was supposedly dashed to the floor did not die or sustain treatable injuries, although the child grew up without hearing in one ear. None of the other Cranford children seemed the worse for wear. Significantly, no one offered an explanation as to why Alfred Cranford's body was discovered near the woodshed and not in the house. The episode is remarkably reminiscent of the Tom Robinson trial in Harper Lee's novel *To Kill a Mockingbird*, although here no Atticus Finch was available to attempt to vindicate the accused. Le Vin concluded that Sam Hose had acted in self-defense, and that the story printed in the newspapers was an almost complete fabrication. He ended his report by noting, "I made my way home, thoroughly convinced that a Negro's life is a very cheap thing in Georgia." Le Vin's entire report, as well as the newspaper citations, are included in Ida B. Wells-Barnett's pamphlet *Lynch Law in Georgia: A Six-Weeks' Record in the Center of Southern Civilization, as Faithfully Chronicled by the "Atlanta Journal" and the "Atlanta Constitution"* (Chicago: Chicago Colored Citizens, 1899).

Palmetto, had its own jail. He was repeatedly questioned, both at the time of his arrest and during the train ride. Described later by white deputies as "free from excitement or terror," he "told his story in a straightforward way, said he was sorry he had killed Cranford [in self-defense], and always denied that he had attacked Mrs. Cranford."[4]

On the night of April 22, Sam Hose was again questioned, this time in the Newnan jail. There are no witness accounts of this session, but, at its conclusion, the white jailers reported that "Hose made a partial confession, acknowledging that he killed Mr. Cranford, and said that the murder had been instigated by a colored preacher [Lige Strickland] who had paid him $12 to commit it."[5] A later investigation by the Chicago private detective found this to be hogwash. "I did not talk with one white man," the investigator reported, "who believed that Strickland had anything to do with [Hose]. I could not find any person who heard [Hose] mention Strickland's name. I talked with men who heard [Hose] tell his story, but all agreed that he said he killed Cranford because Cranford was about to kill him, and that he did not mention Strickland's name."[6]

Word of Sam Hose's capture spread through Georgia with remarkable speed. By early the next morning, Sunday, April 23, plans for his execution were complete. Such was the demand to witness the spectacle that a special excursion train was arranged to carry eager Georgians from Atlanta to the promised execution. In the meantime, Lige Strickland had been snatched up in Palmetto.

As noon approached, a huge crowd had gathered in an open green, one mile from the Newnan town square. At least 2,000 were present, although a dispatch to the *New York Times* claimed "one special and two regular trains brought nearly 4,000 people to Newnan."[7] At the station in Atlanta, conductors cried out, "Special train to Newnan! All aboard for the burning!"[8] The *Constitution* noted that "the spot selected was an ideal one for such an affair, and the stake was in full view of those who stood about with unfeigned satisfaction."

Into this festive atmosphere, men arrived in Newnan accompanied by their wives and even their children. "Ladies clothed in their Sunday finery watched from carriages, gazing excitedly over the heads of men carrying small children on their shoulders as the ritual began."[9] Not every white citizen was in favor of what was to take place. Former Georgia governor William Y. Atkinson, a Newnan native who had recently completed his second term before being replaced by Allen Candler, was appalled. He rode to the site and stood in a buggy, pleading for the crowd to leave and let the law take its course. Atkinson was shouted down.

Finally, Sam Hose was brought in a wagon from the jail. He was dragged to the center of the mob of thousands of jeering whites. He was stripped of his clothing and tied to a small sapling. Wood was stacked around him and soaked with kerosene. Hose himself was smeared with oil. Before the match was struck, however, one of "the cool, determined men who went about arranging to burn him" walked up to Sam Hose and sliced off his left ear. Then his right. His fingers were cut off, then his genitals. Still before the fire was lit, one of these cool, determined men stood next to Sam Hose and skinned his face. (Reports filtered out that during this process Sam Hose made a full confession, admitting to both the rape of Mattie Cranford and the complicity of Lige Strickland, but a subsequent investigation proved this to be a fabrication as well.)[10]

Finally, a match was thrown on the pyre.

"The stake bent under the strains of the Negro in his agony and his sufferings cannot be described, although he uttered not a sound," the *Constitution* faithfully reported. As the heat rose, Sam Hose's eyes popped from their sockets and his veins burst. "At one juncture, before the flames had begun to get in their work well, the fastenings that held him to the stake broke and he fell forward partially out of the fire." The men around him extinguished the flames, retied the victim, again doused him with oil, after which Sam Hose "was kicked back and the flames renewed. Then it was that the flames consumed his body and in a few minutes only a few bones and a small part of the body was all that was left of Sam Hose."[11]

Before the body had cooled, the crowd was upon it. According to the *New York Tribune*, "It was cut into pieces, the bones were crushed into small bits and even the tree upon which the wretch met his fate was torn up and disposed of as souvenirs. The Negro's heart was cut into several pieces, as was also his liver. Those unable to obtain ghastly relics directly, paid more fortunate possessors extravagant sums for them. Small pieces of bone went for 25 cents and a bit of liver, crisply cooked, for 10 cents."[12] Proper southern Christians deposited their souvenirs in pickle jars or handkerchiefs, later to be displayed as trophies in places of business or private homes.

That night, it was Lige Strickland's turn. "Just after dusk," another group of white men gathered at the town square, and soon the preacher was brought forward, hands tied and a noose hung around his neck. Strickland's employer, a Confederate war veteran and former state senator, Major W. W. Thomas, argued with the mob that Strickland was innocent, and he would not leave until the men promised that they would hand the black man over to local authorities until the charges could be investigated. Finally, after threat and argument failed, the mob reluctantly agreed. But Strickland, married and the father of five children, had aroused the enmity of local whites with some outspoken remarks; "had inflamed negroes in the neighborhood," as a newspaper report phrased it.[13] As soon as Major Thomas departed to return home, the men loaded Strickland into a wagon, tightened the noose, and drove him out of town.

They stopped about a mile away, then dragged Strickland from the wagon to a sturdy tree. They threw the rope over a branch and pulled until it was taut. They demanded that Strickland confess. When he did not, they pulled him up. How long they left him off the ground is not known, but the white men eventually lowered him down and once again demanded a confession. Once again, Strickland refused. The white men again pulled on the rope.

When they were done, Lige Strickland had been hoisted three times into the air. Before being raised the third and last time, his ears and little finger on one hand were sliced off. Given one final opportunity to own up to his crime, he reportedly said, "I have told you all I know, gentlemen. You can kill me if you wish, but I have nothing to tell."[14]

When Lige Strickland's body was discovered the next morning, "swinging from the limb of a tree," the New York Times reported:

On the chest of the negro was a piece of blood-stained paper attached by an ordinary pin. On one side of the paper was written:

"New York Journal:
      We must protect our ladies

                                                  23-'99"
The other side of the paper contained a warning to the negroes of the neighborhood. It read as follows.

"Beware all darkies. You will be treated the same way."[15]

In the wake of the executions, Governor Candler issued a statement, printed verbatim in the Chicago Daily Tribune: "The whole thing is deplorable," the governor began. Lest anyone think that he was about to indict those who had perpetrated the torture and execution, Candler quickly added, "Hose's crime, the horrid details of which have not been published, is the most diabolical in the annals of crime. The negroes of that community lost the best opportunity they will ever have of elevating themselves in the estimation of their white neighbors . . . the perpetrator was well known and they owed it to their race to exhaust every means of bringing Hose to justice. I want to protect them in every legal right and against mob violence, and I stand ready to employ every resource of the State in doing so, but they must realize that in order to inherit and receive the protection of the community, they must show a willingness to at least attempt to protect the community from lawless elements of their own race . . . To secure protection against lawless whites, they must show a disposition to protect white people against lawless blacks."[16]

Both the burning of Sam Hose and the lynching of Lige Strickland were reported throughout the nation, front-page news in most northern and western newspapers. Although few other northern newspapers carried Governor Candler's statement, the incidents were, by and large, reported with a complete lack of outrage. The New York Times, which had been ferocious in its editorial condemnation of the Civil Rights Act of 1875,* spoke not a word of genuine disapproval against the burning of Sam Hose.[17] As for Lige Strickland, the Times headline did read GEORGIA MOB KILLS INNOCENT MAN? as though, had Strickland been guilty, the actions of the mob would have been appropriate. The Brooklyn Daily Eagle, in an editorial, decried the killings, noting, "On this occasion, white humanity disgraced itself . . . behaving quite as badly as Indians were ever known to behave." But the Daily Eagle added, "The black man is even more ignorant and passionate, and when he gives way to temptation he becomes indeed a terror to the community. As to the result of a lynching, it is without doubt restraining."[18]

Nor were the identities of those who perpetrated the crime a secret. In

---

* As will be discussed in chapter 8, the Civil Rights Act of 1875, perhaps the most far-reaching legislation of its kind in the nation's history provided "that all persons within the jurisdiction of the United States shall be entitled to the full and equal enjoyment of the accommodations, advantages, facilities, and privileges of inns, public conveyances on land or water, theaters, and other places of public amusement; subject only to the conditions and limitations established by law, and applicable alike to citizens of every race and color, regardless of any previous condition of servitude," and provided vigorous penalties for violators.

the case of Sam Hose, the names of prominent witnesses and even those who incited the murder of the black man were widely reported. (Clark Howell had made his sentiments known to everyone who read his newspaper.) In fact, the reason for the wealth of material on these crimes was the utter lack of timidity by those involved to brag about it.

With all that, not one person was ever detained, arrested, or even officially questioned about either incident. When United States attorney general John W. Griggs, from New Jersey, was asked if he planned to investigate the lynchings, he said that "the case had no federal aspect, and therefore the government would take no action whatever in regard to it."[19]

State pride for these crimes was certainly not unanimous among Georgia's whites. Some voices were raised in outrage. The *Savannah Morning News* wrote, "The method of [the lynching] was in keeping with the spirit of a savage rather than a civilized and Christian community. It provokes a spirit that is likely to lead to other crimes." The Savannah city attorney called the incidents "unspeakably horrible and shameful." A local judge added, "The whole thing is too horrible to think of. I don't want to talk about it. It is terrible in all its hideousness. I am sorry it happened in Georgia."[20]

The day after the incidents, Governor Candler paid $600 of the reward to J. B. Jones, a farmer who had spotted Sam Hose and organized the posse that captured him. Later that day, "a man named Moss" presented a "good-sized piece of Hose's heart" to the governor as a trophy.

Two days after the killings, W. E. B. DuBois, then teaching at a black college in Atlanta, wrote out "a careful and reasoned statement concerning the evident facts," including a plea for racial reconciliation. He set out for the offices of the *Atlanta Constitution* to deliver the letter to Joel Chandler Harris, author of the popular "Uncle Remus" stories, whose work appeared in the newspaper. On his way, he was told that just down the street was a grocery store in which, on prominent display in the front window, were Sam Hose's severed knuckles.

DuBois turned back and headed home.[21]

More than a century earlier, in June 1788, Alexander Hamilton, in an essay published in the *New York Independent Journal* that would become known as Federalist 78, extolled an independent national judiciary as the ultimate guardian of the rights of the common citizen.

Independence of the judges is equally requisite to guard the Constitution
and the rights of individuals from the effects of those ill humors, which the
arts of designing men, or the influence of particular conjunctures, sometimes disseminate among the people themselves, and which, though they
speedily give place to better information, and more deliberate reflection,
have a tendency, in the meantime, to occasion dangerous innovations
in the government, and serious oppressions of the minor party in the
community . . . These sometimes extend no farther than to the injury of
the private rights of particular classes of citizens, by unjust and partial laws.

Hamilton went further, insisting that the judiciary was the one branch of
government that represented "the people" themselves. "It is far more rational
to suppose that the courts were designed to be an intermediate body between the people and the legislature, in order, among other things, to keep
the latter within the limits assigned to their authority." Although Hamilton
did note that the judiciary would be the "weakest of the three" branches of
government, he envisioned a Supreme Court in which, once an appeal was
brought by a citizen, the justices might supply protection or relief unique in
history.

That the judicial branch would be the guarantor of the rights of free men
was not confined to Hamilton. Many of the Founders—James Wilson, Gouverneur Morris, James Madison, even future chief justice John Marshall—
extolled the federal judiciary as the guarantor of individual liberties against
despotism and tyranny by the legislature.

Opponents of the proposed Constitution, men like "Brutus," a competing
essayist in New York, demurred, asserting that the judiciary would be a
source of despotism. "Courts of law," Brutus warned, "will give the sense of
every article of the constitution that may from time to time come before
them. And in their decisions they will not confine themselves to any fixed or
established rules, but will determine, according to what appears to them, the
reason and spirit of the constitution. The opinions of the supreme court,
whatever they may be, will have the force of law; because there is no power
provided in the constitution that can correct their errors or control their
adjudications. From this court there is no appeal."[22] The Supreme Court, to
Brutus, promised to be no less a political body than the legislature, and
granting the Court broad and sweeping powers would hardly protect the
common citizen from the excesses of popular prejudice. Quite the reverse.[23]

Hamilton was ready with a reply. He dismissed the danger, seeking to assuage the fears of New Yorkers apprehensive about the threat of judicial despotism. In doing so, he balanced on the edge of the debate today defined as strict versus broad construction.

> It can be of no weight to say that the courts, on the pretense of a repugnancy, may substitute their own pleasure to the constitutional intentions of the legislature . . . The courts must declare the sense of the law; and if they should be disposed to exercise WILL instead of JUDGMENT, the consequence would equally be the substitution of their pleasure to that of the legislative body.

Although Hamilton sloughed over what recourse would be available under the new Constitution if the courts *did* "substitute their pleasure" to the "constitutional intentions of the legislature," he ultimately prevailed and Brutus's objections were swept away with ratification. Americans had been persuaded, in New York and elsewhere, that a national tribunal would guarantee their freedoms, not take them away.[24]

But which Americans? Hamilton, in anointing the courts as "the people's branch of government," had surely implied that the judiciary was where the weak would be protected from the strong, the common man from the political insider, the poor and honest from the rich and corrupt. Problematic even as these goals were, neither Hamilton nor his fellow Federalists—John Marshall and James Madison from Virginia, New Englanders like Roger Sherman, Nathanial Gorham, and Rufus King, and even indefatigable defenders of individual liberty like Gouverneur Morris and Benjamin Franklin—conceived of those protections extending beyond white men.[25] Blacks in America, even free blacks of wealth, property, and education, were seen in the Founding period as a different species, one which resided in the United States under a different set of standards. Whether those standards even acknowledged African-Americans' fundamental humanity was open to question.

After 1865, however, with ratification of the Thirteenth Amendment, followed soon afterward by the Fourteenth and Fifteenth, the definition of "the people" was radically altered, as was the notion of "equality," both under the law and in Americans' everyday lives. For much of the nation, the war had been fought to preserve the Union, not to free slaves, and certainly not to

elevate black Americans to an equal place in society. The notion of extending the promise of liberty and the protections of the Constitution was as repugnant to many in the North as it was in the South. Despite what personal
feelings they may have had to the contrary, however, the nation—and the
Supreme Court—had been charged with protecting the rights of this new,
fragile class of citizens.

Beyond the philosophical tensions, the practical problems of assimilating
four million newly freed slaves were vast. The overwhelming majority were
illiterate and utterly unsophisticated in either self-maintenance or self-
governance. They lacked even rudimentary knowledge of social organization. Many came from family units torn asunder by owners who sold off
men, women, and children piecemeal as need and profit dictated. No task of
integrating such a large and unprepared population into the political and
economic mainstream had ever been undertaken by any society in history.

But passage of the postwar amendments had left no doubt of either the
nation's intention or its commitment to do just that. Constitutional amendments, because they are so difficult and cumbersome to enact, requiring a
two-thirds majority in both houses of Congress and ratification by three
quarters of the state legislatures, are, more than any other piece of national
legislation, a reflection of the inexorable will of the American electorate.
And unlike a piece of ordinary legislation, a constitutional amendment is
not, at least in theory, subject to review in the courts. Something cannot be
unconstitutional that is *in* the Constitution. "Equal protection of the laws,"
the guarantee of "due process" for all Americans, and equal access to the
ballot box had therefore become, as Article VI proclaimed, "the supreme law
of the land."

After the amendments had been ratified, Congress passed a series of "enforcement acts," legislation to empower the courts, the enforcement branch
of government, to guarantee that the provisions of the amendments were
adhered to. Stiff criminal and civil penalties were to be applied to any
persons or institutions who thought themselves above the law.

Here was the manifestation of Hamilton's vision, an independent judiciary, men serving virtually without oversight from the other branches, accountable only to the rule of law, upholding the rights of society's most
vulnerable. Precisely because federal judges were not subject to the vagaries
of shifting moods or popular sentiment, they could use their power under the
Constitution to protect the freedoms of four million new citizens, despised

and downtrodden as most black Americans might be. And if the zeal to further the social integration of newly emancipated African-Americans waned as time went on, the judiciary would be there to prevent any erosion of civil rights. As Hamilton himself had said:

> If, then, the courts of justice are to be considered as the bulwarks of a limited Constitution against legislative encroachments, this consideration will afford a strong argument for the permanent tenure of judicial offices, since nothing will contribute so much as this to that independent spirit in the judges which must be essential to the faithful performance of so arduous a duty.

In 1867, the role of the Supreme Court in post–Civil War America was further enunciated in an editorial in one of the nation's preeminent law journals.

> For what is the Supreme Court mainly established but that it may be a tribunal of last resort, composed of men uninfluenced by executive or Legislative power or popular impulse, who may do justice, free, as far of the lot of humanity admits, from party passion or political expediency?[26]

Yet, with three constitutional amendments and myriad enforcement acts on the books, after the unstinting efforts of leaders in the Congress, after the impeachment in 1868 of a president who attempted to subvert equal rights for emancipated slaves, by the dawn of the twentieth century the United States had become the nation of Jim Crow laws, quasi slavery, and precisely the same two-tiered system of justice that had existed in the slave era. Throughout the South, black Americans could not go to school with whites, could not ride next to them in streetcars, sit next to them in theaters or restaurants, could not be buried in the same cemeteries, could not use the same public toilets; black Americans were denied the right to vote, to sit on juries, and often, as in the case of Sam Hose, were denied the right to have a trial at all.

The descent of the United States into enforced segregation, into a nation where human beings could be tortured and horribly murdered without trial, is a story profoundly tragic and profoundly American. And the Supreme Court was a central player in the tale.

If the Court's complicity in the subversion of equal rights had been due to rogue justices, or was an aberration of jurisprudence, Americans of the current day might merely shake their heads, deplore a shameful episode in their history, and congratulate themselves that the United States was no longer that nation. If, however, the Court's actions were not aberrant at all, but simply examples of ongoing practice, in which justices subordinate the role that Hamilton espoused for them to the exigencies of popular politics—or worse, their own personal beliefs and prejudices—the equal rights decisions of the latter decades of the nineteenth century become expressions of issues deeper, more disturbing. For then the United States Supreme Court would have, in a very real sense, eschewed the dispassion that the Founders thought so vital and become merely a third political arm of government. The long-maligned and discredited Brutus then becomes the more effective prognosticator of the pitfalls inherent in Article III, which allows Supreme Court justices to serve for life, virtually without oversight or supervision.[27] Lack of accountability does not, as Hamilton insisted, constitute a bedrock of liberty, but rather a profound defect in our constitutional fabric.

ONE

CONSTRUCTION AND RECONSTRUCTION: TWO GREAT EXPERIMENTS

BEFORE 1860, MOST AMERICANS had grown up in a nation dominated by agriculture, ruled by a national government that was limited and often invisible. At the time of Abraham Lincoln's election, "the federal government's . . . conception of its duties [were] little changed since the days of Washington and Jefferson. Most functions were handled on the state and local level; one could live out one's life without ever encountering an official representative of national authority."[1] Before the Civil War began, the federal government employed thirty-four thousand people, twenty-five thousand of whom were in the army or navy. Postwar America found itself ruled by a far more proactive and pervasive entity. By 1865, in addition to the hundreds of thousands still on the military's payroll, fifty-three thousand men and women in nonmilitary jobs were paid out of the national Treasury. Washington had become the largest employer in the nation.

By both necessity and inclination, the federal bureaucracy did not shrink at war's end. The unprecedented challenge of reuniting the nation, in Lincoln's words, binding up its wounds, demanded an array of services unimaginable four years earlier. But in addition, a president and Congress that, for four years, had been given the opportunity to exercise control over almost every facet of the life of its people were hardly likely to once again retire to the shadows simply because hostilities had ceased. In March 1865, weeks before Lincoln's assassination, for example, Congress established the Bureau of Refugees, Freedmen, and Abandoned Lands, which wielded what many saw as dictatorial powers over the conquered South. Not only did the bureau (placed, significantly, under the aegis of the War Department and headed by a general, Oliver O. Howard) distribute food and clothing, and establish schools and medical facilities for freedmen, as the emancipated slaves were known; the Freedmen's Bureau established a shadow justice system of military courts to deal with offenses against black Americans.

Even those, like the new president, Andrew Johnson, who were committed to reestablishing strong prerogatives and equal status for the eleven defeated secessionist states, understood that, in the short term, a powerful central government was necessary to secure those ends. Where Johnson's primary focus was a return to federalism, for many in Congress the two most urgent priorities were care of the literally millions of returned or returning war veterans, and the integration of nearly four million newly freed slaves into the mainstream of American life.

For a radical segment of the Republican Party, led in the House of Representatives by Thaddeus Stevens of Pennsylvania and in the Senate by Charles Sumner of Massachusetts (who, for his abolitionist stance, had once been beaten nearly to death by a cane-wielding South Carolina colleague on the Senate floor), this latter goal was sine qua non to the restoration of the Union. The Radicals held firm to a ferociously aggressive political, social, and economic agenda. They demanded that African-Americans in the conquered South be granted full and equal citizenship with whites. They then insisted that the United States confiscate the assets of Confederate leaders, applying any cash proceeds to the payment of the war debt and to the pensioning of Union soldiers, and distributing the land to freedmen. Stevens's plan was to nationalize any estates whose lands exceeded two hundred acres or were worth $10,000 or more. Each adult freedman would then be given "forty acres and a mule," an expansion of the program William Tecumseh Sherman had initiated during the war. Of the remaining acreage, which would be worth approximately $3.5 billion, Stevens wanted $300 million invested in 6 percent government bonds, with the interest applied to pensions of war veterans and their dependents; $200 million used to reimburse Union loyalists for property damages; and the remaining $3 billion applied to pay down war debt.[2] If enacted, this program would have represented the most socialist initiative of any government in history, save perhaps the forced redistribution of wealth during the French Revolution.

Stevens's rationale for such drastic action was plain. No issue was more vital than establishing parity under law for all Americans.[3] Equality for the freedmen transcended party or politics; it was a paramount ethical issue, one that would define the very character of the United States. Without redress for the evils of slavery and the successful integration of the freedmen into American society, the United States would remain a damned nation. Stevens proclaimed:

> We have turned or are about to turn loose four million slaves without a hut to shelter them or a cent in their pockets. The infernal laws of slavery have prevented them from acquiring an education, understanding the commonest laws of contract, or managing the ordinary business of life. This Congress is bound to provide for them until they can take care of themselves. If we do not furnish them with homesteads, and hedge them around with protective laws; if we leave them to the legislation of their late masters, we had better have left them in bondage.[4]

Unlike Abraham Lincoln, whose main goal had been preservation of the Union, and who had counseled restraint when the Confederacy was finally vanquished, Radicals were determined to remake the South to a new set of political, socioeconomic, and especially moral specifications—to forcibly abolish not only slavery, de facto as well as de jure, but all vestiges of racial discrimination. Blacks, therefore, for the first time, were to go to school, hold public office, sit on juries, own businesses, and walk or ride freely in any state in America.

To fully remake the South, however, lifting up the Negro represented only a portion of the agenda; alteration of whites' attitudes was equally important, either by persuasion or, if necessary, coercion. Of his program, Stevens offered, "It is intended to revolutionize their feelings and principles. This may startle feeble minds and shake weak nerves. So do all great improvements."[5]

That these aims in no way represented a priority for most Americans, and were not even the reason the vast majority of northerners had gone to war, was not lost on the Radicals. Nor were they unaware that postwar industrial expansion in the North would be less likely to spread south if energies in the former Confederacy were occupied in absorbing a massive, uneducated, unskilled, newly freed black population. (As such, many northern businessmen were antipathetic to their program.) But Stevens and his brethren were simply unwilling to delay or dilute their morality to accommodate practicalities. Such zealotry created a certain queasiness in all but small knots of supporters, although, in the immediate wake of the war, with most Americans desirous of moving toward *some* measure of equality of citizenship, insufficient political clout existed to marginalize the Radical agenda.

Both Stevens's intensity and his frustration also had sprung from an awareness that the Confederacy's unconditional surrender had provided a unique window of opportunity. For the first time since America had become a nation, the size, scope, and influence of the national government might allow Washington to exercise authority over state governments, particularly in those states that would be reconstituted as a condition for readmission to the Union. Well before the war ended, eager reformers, both church and lay, were moving from north to south, preparing to launch perhaps the greatest experiment in social engineering ever attempted. They would teach, feed, and organize the freedmen. Not only could millions of erstwhile Negro slaves be integrated into society as full and equal citizens, but the entire fabric of the plantation economy, the values under which a society had lived for well over a century, would be forged and hammered into a new, progressive, egalitarian order. Those who accepted the new order—white as well as black—would enjoy the fruits of prosperity and justice. Those who opposed would be broken. This experiment would be termed "Reconstruction," but the prefix was misplaced. This was not so much "Re-construction" as "New Construction." To grasp the reins of that movement, provide it with the government's imprimatur, and transform it into official national policy was Stevens's quest.

The path was not without serious obstacles. Standing in the road to progress were intransigent Democrats; moderate, less ideological members of Stevens's own Republican Party; President Johnson; and, most of all, an American public that might be willing to support equality for the Negro in principle but was markedly unenthusiastic about extending the practice to their daily lives. Black Americans did not emerge from slavery into a nation eager to embrace their new status as free men, but rather, to most whites, as a perceived burden on the society that had countenanced their enslavement for the previous two centuries. That black Americans would be granted fundamental rights that few Americans thought were either advisable or even deserved would constitute "the incubus with which the Negro was burdened before he was ever awakened into political life."[6] "'Slavery is dead,' the *Cincinnati Enquirer* announced at the end of the war, 'the negro is not. There is the misfortune. For the sake of all the parties, would that he were.'"[7]

True equality demanded a provision too radical for many Radicals: granting freedmen the right to vote. Even those northerners who supported (or seemed to support) the effort to raise African-Americans to the level of whites balked at the notion of hundreds of thousands of illiterate, socially and politically backward black men flooding to the polls. "When was it ever known that liberation from bondage was accompanied by a recognition of political equality?" asked one. "According to the laws of development and progress, it is not practicable . . . as soon as the state was organized and left to manage its own affairs, the white population, with their superior intelligence, wealth, and power, would unquestionably alter the franchise in accordance with their prejudices."[8] The speaker was no conservative, but rather William Lloyd Garrison, publisher of the *Liberator* and the man who termed the United States Constitution "a Covenant with Death and an Agreement with Hell," for its failure to end slavery in America.

Charles Sumner, as late as 1866, favored a literacy requirement for African-Americans, a restriction that, even if applied without contrivance (as opposed to the approach southern states took later), would guarantee that only a tiny portion of the black population would qualify to vote. Even Thaddeus Stevens, the ultimate firebrand, was hesitant to allow freedmen immediate access to the voting booth. Nor could those few in favor of granting the franchise to African-Americans point to their more emancipated status in the North. Only five northern states extended the franchise to blacks; one of the states that did not was Yankee Connecticut. Whatever one's political sensibilities, abundantly clear was that Negro suffrage, especially if guaranteed under federal law, would profoundly and permanently alter the United States.

In the end, this most volatile of all postwar issues would come to the fore not as a result of any effort to gain the franchise for blacks, but because of a strategy specifically designed to prevent it.

Across the political spectrum, the fundamental aims of Reconstruction were not in dispute. In addition to devising the appropriate provisos and caveats to assimilate freedmen into mainstream society, any successful program would need to satisfy two other main goals. State governments in the South needed to be reconstituted, with some mechanism devised to enable their return to the Union. (Although, as will be seen, some substantial question remained as to whether they had ever left.) And those individuals who had taken part in the rebellion would eventually need to be readmitted into political society, all the while ensuring that they forswore future fomenting of insurrection.

Radical Republicans saw both of these in the simplest of terms. By seceding, southern states had abrogated the terms under which they had joined the Union and nullified whatever privileges the Constitution had bestowed. They might apply for readmission, certainly, but under the terms dictated by the government of the United States, from which they were, at that moment, excluded. As to the second, while Radicals might be leery of granting the vote to blacks, they had no hesitation in taking it away from whites. Anyone who had fought for or abetted the rebels had forfeited the privileges of citizenship. They, like the states in which they lived, might be reinstated at some point, but only after some appropriate penance and a pledge to never do it again. At the very least, they should be denied the vote until 1870. Unspoken but understood was that readmission on both an individual and state level would require acquiescence in the Radical program, including confiscation, redistribution, and full—or almost full—civil equality for African-Americans. If Lincoln had lived, Stevens and his ilk would have had little hope of seeing such a draconian approach adopted.[9] But Lincoln was dead, and Andrew Johnson commanded nowhere near the political clout of his predecessor.

Still, Johnson was Lincoln's successor, and when he announced that he intended to follow through on the martyred president's wishes, he bought himself time while the nation waited to see how, specifically, he intended to do so. Every Democrat and all but the most radical Republicans were pleased to allow the new president sufficient leeway to strike the proper, if delicate, balance between punishment and charity. Those who did not were forced to sit on the sidelines and content themselves with moral pronouncements that were largely ignored by a Congress anxious to achieve rapprochement with a minimum of animus.

But Andrew Johnson was hardly the right man for a task that demanded incisive intellect, a keen sense of proportion, a flair for problem solving, and a deft political hand. Cloistered, stubborn, and opinionated, utterly lacking in nuance, Johnson within weeks attempted to impose on the nation a muddled program of Reconstruction, based on muddled, often contradictory, notions of law and justice. As 1865 wore on and Johnson's plan began to crystallize, consensus turned to conflict, then acrimony, and, as 1866 dawned, all-out internecine conflict.

Johnson seemed to be guided by two fundamental principles, which, happily for him if not the nation, dovetailed nicely with his own vision of Reconstruction. The first was a deep commitment to federalism, a belief that the central government's authority over the states was severely limited. Except in those functions specifically prescribed by the Constitution, states should be free to act in whatever manner they pleased. Although, for example, after ratification of the Thirteenth Amendment in December 1865, states might no longer countenance slavery, nothing in the Constitution prevented a state from enacting laws—Black Codes, as they came to be known—that were blatantly discriminatory and allowed the white population to maintain virtually the same degree of control over African-Americans that they had before 1860.*

Johnson also subscribed to the quaint notion that, since secession was illegal, the Civil War had merely been a police action. The eleven states that had left to fight had actually never left the Union. "It is clear to my apprehension," he wrote in a letter to Congress, "that the States lately in rebellion are still members of the national Union . . . The 'ordinances of secession' adopted by a portion (in most of them a very small portion) of their citizens, were mere nullities . . . Were those States afterwards expelled from the Union by the war? The direct contrary was averred by this government to be its purpose, and was so understood by all those who gave their blood and treasure to aid in its prosecution. It cannot be that a successful war, waged for the preservation of the Union, had the legal effect of dissolving it."[10]

To Johnson, therefore, no petition or readmission procedure was necessary. (With typical ambiguity, he seemed to find nothing contradictory in another of his pronouncements that, as a precondition to rejoining the Union, the eleven states could be made to renounce both slavery and future rebellion, and provide for the welfare of the freed slaves.) In any case, his position was anathema to the Radicals and none too popular with even the most moderate Republicans. That southern states might simply return to the fold and send representatives to Congress just as soon as the practicalities

---

* Black Codes mandated such contrivances as forced labor contracts, binding a worker to an employee on pain of criminal penalty or forfeiture of a year's back wages, forbidding blacks to carry knives or guns, setting sunup to sundown working hours, allowing corporal punishment of workers, and creating standards for vagrancy that would apply to virtually every black agricultural worker not tied to a white employer. Under Black Codes, strict racial segregation was also required in schools, public buildings, and cemeteries.

could be worked out was blatantly unacceptable. When southern states did, in fact, send representatives to Congress in late 1865, they were refused seats.

The other pillar of Johnson's philosophy was a profound and abiding racism. His antipathy to slavery was not as a moral evil, but that it facilitated an arrogant landed aristocracy, a "slaveocracy" as he put it. From poor origins himself, Johnson loathed the planters and remained convinced, incredibly, that freed slaves were so childlike that they would identify with, support, and vote for their former masters over the white working class or even other blacks.

The president's public pronouncements on African-Americans could be astonishing. In that same message to Congress in which he discussed the nullity of secession, the president observed:

> If anything can be proved by known facts, if all reasoning upon evidence is not abandoned, it must be acknowledged that in the progress of nations negroes have shown less capacity for government than any other race of people. No independent government of any form has ever been successful in their hands. On the contrary, wherever they have been left to their own devices they have shown a constant tendency to relapse into barbarism . . . I repeat the expression of my willingness to join in any plan within the scope of our constitutional authority which promises to better the condition of the negroes in the south, by encouraging them in industry, enlightening their minds, improving their morals, and giving protection to all their just rights as freedmen. But the transfer of our political inheritance to them would, in my opinion, be an abandonment of a duty which we owe alike to the memory of our fathers and the rights of our children.[11]

Johnson's abstruse views on state sovereignty and immoderate racial attitudes were of no particular consequence when he took office in April 1865. The status of the defeated Confederacy would be decided in due course, and racism was hardly unheard of in the nation's capital. Even when he aroused the antipathy of Radical, then moderate Republicans, by appointing interim governments in the South that promised to, if not reinstitute slavery, then de facto replicate it, most of his enemies shied from direct confrontation.

In December 1865, however, with the ratification of the Thirteenth Amendment, everything changed.

The Apportionment Act of 1862, by which the Thirty-ninth Congress had been constituted, had assigned 57 of the 241 seats in the House of

Representatives to the eleven states that had seceded, a distribution that had been arrived at using the old three-fifths rule.[12] By ending slavery, however, the Thirteenth Amendment rendered that formula extinct. Since there were no longer "other persons" (as slaves had been denoted), any future apportionment had to be based on a full counting of African-Americans. If the eleven slave states could simply retake their places in Congress—as Andrew Johnson insisted—they would do so in a stronger position than when they had left. The South, "as a result of *losing* the Civil War," would gain apportionment and "be entitled to an *increase* in membership in the House of Representatives and the Electoral College."[13]

And so the philosophical niceties concerning Negro suffrage became moot. Enfranchising freedmen became a matter of necessity rather than morality. If blacks were counted for apportionment but could not themselves go to the polls, white Democrats would dominate in the South and wield more power in Congress than they had before the war. That prospect, coupled with Johnson's growing combativeness, shook moderate Republicans out of their quiescence, altered the balance of power, and, soon afterward, ushered in one of the unique experiments in a nation that itself had been formed as a unique experiment.

Andrew Johnson's effort to restore the Union has been dubbed "Presidential Reconstruction" and was marked not only by accommodation to all but the most prominent of the former Confederates and passage of Black Codes, but also, perhaps most fatally for Johnson, by presidential vetoes of two key bills. The first, to thwart an extension of the life and influence of the Freedmen's Bureau, stood; the second, to prevent enactment of the Civil Rights Act of 1866, was overridden.

Johnson's veto and Congress's subsequent override altered the course of American history. Because of the acrimony its ultimate passage engendered—this was the first time that a major piece of legislation was enacted over a presidential veto—the Civil Rights Act, instead of charting the moderate course through extremes as was its intention, enabled those extremes. When Johnson dug in his heels—or tried to—in promoting racist governments in the conquered South, the Radicals gained sway over more moderate factions of the Republican Party.

The legislation itself, while considered excessive, even fanatical, by Democrats and Andrew Johnson, was actually moderate given the new requirements for congressional and electoral apportionment engendered by the Thirteenth Amendment. Conspicuously absent from the bill was a provision for guaranteeing African-Americans the right to vote. White southerners would be free, therefore, if they forswore insurrection, to eventually wield significant clout both in Congress and in presidential elections.

The bill, aimed unapologetically at Black Codes, provided substantial guarantees for the rights of freedmen, starting with the most fundamental right of all. "All persons born in the United States and not subject to any foreign power, excluding Indians not taxed, are hereby declared to be citizens of the United States." Also guaranteed were the right of contract, access to the legal system, and the right to employment for all citizens, black and white, and to "full and equal benefits of all laws and proceedings for the security of person and property."[14] Denial of any of these rights became a federal crime, enforceable according to federal law, in federal courts. With the exception of the removal of jurisdiction to federal courts, the bill's guarantees were pretty much in line with what a majority of the nation thought was fair. Democrats, of course, particularly in the South, demurred, complaining that the bill was a gross violation of states' rights and a betrayal of the principles under which the United States was founded.

Secession no longer being an option, however, Democratic grousing might have been merely shunted aside were it not for the presidential veto. But Johnson, in announcing his unyielding opposition to the bill—which he insisted was on the basis of the states' rights argument, a claim that elicited snickers from his enemies—demonstrated to its supporters that the mandates embodied within it might well be transitory, subject to the whim of whoever sat in Congress or the White House.[15] Thus Republicans, now moderate as well as Radical, quickly saw the necessity of situating these principles in a place where Johnson and the Democrats could never get at them.

The Constitution.

Over seventy amendments were proposed and discussed in the first session of the Thirty-ninth Congress. Only one emerged. Debate was fierce, and so many changes were made to the text after so many rounds of horse-trading, both in the joint committee that drafted the amendment and on the floors of both houses, that a complete and thorough analysis of the process that led to the final draft is impossible.

Nor would this amendment pass quickly into law. Unlike the Thirteenth Amendment, which had been ratified a mere ten months after first being introduced in Congress, ratification of the Fourteenth Amendment was to take more than two years. From the standpoint of embedding the language of the Civil Rights Act into the Constitution, the amendment was a success; from the standpoint of guaranteeing the fundamental rights of African-Americans, it was decidedly less so.

Section 1, from which reams of jurisprudence have emanated, was essentially a recapitulation of the Civil Rights Act.

> All persons born or naturalized in the United States, and subject to the jurisdiction thereof, are citizens of the United States and of the State wherein they reside. No State shall make or enforce any law which shall abridge the privileges or immunities of citizens of the United States; nor shall any State deprive any person of life, liberty, or property, without due process of law; nor deny to any person within its jurisdiction the equal protection of the laws.

The second section went to the heart of the pragmatics of black voting.

> When the right to vote at any election for the choice of electors for President and Vice President of the United States, Representatives in Congress, the Executive and Judicial officers of a State, or the members of the Legislature thereof, is denied to any of the male inhabitants of such State, being twenty-one years of age, and citizens of the United States, or in any way abridged, except for participation in rebellion, or other crime, the basis of representation therein shall be reduced in the proportion which the number of such male citizens shall bear to the whole number of male citizens twenty-one years of age in such State.

Thus any state that chose to deny freedmen the right to vote would lose the bonus representation that had accrued to them through their nonvoting black population. At one point, Charles Sumner presented a "petition of colored citizens" asking that the second section be revised to require a congressman to attain the votes of "at least half of the loyal men of his district, without regard to color," before being seated, but Negro suffrage had no real chance of being incorporated into this amendment.[16]

The third section barred former Confederates from serving in state or national government, the criteria being broad but vague, and capable of, on a case-by-case basis, being set aside by two-thirds majority of both houses of

Congress.[17] The fourth voided any claims against the United States for loss of slaves or other Confederate property; and the fifth empowered Congress to pass legislation to enforce any of the other provisions.

Significant in both the gist and the wording of the amendment was the enforcement role of the courts, the reliance Congress had placed on the federal judiciary as the avenue through which those whose civil rights had been violated might seek redress. In this, Congress affirmed Hamilton's idealistic vision in *Federalist 78*. For the first time in American history, laws enacted by state legislatures seen to be discriminatory could be overturned in federal court. By investing the judiciary with this guardianship role, which party was dominant in Congress would no longer be relevant. Civil rights enforcement would have been constitutionally removed from partisanship.

The House endorsed the Senate version of the amendment on June 13, 1866, in a strict party line vote of 120–32.[18] The mood was as much relief as exhilaration. The *New York Times* observed, "The adoption by the House of the proposed Constitutional Amendment, as modified by the Senate, will, we trust, terminate all irritating discussion on the question of reconstruction."[19] The *Hartford Courant* noted that "the amendment has been cleansed of Mr. Stevens' obnoxious ideas and is in good shape . . . Let Connecticut be the first state to ratify it."[20] Although its sponsors were given the serendipitous advantage that, constitutionally, the president plays no role in the amendment process—Johnson reacted with a harrumph and by calling a convention of his supporters to take back the government in the coming elections—the amendment still needed to be ratified by three fourths of the states.

But the pool of states from which the three fourths would be drawn was in some doubt. Whether or not the secessionist states were to be included in the ratification process depended on one's view of the legality of their secession. Andrew Johnson's view that they were still part of the Union had been repudiated when southern congressmen were denied their apportioned seats by this very same Thirty-ninth Congress in 1865. Yet to ignore the eleven states entirely seemed equally unpalatable. When Thaddeus Stevens proposed limiting ratification to northern states, even his fellow Republicans balked at what they saw as a blatant power grab.

Computing the three fourths with Andrew Johnson's governments in place in the South, however, presented what seemed an unconquerable obstacle to ratification. Once the amendment was in place, southern states would be faced with two extremely distasteful options: accept black voters and gain representation but risk that the added representatives would be Republicans or, even worse, Negroes; or deny freedmen the vote and accept diminished influence, possibly in perpetuity.[21] If there was no carrot, neither was there a stick. The only means to coerce southern state legislatures into accepting the amendment was to make ratification a precondition for readmission to the Union, which, at that point, could not be achieved under the law.

And the stakes were immense; thirty-seven seats in the House of Representatives throughout the South and thus thirty-seven electoral votes in every presidential election. Compounding the urgency for Republicans was a long-standing alliance between southern and northern Democrats. Southern states would be readmitted at *some* point; there were no illusions on that score. If all the congressional seats of the readmitted states were filled by whites elected by whites, Stevens, Sumner, and their allies had little hope of seeing their Reconstruction program adopted. Without Negro suffrage, sufficient votes would not be present to override a presidential veto. And without the Fourteenth Amendment, there would be no Negro suffrage. As the elections approached, only a woeful five states had ratified.

But the Radicals were saved at the ballot box. The elections of 1866 were a disaster for Andrew Johnson. Rather than take back the government, Johnson's allies, virtually all of whom were Democrats, lost sufficiently that Republicans had veto-overriding two-thirds majorities in both houses of Congress. Republicans made immense gains in state legislatures as well. The Fourteenth Amendment, while still vital to the Radical program, no longer represented the balance of power. Although the new Congress would not sit for five months, Presidential Reconstruction had effectively come to an end. The era of Radical Reconstruction was about to begin.

Johnson's extremism, as extremism is wont to do, had merely pushed his opponents into a more intractable position of their own. The notion of freedmen at polling stations had begun to gain surprisingly widespread acceptance. Many previously antipathetic congressmen seemed to have changed positions simply to avoid identification with Johnson.[22] Whatever the reason, when the Thirty-ninth Congress convened for its final, lame-duck session in December 1866, black suffrage was a topic of discussion in both houses.[23]

Whether or not African-American voting was imminent, the Fourteenth Amendment certainly was not. Most southern states had flatly rejected the measure, and, under their legislatures as then constituted, little likelihood existed that they would alter their stance. The solution was clear. If one could not persuade sitting governments to ratify the amendment, it would be necessary to change the governments.

So, while the Thirty-ninth Congress did not actually take on the thorny issue of African-American voting, it did pass "An Act to Provide for the More Efficient Government of the Rebel States," dubbed almost immediately the "Reconstruction Act." Its opening sentence read, "Whereas no legal State governments or adequate protection for life or property now exists in the rebel States of [all secessionist states were listed, except Tennessee, which had ratified the Fourteenth Amendment]; and whereas it is necessary that peace and good order be enforced in said States until loyal and republican State governments can be legally established . . ."[24] A more direct slap at the Andrew Johnson appointments would be difficult to conjure up. The law went on to divide the ten secessionist states into five military districts, each commanded by no less than a brigadier general, and directed the district commanders to "protect all persons in their rights of person and property, to suppress insurrection, disorder, and violence, and to punish, or cause to be punished, all disturbers of the public peace and criminals." To achieve this, a commander could empower civil courts or, if he chose, military tribunals to deal with the offenders. Only death sentences were subject to review, and those by the president.

Section 5 of the law required each of the ten states to "form a constitution . . . in conformity with the Constitution of the United States in all respects." State constitutions were to be drafted by "male citizens, twenty-one years old and upward, of whatever race, color, or previous condition."[25] The resulting document would then need to be approved by Congress. When a state's constitution had been approved and a legislature formed, the state would be required to ratify the Fourteenth Amendment. Ratification thus became a de jure condition for readmission to the Union.

Although the law appeared to insist on color-blind male suffrage, there was no prohibition on states demanding certain qualifications for the franchise, as long as those qualifications were applied evenhandedly to all applicants. Literacy, lineage, poll taxes; all of these would be permissible under the law, as they would be under the Fourteenth Amendment. Of course, any attempt to skirt past the intent of this law, to disenfranchise potential voters based only on race, would, so its sponsors believed, be given short shrift by the federal courts.

As everyone in America assumed he would, Andrew Johnson vetoed the bill virtually the moment it arrived at his desk. (He had complained to a newspaperman that whites "were being trodden under foot to protect niggers.")[26] Just as quickly, Congress overrode the veto.

By March 4, 1867, when the Thirty-ninth Congress was replaced by the Fortieth, an additional fifteen states had ratified the Fourteenth Amendment. Still, with the secessionists included, twenty-eight states were needed for ratification, and Tennessee was still the only former slave state to approve the measure (and, as a result, was allowed to rejoin the Union). Other southern states showed no inclination to knuckle under.

The Fortieth Congress immediately began work on a supplement to the Reconstruction Act designed to ratchet up pressure on both the secessionist states and the president.[27] Within three weeks, both houses had passed a bill requiring that by September 1, 1867, the commanding general of each of the five military districts register every male twenty-one or over who was not disqualified from voting under section 3 of the Fourteenth Amendment to vote on whether or not to hold a constitutional convention. The bill further laid out specific rules of how these conventions would be elected, and the procedures for having new state constitutions drafted and approved. Significant was that the entire process was to be overseen by the army, so that no artificial impediments to registration might be erected. Implicit was that, for the first time, African-Americans—the men at least—would have unfettered access to the ballot box.

Predictably, Andrew Johnson vetoed the measure and both houses promptly overrode the veto, the House by a vote of 114–25 and the Senate by 40–7. Congress did not even give Johnson the courtesy of a hearing. "Not a word of debate; merely the reading of the [president's] message, the recording of the yeas and nays, and the business ends."[28]

With victory in their nostrils, Stevens and Sumner pushed for even more radical measures, chief among them the program of confiscation and redistribution of southern plantation and farm land. But, with pronouncements that they had no intention of participating in a "revolution," moderate Republicans, and even some heretofore Radicals, stopped confiscation in its tracks. And although he had been soundly trounced in his war with Congress, Andrew Johnson remained commander in chief and thus was the man who appointed the commanders of the five military districts. Two expressed outright opposition to the Reconstruction Acts and two were more or less neutral. Only Phil Sheridan, in charge of the Louisiana and Texas district, actively aided the freedmen, and Johnson soon replaced him.

Nonetheless, the Reconstruction Acts transformed the Confederacy. Union Leagues, which promoted African-American political activity, sprang up throughout the South. Blacks registered to vote, asserted their civil and property rights, and attended schools sponsored by either the Freedmen's Bureau or private agencies. Blacks and whites traveled from the North to participate in the transition, some for monetary gain, some because of altruism. "Carpetbaggers" were a far more diverse and layered group than is often indicated in popular folklore.

Although the Reconstruction Acts did not specifically enfranchise blacks, nothing prevented army commanders from granting the vote to freedmen on their own authority. Which they did. Within months, thousands of black Americans gained access to the ballot box for the first time. Virtually all registered as Republicans. In addition, the terms of the legislation were such that military governments could not help but *disenfranchise* large numbers of whites. Anyone who had been deemed a "rebel" could be denied the vote. Virtually all of these were Democrats. Under the watchful eye of the army, the state constitutional conventions were approved, newly enfranchised African-Americans voting "aye" almost unanimously. New constitutions were then drafted and approved. The Johnson-appointed governments were kicked out, replaced by Republican-controlled state legislatures that represented only a small minority of the white population but almost every black.

The Fourteenth Amendment was, as required for readmission into the Union, ratified under these new state constitutions and thereby incorporated into the United States Constitution. As a result of the Reconstruction Acts (and eventually the Fifteenth Amendment), the prospect that the additional seats in the House of Representatives the South received would be filled by Democrats had been eliminated. As the *New York Times* reported on July 10, 1868, the day after ratification of the Fourteenth Amendment, the measure "settles the matter of suffrage in the Southern States beyond the power of the rebels to change it, even if they had control of the government. Its potent provision is that where any portion of the citizens of a state are denied the right of suffrage for any cause but crime, duly established, said citizens will not be counted in the basis of representation. If South Carolina concludes to return to a white man's government, she reduces her representation from five to two."[29]

Yet with all the cataclysmic change, Reconstruction was overhung by not one set of storm clouds but two. First, there were no illusions in either the

North or the South that these Reconstruction governments could survive without the army to back them up. But the army could not remain in the South forever. Radicals could only hope that, with time, white southerners would grow accustomed to power sharing with African-Americans; that freedmen would assimilate sufficiently that their presence in government, schools, theaters, and business would gain at least tacit acceptance. Second, while Republicans were in ascension in the South—artificial though their rise may have been—Democrats had begun to eat into their overwhelming majorities in the North. Not everyone was pleased at the immense expenditure of time, money, and matériel to create a series of experimental governments in the old Confederacy. In addition, the notion of Negroes lording it over whites in state governments—and eventually in Congress—was as distasteful to most northerners as to southerners. Reconstruction was an experiment that would surely have an end point, at least at the ballot box. Once the army withdrew, the only place black Americans would be able to find justice was in the federal court system.

TWO

BEYOND PARTY OR POLITICS:
THE CAPITALISTS ASCEND

T HE CIVIL WAR WAS AN AMERICAN watershed not simply because slavery ended and the national government established a predominance that had been in question since the drafting of the Constitution. At least as significant to the nation's future, the war—and its aftermath—enabled the release of volcanic economic forces, the pressure of which had been building for decades. America's economy, stoked by the voracious appetite of fraternal conflict, was remade. Four years of fighting not only had generated immense profits for industrialists but, for the same reasons as centralized authority was necessary in government, had created an environment in which the business class could assert extraordinary postwar influence. The prosecution of the Civil War not only altered the political relationship between the federal government and the states, but also widened the economic gaps between North and South, and between capitalist industry and small artisans.

After four years of record prosperity in the North, businessmen had a unique base on which to build. Fortunes had been acquired; profit potential seemed unlimited. Textile mills, foundries, arms manufacturers, railroads, shoe factories, lumberyards, farms, even casket makers had all strained to meet the demands of the engine of war. With a population large enough to replace its army many times over, the North could absorb the increased demand without deteriorating its efficiencies of scale. Most important, the boom in demand presented an opportunity for continued growth once the war ended, a prospect not lost on the great entrepreneurial class of the second half of the nineteenth century. Thus the war changed business as much as business affected the war. "Neither manipulation of governments and corporations by promoters, with attendant corruption and betrayal of fellow stockholders, nor attempts to substitute monopoly for competition were dominant features of business before secession."[1]

The men who would forge and shape America in the coming decades were initiated by the conflagration, although not in battle; men in their twenties to early thirties, the perfect age to direct men in the field, who preferred to remain civilians, directing lawyers and politicians instead of soldiers, growing their businesses and their fortunes while others did the dying for them. The list of entrepreneurs born in the 1830s (when James Madison died) is nothing short of stunning. No decade in American history has produced so many who went on to such astounding success: Andrew Carnegie, Philip D. Armour, Marshall Field, John D. Rockefeller, John Wanamaker, Frederick Weyerhaeuser, Clement Studebaker, Charles Deere, Augustus Juilliard, Frederick Pabst, George A. Pullman, A. J. Cassatt (Pennsylvania Railroad), Gustavus Swift, James J. Hill (Great Northern Railway), Jay Gould, J. P. Morgan, and Charles A. Pillsbury (born in 1842) were just some of the more recognizable figures. The 1830s also produced titanic figures in nonfinancial endeavors who avoided service in the Army of the Potomac; men such as Andrew Dickson White (cofounder of Cornell) and Daniel Coit Gilman (first president of Johns Hopkins).

Unlike Thaddeus Stevens and Charles Sumner, who viewed the old Confederacy as a social laboratory, capitalists looked south and saw vast potential of a different sort, the same sort as England once felt looking across the Atlantic to the colonies. And the humbled Confederacy was in no position to blunt the capitalist ax. The South, desperate for both enlisted men and officers, had not had the luxury of exempting members of the intelligentsia or business class from active service. The greatly diminished number of southern leaders who did straggle home in 1865 were largely of the same agricultural class as had begun the war four years earlier.

Both in their heyday and since, the northern entrepreneurs have evoked an almost rabid degree of either admiration or antipathy. Historians and economists on the right have lauded these men for "making America," launching the nation into global preeminence; those on the left have seen only exploitation, profiteering, and moral bankruptcy. "As the idealists in the North joined the colors," wrote one particularly harsh critic on the left, "the unprincipled, the bigoted, and the corrupt reached for the reins of political power, and the unscrupulous in a number of cases seized leadership in important fields of business. Before the war ended, the corrupt alliance that opened the door wide to the 'robber barons' had been fashioned not only in Washington and New York City, but in the states that ranged from the Berkshires to San Francisco Bay. Castigated by Walt Whitman in his *Democratic Vistas* (1871) this regime of business politics and of entrepreneurs who sought special advantage through government favoritism or other forms of privilege lasted until it was terminated by Theodore Roosevelt's accidental rise to power."[2]

Whether loved or loathed, however, the growth of America's industrial base was undeniable. In 1860, the United States held 30,626 miles of railroads. By 1877, that number had increased more than two and a half times to 79,208. Despite generous offers of subsidies by southern states in the war's aftermath, that growth was almost entirely in the North and West. In 1860, no railroad stretched past the Missouri River. In 1877, Nevada, California, and Oregon alone held 3,000 miles of track. In 1865, southern states, by comparison, contained 8,562 miles of railroad; by 1877, the number had grown to only 12,331. Illinois alone added more track in the period than the entire South.[3] From 1867 to 1878, production of pig iron almost doubled from 1.2 million tons to 2.1 million, sufficient for the United States to export 10,000 tons, where a decade before, exports were only 628 tons.[4]

The South, weighed down by the diseconomies of slavery—the war did not put an end to the institution as much as hasten its already inevitable demise—was unable to move effectively toward integrating industry into its economy. Dependent as it was on outside factors for virtually every aspect of pre- and postproduction, southern states were unable even to maintain profit margins in agriculture. The war devastated southern ability to grow crops on more than a subsistence scale.

Population growth in the Confederacy was virtually halted by the war. Where the population of Illinois, for example, grew by almost 800,000 between 1860 and 1870, to more than 2.5 million, Louisiana's grew by only 15,000 to 726,000. New York had half a million more inhabitants after the war than before it; Missouri 600,000; and even Connecticut, starting from a base of only 400,000, grew by over 100,000 during the 1860s. Georgia, with more than 1.1 million inhabitants in 1860, had virtually the same number in 1870. Mississippi, Alabama, Tennessee, and South Carolina all had no real growth. Virginia lost almost 400,000 inhabitants to go from the fourth most populated state in the nation to the tenth. Overall, the United States grew in population by almost seven million between 1860 and 1870, almost all in the North and West.[5]

The South's qualitative loss was more devastating than the quantitative. An entire generation of young men was decimated. Young white men. Europe has occasionally experienced such a cataclysm, but the depletion of the most productive segment of southern society during the Civil War was unique in American history. The North had suffered huge casualties as well, of course, but the North, as with its capital base, could quickly replenish its losses, while for the South, the diminution of resources was, if not permanent, at least certain to provide massive impediments to growth for decades to come.

Without industry and postproduction factors of its own, the South had traditionally relied on northern and foreign shippers, bankers, and distributors to ensure profit from its crops. But this "merchant-planter-agrarian alliance" was shattered by the war, "leaving its separated elements helpless during a chaotic epoch of Reconstruction."[6] By the war's end, the North was poised to become an economic empire, while the South would struggle to feed and clothe its population. The North, then, at least from an economic standpoint, emerged in 1865 a society wanting only to perpetuate what war had wrought; the South a society needing to emerge from desolation.

Early indications were that, for the victors at least, prosperity would be quick in coming. In 1863, the Treasury collected $113 million in revenue but spent $714 million. In 1864, $265 million came in, while $865 million went out. In 1865, the national debt grew by almost $1 billion as the nation spent $1.3 billion while taking in only $334 million. Yet the very next year, the first full year of peace, the United States had a $37 million surplus. That surplus grew to $133 million in 1867, and the nation ran a surplus for each of the next dozen years.[7] In all, the national debt exploded from $65 million in 1860 to $2.7 billion in 1865, but then remained either stable or decreased for the next thirteen years. While the details of revenues and expenditures are not broken out by state, to postulate that this turnaround was not engendered in the South would not be unreasonable.

A fundamental belief common to virtually all capitalists is that business, if left free of the intrusions of government or well-meaning but ultimately misguided social reformers, will create wealth and benefit not simply for those at the top of society's pyramid, but prosperity that will permeate down to the bottom as well. Call it the invisible hand or supply-side economics, entrepreneurs seek an environment in which they are free to operate and therefore gravitate to whichever point on the political spectrum will maximize that freedom. (That after they've made their fortunes they want government to protect their interests tends to be brought up less.)

In the immediate aftermath of the war, businessmen gravitated to the Republicans. The impact on both economy and government was profound. Paper currency, a national banking system, and a national debt to match were direct offshoots of the war effort. Tariffs and taxes were increased, immigration was encouraged, and infrastructure and railroads were improved. Free homesteading was offered on public lands, and colleges were established to teach "agricultural and mechanical arts."

For a while, the Radicals and financiers did well by one another. An editorial on Abraham Lincoln's birthday in 1867, commenting on "the evident understanding between the stock jobbers and legislators," noted:

> Gold perhaps steadily declines for a week or two . . . and [market] prices begin to decline, to the alarm of speculators, when Thad Stevens . . . comes to their rescue with a series of destruction resolutions or a bill to place the South under martial law. Up goes gold and market prices and down go government securities. The speculators having sold out on the rise desire a decline; the Radicals in Congress temper their wrath; Thad Stevens's bill is tabled or sent to a committee, and there is "returning confidence" in Wall Street. This game of battledore and shuttlecock has been kept up through the present session of Congress . . . Congress has been playing into the hands of all the monied interests in the country . . . The Radicals seek a partisan justification for the suffering they are inflicting on the South, but the evils their policy entails cannot be confined to any one section of the country . . . The Radicals are allied with the capitalists and speculators, because they have an interest in common—both profit by the distractions of the country.[8]

But as the Republican Party tilted increasingly toward the Radicals, the business community began to experience disillusionment. The insistence by the Radicals in forming a southern society in their image had deep consequences not just for the South but for the nation as a whole. Resentment of what came to be seen as a ham-fisted attempt to legislate attitudes and points of view, to define righteousness—and iniquity—created a backlash that only deepened over time. Social reforms of any kind would come to be thought of as exercises not only in futility but in despotism. Allowing a state or a region to live by its own standards, even if those standards included lynching, would eventually predominate in American thought. The foolhardiness of attempting to legislate racial equality—or even tolerance—would find its way into Supreme Court opinions and, in some cases, provide justification for the Court's refusal to intercede to prevent even the most egregious injustices.

Thaddeus Stevens died in 1868. The *New York Times* eulogized him as "an able and intrepid leader of the most radical wing of the Republican Party . . . noted for his indomitable will and wonderful energy . . . and even those who in the past have been swift to condemn the measures he has advocated will not hesitate to admit that the objects he aimed at were as he conceived redound to the advancement of the nation and the lasting good of all its people."[9] Stevens had a less complimentary view of his achievements. On his deathbed, he told a reporter, "I have achieved nothing in Congress . . . Some of the papers call me 'Leader of the House.' I only laugh at them. I lead them, yes; but they never follow me or do as I want them until public opinion has sided with me."[10]

Stevens's cynical self-appraisal was not shared among the general public. When he lay in state in the Capitol, he attracted a stream of mourners outstripped only by Abraham Lincoln. And Stevens was also incorrect about his perceived lack of influence among his peers. With his passing, the Republican Party began its inexorable drift to the right. "The Radical generation was passing, eclipsed by politicos . . . 'the struggle over the Negro,' the party's rising leaders believed, must give way to economic concerns."[11] But political parties, like great ships, do not turn on a dime, and Republicans would not be completely recast for almost a decade.

So in 1869, in the face of almost universal white skepticism about black voting, the Fifteenth Amendment was passed by a Republican Congress and ratified in the states the following year. "The right of citizens of the United States to vote shall not be denied or abridged by the United States or by any State on account of race, color, or previous condition of servitude" became part of the Supreme Law of the Land. In the South, curiously, the issue had become largely moot. Even before the amendment was introduced in Congress, Negro suffrage had been imposed throughout most of the South by the military governments of occupation in the old Confederacy. But military governments, even to the Radicals, were only a stopgap until a more just and equitable society could grow in the South from the seeds of Reconstruction.

As a result, to include in the Constitution a guarantee that color or race could not be a bar to the ballot box seemed to many the coup de grâce to racial inequality. William Lloyd Garrison gushed that over four million human beings transferred from "the auction block to the ballot box."[12] The American Anti-Slavery Society disbanded in March 1870, feeling there was no longer any reason for its existence. President Ulysses Grant, in a message to Congress, called the amendment "a measure of grander importance than any other one act of the kind from the foundation of our free Government to the present time."[13] Finally, the amendment infuriated Democrats, which in and of itself seemed ample justification to many for its inclusion in the Constitution.

Ratification of the amendment engendered a good deal of relief as well. The nation might finally have moved past "the Negro question," as it was called. Ohio congressman and future president James A. Garfield asserted that the amendment "confers upon the African race the care of its own destiny. It places fortunes in their own hands."[14]

Others, however, took a more circumspect view. The wording of the amendment to them gave indication of an increasingly lukewarm commitment among white Americans to ensuring equal rights for African-Americans. Unlike the Fourteenth Amendment, whose provisions were sweeping, the Fifteenth contained no guarantee that black Americans could *hold* office. Nor were uniform standards of eligibility included, which would prevent white governments from excluding potential voters through arbitrary literacy tests, or grandfather clauses, or tortuously formulated property requirements. These omissions were not lost on the shrinking contingent of northern Radicals, who decried the "lame and halting language" or noted that the amendment was "more remarkable for what it does not than for what it does contain."[15]

Negative sentiment came from other quarters. An editor at the *New Haven News* wrote portentiously, "The question of the elective franchise is one that [the states] will never surrender at the dictation of congress or any other power seeking to arbitrarily wrench it from [their] constitutional grasp."[16]

But for most, both the intent and the impact could not have been clearer; the Fifteenth Amendment was to add cement to an edifice of democracy built of American virtue. Naysayers, like the New Haven editor, were re-minded that any attempt by unscrupulous white legislators to end-run the Fifteenth Amendment through, say, bogus literacy tests, would certainly run afoul of the equal protection clause of the Fourteenth. And to ensure that the Constitution was adhered to by any who would seek to contort its aims were the justices of the Supreme Court.

THREE

Another Reconstruction:
The Lincoln Court

In addition to presiding over a nation to be politically and socially transformed, Abraham Lincoln, although in effect only a one-term president, nonetheless had the opportunity to transform the Supreme Court.* Although Roger Brooke Taney remained as chief justice, the death of Associate Justice Peter Daniel had created a vacancy even as Lincoln took office on March 4, 1861. On April 4, Associate Justice John McLean died, and three weeks after that, in the wake of the attack on Fort Sumter, John A. Campbell reluctantly tendered his resignation, his efforts to mediate between Lincoln and his native South having come to naught. Thus, barely seven weeks into his term of office, Lincoln was afforded the opportunity to appoint fully one third of the Court. No president since Washington had been in such an enviable position.

But Lincoln's prerogative was limited by both practical considerations and the president's own sense of fairness. The Court in 1861 was composed of nine justices. This number was neither arbitrary nor mandated by the Constitution. Supreme Court justices, in addition to their service on the high tribunal, were also required to serve as a member of a United States circuit court—to "ride circuit"—an unpleasant and anachronistic task left over from the days when the United States was young, broke, and stretched only to the Mississippi. The nation, before secession, had consisted of nine circuits, and so nine justices were required. Although there was no requirement to do so, custom dictated that an associate justice would be appointed

---

* Although Lincoln was reelected in 1864, his actual term of office lasted from March 4, 1861, to April 14, 1865, when he was assassinated, giving him a term in office of four years and five weeks.

from within the circuit over which he would then preside while on the Court.

With secession, of course, the old circuit court map was out the window. Or was it? As Andrew Johnson was so fond of pointing out, the Union didn't recognize the Confederacy. In Washington, these were, officially at least, simply rebels, still accountable under the laws of the United States. In theory, then, the nine circuits should have remained unchanged, and President Lincoln should have filled the vacancies from the southern circuits with southern judges. (Justice Campbell, for example, had been from Alabama.) Practically speaking, of course, this was an absurdity. No secessionist state was likely to allow a United States Supreme Court justice to ride into town and preside over legal proceedings it no longer recognized as legitimate. But what if Lincoln packed the Court with northern justices, and the war, as many predicted, was short? The resentment from the southern portion of the reconstituted Union would be intense.

Lincoln chose to wait. He decided to leave all three seats vacant, at least until Congress redrew the circuit map. But six justices or nine, Roger Taney remained on the Court, and anyone who thought the chief justice had been chastened by the execration to which he had been subjected in the wake of *Dred Scott* was to be severely disappointed.[1] At the first opportunity, Taney produced the same sort of gauntlet-throwing jurisprudence that had caused him to be earlier branded a national disgrace. (That opprobrium had become near unanimous with the southern states no longer in the polling sample.)

In May 1861, Taney was sitting as a circuit court judge in his native Maryland when he received a petition from one John Merryman for a writ of habeas corpus. This was no ordinary request but represented a direct challenge to President Lincoln's authority in time of war.

In the weeks after Lincoln's inauguration, Maryland had become the most important state in the Union. Virginia had seceded, and if Maryland followed suit, Washington, D.C. would lie within the core of the Confederacy. Agitation for secession was strong. On April 27, in response to a series of riots and guerrilla actions, Lincoln sent an order to General Winfield Scott. "You are engaged in repressing an insurrection against the laws of the United States. If at any point on or in the vicinity of the military line which is now used between the city of Philadelphia via Perryville, Annapolis City and Annapolis Junction you find resistance which renders it necessary to suspend the writ of *habeas corpus* for the public safety, you personally or through the officer in command at the point where resistance occurs are authorized to suspend that writ."[2] Habeas corpus is the fundamental right of an accused to appear before a judge and demand justification for arrest or imprisonment. Suspension of that right effectively established martial law, empowering the army to summarily arrest and imprison, without trial, anyone its commanders deemed involved in sowing sedition.[3]

One of those arrested was John Merryman, an officer in the Maryland cavalry, who seemed a ringleader in anti-Union activities. Merryman was arrested in his home, without a warrant, at two A.M. on May 25, 1861, by armed soldiers; dragged off while his wife and children helplessly stood by. His lawyers promptly petitioned the circuit court for a writ of habeas corpus, as authorized under the Judiciary Act of 1789. Taney granted the writ, and a United States marshal presented it at Fort McHenry, where Merryman was incarcerated. But the commandant at the fort refused to release the prisoner on the grounds that the commander in chief had suspended habeas corpus. Taney tried once more, issuing an order for contempt to the commandant, but this time the marshal could not even get past the fort's front gate.

Reduced to hurling brickbats, Taney issued an opinion in what would become known as *ex parte Merryman*, stating in harsh terms that the president had overstepped his authority. Only Congress, Taney asserted, citing unambiguous language in Article I, Section 9 of the Constitution, has the power to suspend habeas corpus. "I had supposed," he added, "[this] to be one of those points of constitutional law upon which there was no difference of opinion." Taney went on to note, "The only power, therefore, which the president possesses, where the 'life, liberty or property' of a private citizen is concerned, is the power and duty prescribed in the third section of the second article, which requires 'that he shall take care that the laws shall be faithfully executed.' He is not authorized to execute them himself, or through agents or officers, civil or military." In short, "The president, under the constitution of the United States, cannot suspend the privilege of the writ of *habeas corpus*, nor authorize a military officer to do it."[4]

Although on this occasion Taney turned out to be on the right side of history as well as the law, his political instincts remained as woeful as ever.[5] In the spirit of Andrew Jackson, who declared famously of Taney's predecessor, "Mr. Marshall has made his ruling. Now let him enforce it," Lincoln proceeded to ignore the chief justice and went about his business as commander in chief as he saw fit. The president's first draft of a message to Congress in special session on July 4, 1861, contained references to his eighty-five-year-old adversary, but Lincoln struck them out, preferring to treat the ancient chief justice as if he did not exist.

Taney certainly anticipated Lincoln's response, as he closed his opinion noting, "In such a case, my duty was too plain to be mistaken. I have exercised all the power which the constitution and laws confer upon me, but that power has been resisted by a force too strong for me to overcome."[6] That by taking such a stand, proclaiming the Court's impotence, he might be further eroding the authority of a Court still reeling over *Dred Scott* did not seem to enter his thinking.[7]

Although critics of the president decried the arbitrary destruction of the rule of law, the vast majority of Americans agreed with Lincoln's assessment, which he presented in the final version of his July 4 address to Congress.

> The whole of the laws which I was sworn to [execute] were being resisted . . . in nearly one-third of the States. Must I have allowed them to finally fail of execution, even had it been perfectly clear that by the use of the means necessary to their execution some single law, made in such extreme tenderness of the citizen's liberty, that practically it relieves more of the guilty than the innocent, should, to a very limited extent, be violated? Are all the laws but one to go unexecuted, and the Government itself go to pieces, lest that one be violated?[8]

When the Court convened for the December 1861 term, Taney had become quite ill, as had Justice John Catron. The prospect of a nine-member Court reduced to four was untenable, so Lincoln filled one of the existing three vacancies by nominating the Ohio lawyer Noah Swayne, a Quaker, abolitionist, and the Court's first Republican. When Congress finished the process of realigning the circuits in mid-July 1862, maintaining the southern states, although not in separate circuits, Lincoln immediately appointed Samuel Freeman Miller to the Court. Miller, a westerner raised in Kentucky, was a Unitarian who, like Lincoln, abhorred slavery, and who also supported the president's decision to suspend habeas corpus.

Lincoln left the final seat, the Michigan-Wisconsin-Illinois circuit, vacant. Fierce lobbying from party regulars in the various states made certain that the president would ruffle feathers no matter who his choice. Lincoln settled on David Davis from Illinois, a close friend and someone whose personal integrity was sufficiently respected that, fourteen years afterward, he would be proposed as the man who, on his say alone, would choose a president of the United States. Each of Lincoln's appointees thus possessed impeccable antislavery credentials and could be expected, if the war was prosecuted to a successful conclusion, to champion the rights of millions of freed slaves.

The three new justices arrived on the Court just in time to sit on another test of the president's war powers, this with a more far-reaching impact than *Merryman*. These were a group of cases lumped together as the *Prize Cases*, arising out of the naval blockade of southern ports that Lincoln had instituted. As such, vessels flying the flags of neutral nations attempting to sail to blockaded ports became subject to seizure. International law dictated that certain rules and laws of salvage be followed with seizures of vessels heading for "declared belligerents." But did the North and South qualify under those terms? The Lincoln administration had taken the same position as would Andrew Johnson: that the secession of the eleven southern states was a rebellion, in effect an internal matter. Although Congress had authorized Lincoln to declare "a state of insurrection," no formal declaration of war had ever been issued. If a state of war did not exist, all seizures of neutral vessels by the United States Navy were illegal, qualifying as piracy under maritime law.

The Court was in something of a bind. The lack of a formal state of war was not due to an oversight by a foreign government, but to the failure of the Congress of the United States to issue the appropriate declaration. Strict reading of the Constitution seemed to leave little doubt that the president had exceeded his powers. The Court had faced a similar conundrum in the 1790s, when a group of prize cases arising from "the phony war" with France had put President John Adams's war powers to the test. Then, the Court had danced around the issue in a series of rulings, the most important of which was *Bas v. Tingy*, which established the murky concept of "partial war" in order to avoid a confrontation with the executive.[9]

The *Prize Cases* were argued for twelve days, and the Court rendered its decision a mere two weeks later. By a 5–4 vote, with Lincoln's three new appointees in the majority, the justices ruled that the president was within his rights to order a blockade and to seize neutral vessels, even in the absence of a formal declaration of war.

Justice Robert Grier, writing for the majority, began by noting, "The right of prize and capture has its origin in the *jus belli*, and is governed and adjudged under the law of nations. To legitimate the capture of a neutral vessel or property on the high seas, a war must exist *de facto,* and the neutral must have knowledge or notice of the intention of one of the parties belligerent to use this mode of coercion against a port, city, or territory, in possession of the other." Grier having inserted *"de facto"* into the equation, thus conveniently sidestepping a need for declaration, the leap to demonstrating that the conflict between the northern states and the southern qualified was a good deal more manageable. As he observed a bit later in his opinion, "As a civil war is never publicly proclaimed, *eo nomine,* against insurgents, its actual existence is a fact in our domestic history which the Court is bound to notice and to know." Continuing the argument, Grier wrote, "It is not the less a civil war, with belligerent parties in hostile array, because it may be called an 'insurrection' by one side, and the insurgents be considered as rebels or traitors. It is not necessary that the independence of the revolted province or State be acknowledged in order to constitute it a party belligerent in a war according to the law of nations. Foreign nations acknowledge it as war by a declaration of neutrality." Then, in conclusion, "Whether the President, in fulfilling his duties as Commander-in-chief in suppressing an insurrection, has met with such armed hostile resistance and a civil war of such alarming proportions as will compel him to accord to them the character of belligerents is a question to be decided by him, and this Court must be governed by the decisions and acts of the political department of the Government to which this power was entrusted." Grier did not cite *Bas* in his opinion, nor any other precedent for upholding Lincoln's right to commit to an act of war in the absence of a declaration of war.[10]

Justice Samuel Nelson, in dissent, took a more traditional—and accepted—view of war. "The legal consequences resulting from a state of war between two countries at this day are well understood, and will be found described in every approved work on the subject of international law. The people of the two countries become immediately the enemies of each other—all intercourse commercial or otherwise between them unlawful—all contracts existing at the commencement of the war suspended, and all made during its existence utterly void." He was equally unequivocal as to the powers of the president under the Constitution. In the end, Nelson concluded, in an opinion in which Taney joined, the president might contort the Constitution for political expediency or even necessity, but in doing so he was violating both the law and his oath.

But Nelson and Taney were railing against the wind. They had lost not simply in the *Prize Cases* but in the attempt to use the judiciary to limit rule by what they saw as presidential fiat. The Court, buttressed with three new appointees, had sent a clear message: In times of national crisis, jurisprudence must be subordinate to politics, not the other way around.

For the remainder of the war, the justices eschewed further confrontation with the executive. On matters in which the executive was clearly in the right, the justices affirmed Lincoln's position.[11] With more controversial questions, the Court generally employed the simple yet highly effective strategy of avoidance. The justices merely found some technical reason to deny the Court's jurisdiction when an inflammatory case crossed their path.[12] Thus neither Lincoln's issuance of paper money nor the Emancipation Proclamation was ever reviewed by the Court.[13]

In the spring of 1863, Congress added a circuit for California and Oregon, necessitating an additional associate, the only occasion in the nation's history when the Court contained more than nine justices.[14] To fill the seat, Lincoln nominated a Democrat, Stephen J. Field. Field's legal expertise was uncontested, as were his Unionist sentiments. But Field, who would serve for almost three decades, had a streak of conservatism that, while not affecting Lincoln, would come to the fore in subsequent administrations and have significant impact on the Court's application of the postwar amendments.[15]

In October 1864, after a term of twenty-eight years as chief justice, Roger Brooke Taney died. Thus, in the first thirteen years under the Constitution, the United States had three chief justices and, in the ensuing sixty-three years, only two. Although many spoke highly of Taney's personal qualities, and his tenure was defended by friends, the author of the *Dred Scott* decision was vilified after his death to a degree unprecedented in American history. Newspapers, members of Congress, and even other jurists described the departed chief justice as a blight on American democracy. One editorial observed, "History will expose him to eternal scorn in the pillory she has set up for infamous judges."[16] Another, while praising Taney as "a man of pure moral character and great legal learning," observed that the *Dred Scott* decision was "an act of supreme folly, and its shadow will ever rest upon his memory."[17] A third, generally supportive of the dead chief justice, nonetheless quoted his infamous observation in the *Dred Scott* opinion that blacks were "beings of an inferior order and altogether unfit to associate with the white race either in social or political relations."[18] A move to erect a bust of

Taney mounted next to that of his predecessor, John Marshall, was blocked by outraged congressmen. Almost universal was a desire to return the Court to the position of prestige it had enjoyed during Marshall's tenure.

But a John Marshall is not easily found. Lincoln needed a man of stature, but not one who would strike out on his own at a time when the president was, to put it kindly, skirting a number of constitutional provisions. Many candidates were put forward, representing just about every political and geographic interest in the Union. Lincoln was inundated with recommendations, some subtle, most not so. Whomever he chose was certain to displease more than he satisfied. In the end, Lincoln made what seemed to many an odd choice, Salmon P. Chase of Ohio. Chase's credentials were certainly beyond reproach. Although not an intimate of Sumner, Stevens, and the Republican Radicals, Chase's loathing of slavery was the equal of any man's in the Union. He had been a senator, governor, and secretary of the Treasury.[19] Chase was also a deft and clever politician, an independent thinker, a man who kowtowed to no one, and whose own aspirations to the presidency were well known.

But after Taney, Lincoln wanted a powerful steward for the Court, and one whose ideology comported with his own. A streak of independence, as long as it did not threaten Lincoln's war and postwar agendas, was a price the president was willing to pay.

With Chase's confirmation, Lincoln had succeeded in remaking the Supreme Court, appointing five of the ten justices in four short years. The Lincoln Court, abolitionist and pragmatic, would have seemed the perfect vehicle for the Reconstruction to come, prepared to work hand-in-hand with the president to ensure fair and just treatment for the delicate class of free Americans that a northern victory would create. If any doubt of the Lincoln Court's direction on civil rights existed, Chase dispelled it on February 1, 1865, six weeks after he took the bench, when he personally admitted John S. Rock, a member of the Massachusetts bar, to practice before the Court.

John S. Rock was black, the first African-American to gain that right.[20]

But Lincoln never made it past the first few weeks of his second term. Upon his death, the folly of choosing as his vice president a man not of his party, his ideals, nor even his views on race and slavery became manifest. With Andrew Johnson's ascendancy, a Democrat sat in the White House, and the fragile political balance that Lincoln had fashioned was thrown askew. The Court, its tacit partnership with the presidency at an end, no longer felt the need to rubber-stamp its political initiatives.

Six weeks after Lincoln's death, Associate Justice Catron died at age seventy-nine. Catron was a Tennessean who had opposed secession but supported slavery. With Catron's death, Lincoln appointees now held a clear majority on the Court. Andrew Johnson had already made no secret of his intention to ease the secessionist states back into the Union with its prewar power structure largely intact. When, early the following year, he nominated his attorney general and close friend Henry Stanbery to fill Catron's seat, Congress made sure that Johnson could not shake the new majority. Although Stanbery was above reproach and held racial views a good deal more enlightened than his boss, Congress enacted a bill, over the president's objections, to reduce the Court to seven members, to be achieved by attrition, thus abolishing Catron's seat and leaving, for the moment, a nine-seat Court.[21]

As the president's disagreements with Congress degenerated more or less into open war, the Supreme Court soon found itself in the center of a controversy that resulted in a constitutional crisis perhaps unmatched since John Marshall evaded Thomas Jefferson's wrath in *Marbury v. Madison in 1803.*

The stage was set in 1864, when a southern sympathizer named Lambdin P. Milligan was arrested in Indiana along with four other members of a shadowy group who called themselves the Order of American Knights. Milligan and his fellows were charged with resisting the draft and conspiring both to steal weapons and free Confederate prisoners of war. The freed prisoners would then form an army in the heart of the Union to be commanded by a Confederate raider, General John Hunt Morgan.

As with John Merryman, the arrest was made not by civil authorities but by Union soldiers, and, also like Merryman, did not take place in the Confederacy—in this case, in Indiana. Unlike Merryman, however, Milligan was not simply locked up but brought to trial by military tribunal. There, he was convicted of sedition and sentenced to hang, although, for some reason, the tribunal stayed the sentence until the following year. Milligan waited until the war ended and then, in May 1865, petitioned for a writ of habeas corpus. He sought to set aside both his arrest and conviction on the grounds that the military had no jurisdiction in Indiana, as Lincoln had overstepped his constitutional authority in declaring martial law in a noncombatant state.

While Milligan languished in jail—a more agreeable fate than that prescribed in his sentence—the case slowly wended its way through district court, then circuit court in Indiana. During the process, Andrew Johnson affirmed the legality of military tribunals in noncombatant states. As the case didn't reach the Court until the war had ended, the justices were not forced to rule on the issue until the threat from Milligan and his fellow Knights had been rendered moot, and thus the issue of war powers could be dealt with in the abstract. Even then, the process promised to be awkward, since this very same Court had, just two years earlier, during its avoidance phase, claimed it lacked jurisdiction over military tribunals in another copperhead case, *ex parte Vallandigham*.

In April 1866, the Court finally delivered its ruling.[22] The nine justices ruled unanimously that Milligan should not have been tried in a military court. They split, however, on the larger question of suspension of habeas corpus in principle, and the degree to which military prerogative could supersede civil authority.

Five justices, led by David Davis, claimed that while habeas corpus could be suspended in an emergency, the Constitution forbade suspension of the right of trial by jury unless civilian authority was absent or had broken down. "Martial rule can never exist where the courts are open, and in the proper and unobstructed exercise of their jurisdiction." The president could not authorize such an exception, nor could Congress. "The Constitution of the United States is a law for rulers and people," Davis went on, "equally in war and in peace, and covers with the shield of its protection all classes of men, at all times, and under all circumstances . . . Civil liberty and this kind of martial law cannot endure together; the antagonism is irreconcilable; and, in the conflict, one or the other must perish." Whether Justice Davis would have used such unambiguous language if the decision had been rendered while his old friend Lincoln was still alive is unknown. This wording was aimed directly at Andrew Johnson.

Chief Justice Chase, speaking for the four justices in the minority, disagreed, asserting that in some cases military rule could be instituted even though civilian authority continued to exist. There might be circumstances, he argued, where civilian courts continued to function, but either ineffectively or unreliably, and Congress could therefore legitimately authorize military control.

While *Milligan* represented a direct rebuke to executive overreaching—Lincoln had initiated the policy; Johnson had upheld it—the decision was unwelcome in Congress as well. For Radical Republicans, military rule was essential to guarantee that their Reconstruction program would not be undermined. If interpreted broadly, *Milligan* might forbid the very sort of martial initiatives that Stevens had been promoting and that would be undertaken the following year in the Reconstruction Acts. Once again, the linchpin seemed to be whether or not one viewed the South as conquered territory or merely the site of a suppressed insurrection. If the former, the Court would lack jurisdiction to limit or prohibit military rule; if the latter, and the states were viewed as noncombatant, military rule would violate the Constitution.

Radical Republicans were unconcerned with legal niceties. Their newspapers denounced the decision; their partisans called for impeachment of the offending justices; their congressmen contemplated legislation either to curtail the Court's authority or, precursing Franklin Roosevelt, to simply add a sufficient number of proper-thinking justices so as to constitute a proper-thinking majority. Despite the ominous language, no immediate concrete action was taken, but the Court had little choice but to consider itself on notice.

Democrats, particularly in the South, took a rather different view. Although couched in praise for the Court for upholding the rights of an individual over the arbitrary and crushing power of the state, Democrats' real reason for praising a branch of the hated federal government was the possibility that the Court might again represent a bastion of laissez-faire white government, as it had in Dred Scott.[23] Democrats could only praise from a distance, however, since they had little power in Congress.

Democratic hopes were soon buoyed by Andrew Johnson, who regarded the Milligan decision as "an indorsement [sic] of his policy to put an end to military government in the South as soon as possible."[24] Johnson immediately ordered a cessation of military trials of civilians in southern states and waited for popular opinion to vindicate his decision.[25]

Just the opposite occurred. After the Republican landslide in the elections of 1866, Radicals found themselves in the unique position of being able to stare down both the president and the justices. To the other two branches of government, they cast an implicit threat: block Reconstruction legislation and risk your sinecure.[26] Then, almost daring the Court to interfere, Radicals rammed the Reconstruction Acts through Congress, sweeping aside Andrew Johnson's roadblocks with two-thirds majorities.

While the president would eventually be dealt with through confrontation, the Radicals could take a more measured approach to the Court. Until Milligan, the justices had not especially asserted themselves. Not only had they yet to answer the question of whether the Civil War was indeed a war or simply an insurrection, but their various interpretations seemed to wander about erratically to suit political exigency. In *Merryman*, *Vallandigham*, and *Milligan*, each opinion took a rather different view of the same question, and all were decided within a five-year period. When the justices were willing to take a constitutional rather than a technical position, as they had in *Milligan*, they had seemed to indicate that military rule in civilian areas was questionable at best. But whether or not they would assert that view again, after the thinly veiled threat by the Radicals to drastically curtail their authority, and perhaps even their tenure, remained an open question.

The Radicals would soon have their answer. Within three weeks of the passage of the supplemental Reconstruction Act on March 25, 1867, an extraordinary action by an extraordinary plaintiff was brought before the Court.

FOUR

Siege: Congress Counterattacks

O N APRIL 5, 1867, William L. Sharkey and Robert J. Walker, attorneys representing the state of Mississippi, appeared before the justices "for leave to file a bill in the name of the State praying this court perpetually to enjoin and restrain Andrew Johnson, citizen of the State of Tennessee and President of the United States, and his officers and agents appointed for that purpose, and especially E. O. C. Ord, assigned as military commander of the district where the State of Mississippi is, from executing or in any manner carrying out two acts of Congress named in the bill, one 'An act for the more efficient government of the rebel States,' passed March 2d, 1867, notwithstanding the President's veto of it as unconstitutional, and the other an act supplementary to it, passed in the same way March 23d, 1867; acts commonly called the Reconstruction Acts."[1] The Reconstruction Acts, the plaintiff asserted, "annihilate the State and its government by assuming for Congress the power to control, modify, and even abolish its government—in short, to exert sovereign power over it—and the utter destruction of the State must be the consequence of their execution."

Not only was *Mississippi v. Johnson* the first action in United States history to name a sitting president as party to a lawsuit; never before had "the legal representatives of participants in an organized rebellion . . . been permitted to appear in court" to overturn terms of surrender.[2] If the Reconstruction legislation was enforced, argued the plaintiffs, it would render "the civil power subordinate to the military power, and thus establish a military rule over the States enumerated in the act, and make a precedent by which the government of the United States may be converted into a military despotism in which every man may be deprived of his goods, lands, liberty, by the breath of a military commander or the sentence of the military commission or tribunal, without the benefit of trial by jury and without the observance of any of those requirements and guarantees by which the Constitution and laws so plainly protect and guard the rights of the citizen."

But Mississippi was making an assumption as well, that it was indeed still a state and that its government was therefore protected against annihilation or had recourse against the "breath of a military commander." The old question of the nature of the Civil War had arisen once more, and with *Milligan* on the books, the consequences for whatever decision was made had become more pronounced. If Mississippi was still a state, with a civil government that functioned, military tribunals, and thus military rule, would indeed be unconstitutional. If, however, Mississippi was a conquered territory, the Reconstruction Acts would seem to pass constitutional muster.

The Court's bind was more acute still. By merely agreeing to hear the case, the justices would be acknowledging that the "State of Mississippi" had the right to sue and was, therefore, at least in all likelihood, still a state, thereby (perhaps) agreeing with Andrew Johnson that the secessionist states had remained in the Union. If the Court refused, it had little alternative but to do so on Mississippi's lack of standing, thereby affirming the Radicals' contention that the secessionist states had forfeited membership in the Union.

When the justices agreed to hear the case one week afterward, Radical newspapers shrieked of a Supreme Court that seemed to have elevated itself over the other branches—or at least the legislative branch, since the executive was in none too high repute at the time.[3]

On April 12, perhaps out of interest or perhaps as a hint, the Court chamber was filled with prominent Republican legislators. An adverse decision, a ruling that the Reconstruction Acts were unconstitutional, they seemed to say, could mean a legislative move against the justices, restriction of jurisdiction, the authorization of additional associates, or even impeachment. But after *Milligan*, to rule in favor of the Radicals after agreeing to allow Mississippi to plead its case as a sovereign state would constitute complete capitulation to Radical threats. (*Harper's Weekly* wrote that counsel for the plaintiffs were propounding "the old fallacy, thoroughly exposed and exploded, that once a State, always a State," characterizing the action as "a desperate attempt to undo in a Court the decision of a war.")[4]

So the justices did neither. And they did it quickly. The Court heard oral arguments on Friday, April 12, 1867, and the following Monday, Chief

Justice Chase delivered an opinion for the Court.[5] Familiar with John Marshall's strategic retreat in *Marbury v. Madison* in 1803, in which the chief justice eluded impeachment by coming down on both sides of the same question, Chase not only employed the same tactic but even borrowed from Marshall's *Marbury* opinion in his own.

Any question of whether the justices would rule on either the constitutionality of the Reconstruction Acts or whether the president could be named as a defendant in a lawsuit was dispelled quickly. "We shall limit our inquiry to the question presented by the objection, without expressing any opinion on the broader issues discussed in argument," Chase wrote. "The single point which requires consideration is this: Can the President be restrained by injunction from carrying into effect an act of Congress alleged to be unconstitutional?"*

Effectively dodging the first two questions, Chase then proceeded to dodge the third. In *Marbury*, Marshall had made a distinction between objective "ministerial functions," in which the president (or a cabinet officer) merely carries out a mandated duty without discretion, and subjective "executive functions," in which the president (or a cabinet officer) can use his judgment. To fully elaborate this distinction would in itself be subjective, of course—and therefore "executive"—rendering the entire argument circular. Chase, however, was hardly likely to point that out. Instead, availing himself of the convenient array of choices that such a vague differentiation allows, Chase proceeded merely to shrug and disagree with the plaintiff. Mississippi had been incorrect—Andrew Johnson's role in enforcing the Reconstruction Acts was not ministerial at all. And, since it was executive, the Court had no right to tell the head of another branch of government how to do his job. The motion was thereby denied, leaving both the constitutionality of the Reconstruction Acts and the status of Mississippi for another (hopefully quite distant) day.

But the South was not done. Sharkey and Walker, now representing Georgia, immediately amended their petition, this time seeking to enjoin Secretary of War Edwin Stanton and Generals Ulysses Grant and John Pope

---

* In his argument, Sharkey had claimed "the President of the United States is just as amenable to the process of this Court as any other man in the United States." Attorney General Stanbery had countered that "if the Supreme Court could entertain such a proceeding against the President, it must have the power to enforce its decree by imprisoning him if he did not obey it, which would amount to deposing him." Quoted in the *New York Times*, April 16, 1867.

from enforcing the Reconstruction Acts as, by doing so, Grant and Pope would annul a lawful state government and replace it with military rule. They claimed that Georgia's government, "thus reorganized [by Andrew Johnson,] was in the possession and enjoyment of all the rights and privileges in her several departments—executive, legislative, and judicial—belonging to a State in the Union under the Constitution, with the exception of a representation in the Senate and House of Representatives of the United States." In the wording of this petition, the plaintiffs were more cognizant of the prohibitions set up in *Milligan*, asserting that Georgia's government was in good order, as had been Indiana's. The plaintiffs further argued that "the intent and design of the acts of Congress, as was apparent on their face and by their terms, was to overthrow and to annul this existing State government, and to erect another and different government in its place, unauthorized by the Constitution and in defiance of its guarantees."[6]

Walking the political tightrope in this case promised to be a more delicate operation than in *Mississippi v. Johnson*, but the Court was determined to maintain its distance from both the issue and Congress. In May 1867, the justices ruled, once again unanimously, that, as Attorney General Stanbery had insisted, "the matters involved, and presented for adjudication, are political and not judicial, and, therefore, not the subject of judicial cognizance." Sharkey and Walker tried one more time, this on the basis of property rights, but the Court declined to accept the case. The Reconstruction Acts, it seemed, were not to be subject to constitutional scrutiny and "Congress [would be] left with a free hand."[7] The justices likely breathed a sigh of relief to be done with the issue.

Except they weren't.

In January 1868, the Court received a petition from one William McCardle, a newspaper editor in Vicksburg, Mississippi. McCardle had been arrested by military authorities for publishing material deemed to be promoting insurrection and was being held for trial by the army. He petitioned in federal circuit court for a writ of habeas corpus, citing *Milligan*. When his petition was denied, McCardle appealed to the Supreme Court.

Before 1867, McCardle's plea would have had no basis. The Judiciary Act of 1789, under which the duties of the national court system had been originally laid out, allowed federal courts to issue such writs in only a narrow variety of conditions. In February 1867, however, in order "to protect freedmen who were being reduced to new forms of slavery because of state vagrancy and apprentice laws," Congress had expanded habeas corpus jurisdiction so "that all federal courts and judges could grant a writ of *habeas corpus* to any person restrained of liberty in violation of the Constitution or laws of the United States."[8] The 1867 law specifically prohibited appeals from those in military custody, but with *Milligan* as precedent, McCardle sought to overturn that exception. Although William McCardle represented the very sort of person whom the federal government wished to protect the freedmen *against*, there seemed no legal impediment to his plea.

Once again, this time through the back door, the Court was being asked to determine the status of the secessionist states and, by extension, the constitutionality of the Reconstruction Acts.

Despite pressure by Radicals to decline the case, Chase decided to at least hear arguments on jurisdiction. Even before McCardle filed his motion, the Radicals had concluded that, although the Court had retreated from its *Milligan* activism in the Mississippi and Georgia cases, any chance that the justices would again rise up needed to be eliminated. More moderate Republicans also began to have qualms that the entire Reconstruction program could be eviscerated by eight men against whom Congress had no recourse.[9] A series of initiatives to control or weaken the Court was introduced, the most significant of which was an attack on judicial review, the power of the Court to overturn a duly enacted law as not comporting to the Constitution. A proposal was made that two thirds of the justices, not merely a simple majority, must agree before an act of Congress could be overturned.

In January 1868, just after Chase agreed to hear jurisdictional arguments in *McCardle*, the bill passed the House. As the measure was introduced in the Senate, Republican newspapers broadcast rumors that the Court was finally going to declare the Reconstruction Acts unconstitutional. During Senate debate, Charles Sumner, trying to ram the bill through while sentiment against the Court was high, declared, "I do not think it reasonable that a bare majority of any court should declare an act of Congress unconstitutional. I say it is contrary to reason, almost contrary to common sense." Then Sumner, overreaching as always, went on to suggest "something more than a two-thirds vote of the Supreme Court in order to set aside an act of Congress; consider whether they should not require a three-fourths vote, a four-fifths vote, perhaps a unanimous vote."[10]

Extreme as Sumner seemed to be in advocating such a drastic incursion into separation of powers, there was, in fact, nothing in the Constitution itself to prevent Congress from limiting the Court's power in precisely the manner he suggested. Quite the contrary. Depending how one read Article III, Section 2, the clause "under such exceptions and specifications that Congress shall make" could well be authorization to enact the very legislation that Radical Republicans had proposed. To demonstrate the Court's vulnerability, another bill was introduced, even more severe, denying the justices the right to rule on "political questions at all," assuming a definition of such a hazy term could be agreed on.

On February 10, 1868, the Court finally published its opinions in *Mississippi v. Johnson* and *Georgia v. Stanton*.[11] Moderate Republicans were somewhat assuaged at the finality of the wording and assumed that the Court would thus decline jurisdiction in *McCardle*. In the face of what appeared to be Court compliance, and despite the efforts by Charles Sumner to keep the two-thirds measure alive in the Senate, widespread Republican agreement to take such a drastic step could not be attained and the measure died. (Another inhibition was the disinclination by many senators to take on the constitutional crisis that such a law would inevitably incite. Since, as a result of *Marbury*, the Court itself was the final arbiter on whether or not an act of Congress was constitutional, passage of a two-thirds law could have led to the justices ruling on themselves, either by a majority or by two thirds. The potential of sending the entire government into a legal hall of mirrors was manifest.)

With the two-thirds measure defeated, to the Republicans' surprise, the Court announced that it would hear *McCardle* after all. Arguments began on March 2, and one week later the Court retired to consider the case. (Chief Justice Chase would not be present at the deliberations. He had been summoned to preside over the impeachment trial of Andrew Johnson.)

The Radicals, flushed with self-righteousness, did not wait for the Court's *McCardle* decision. Congress repealed that portion of the 1867 law that "authorized appeals from the judgment of a circuit court to the Supreme Court, 'or the exercise of any such jurisdiction by said Supreme Court on appeals which have been or may hereafter be taken.'"[12] Andrew Johnson, although in the throes of an impeachment proceeding, took the time to craft a carefully worded veto message extolling the sanctity of the Court. (He was extremely attached to the notion of separation of powers at the time.) Congress promptly overrode him.

But the Court had already heard arguments on McCardle's appeal before the repeal bill became law. Unclear was whether or not that case could be covered under the prohibitions of the repeal. The justices once again chose the path of nonconfrontation and postponed the entire case until the following term, at which time they returned to square one and once again heard arguments on jurisdiction.

Finally, in April 1869, with Andrew Johnson out of the White House and Ulysses Grant in, Chief Justice Chase, speaking for a unanimous Court, agreed that Congress had been within its rights to restrict the Court's habeas corpus jurisdiction. Citing the very clause in Article III, Section 2, which would have enabled the two-thirds law—"with such exceptions and under such regulations as Congress shall make;" the very clause John Marshall had neglected to include in his *Marbury* opinion—Chase, while "not at liberty to inquire into the motives of the legislature," admitted that "the power to make exceptions to the appellate jurisdiction of this court is given by express words." It was "quite clear that this court cannot proceed to pronounce judgment in this case, for it has no longer jurisdiction of the appeal."[13] *Ex parte McCardle* was thereby dismissed.

Although their distrust of the justices was unabated, the Radical Congress had again been denied a concrete example of judicial activism to attack. Even so, although the Court had shied away from a confrontation with the legislature—even as Andrew Johnson had not—the justices were every bit as bitter as was Johnson about what they regarded as congressional despotism. Chase, who had been compelled to preside over an impeachment trial in the Senate that he saw as little more than a bald-faced power-grab, loathed the notion of ten states being governed by the army, even though he greatly favored securing the rights of the freedmen. "I hold my old faith in universal suffrage," the chief justice wrote, "[and] in Reconstruction upon that basis . . . but I do not believe in military government for American States, nor in military commissions for the trial of American citizens, nor in the subversion of the Executive and Judicial Departments of the General Government by Congress."[14]

One must wonder why, however, if the chief justice saw the Radicals' actions as subversion, he did so little to stop it. The Court was under attack from the legislature, it was true, but abdication of constitutional responsibility was hardly a response that would protect American democracy. That the Court was merely "following the law" is also difficult to support, particularly since the same justices seem to have interpreted the very same laws differently depending on the strength and direction of the prevailing political winds.

Only after the constitutionality of the Reconstruction Acts had, for all practical purposes, been settled did the Chase Court finally rule on one of its crucial facets. On the same day as it issued its *McCardle* decision, the Court also ruled in *Texas v. White*, a financial case involving a sale of Texas state bonds during the secessionist period that Texas now wished to have returned. The more significant issue, however, was whether or not Texas had the standing to appear as a plaintiff before the Supreme Court at all. Although Article III specifically states that in cases "in which a state shall be party, the Supreme Court shall have original jurisdiction," whether or not Texas had been a state during the Civil War (when the action under consideration had taken place) had never been adjudicated. The Court had equivocated on the subject for four years. Now, with the issue largely moot, the Court's language finally became definitive.

As Chase loftily put it in his majority opinion, "We are very sensible of the magnitude and importance of this question, of the interest it excites, and of the difficulty, not to say impossibility, of so disposing of it as to satisfy the conflicting judgments of men equally enlightened, equally upright, and equally patriotic. But we meet it in the case, and we must determine it in the exercise of our best judgment, under the guidance of the Constitution alone."[15]

After some extensive exposition on the nature of a state and the history of the Union, Chase got to the only point that mattered. "The Constitution, in all its provisions, looks to an indestructible Union, composed of indestructible States. When, therefore, Texas became one of the United States, she entered into an indissoluble relation. All the obligations of perpetual union, and all the guaranties of republican government in the Union, attached at once to the State. The act which consummated her admission into the Union was something more than a compact; it was the incorporation of a new member into the political body. And it was final. The union between Texas and the other States was as complete, as perpetual, and as indissoluble as the union between the original States. There was no place for reconsideration, or revocation, except through revolution, or through consent of the States."[16]

Therefore, Chase concluded, "the ordinance of secession, adopted by the convention and ratified by a majority of the citizens of Texas, and all the acts of her legislature intended to give effect to that ordinance, were absolutely null. They were utterly without operation in law. The obligations of the State, as a member of the Union, and of every citizen of the State, as a citizen of the United States, remained perfect and unimpaired."[17]

So, after four years, an ongoing constitutional crisis, an impeachment trial, and almost unprecedented rancor among the three branches of government, the Court had finally taken a position. The reviled and departed Andrew Johnson, it seemed, had been correct all the time. The Confederacy was a nullity; its members had never ceased being part of the United States. The postwar governments Johnson had created in the South may have been racist and reprehensible, but they were perfectly in comport with the Constitution. The *Milligan* decision, therefore, should have been applied in the secessionist states. And, most significantly, the Reconstruction Acts were quite probably unconstitutional.

But none of this mattered anymore. Those stunning implications of *Texas v. White* were forced to butt up against political reality. By dragging its feet, the Court had allowed a status quo to become cemented in the South. New state constitutions had been drafted and approved; the Fourteenth Amendment had been ratified; the secessionist states were in the process of being readmitted to the Union; their senators and representatives had been elected under the new rules. That all of this would be rolled back, the military authorities withdrawn, and the Johnson governments reconstituted was inconceivable. *Texas v. White* might have application to the next insurrection but was hardly germane to the one just passed.

Texas v. White effectively marked the end of the joust between the Court and congressional Radicals. Although the Court agreed to hear *ex parte Yerger*, another habeas corpus appeal, this one based on the Judiciary Act of 1789, Yerger himself, accused of the murder of a Union soldier, was returned to civil authorities so the justices never ruled on the merits.[18] The most vitriolic congressional Radicals also made one last effort to curb the Court by introducing legislation eliminating its right of judicial review, but the bill got nowhere. In the end, the constitutionality of the Reconstruction Acts was never adjudicated, nor were the specific habeas corpus rights of an accused under extreme circumstances. The Court, which had made such an independent and aggressive postwar start with *Milligan*, had ended with the whimper of *Texas v. White*.

Some scholars have argued that the Court's behavior in the Reconstruction cases was less retreat than "judicial discretion," but from a practical standpoint, little difference seems to exist between the two.[19] Gideon Welles wrote in his diary, "The Judges of the Supreme Court have caved in, fallen through, failed, in the *McCardle* case."[20]

For freedmen, the Court's timidity seemed to constitute a victory. With the imposition of military oversight, equality in schools, civil affairs, and even election to seats of government could be approached unimpeded. But a victory based on politics, on the unwillingness of the Supreme Court to confront a swaggering legislature, was fragile indeed. With Stevens and Sumner holding sway, freedmen's gains were guaranteed. But if the mood in Congress—or in the nation at large—shifted, law or no law, a political Court might well shift right along with it.

FIVE

BAD SCIENCE AND BIG MONEY

WHETHER THEOLOGICAL OR EMPIRICAL, whites in the antebellum South had constantly sought justification for the enslavement of fellow human beings. Citations from Scripture were contorted to show that slavery was actually beneficial to barbaric, childlike Africans. Crackpot theories asserting that Negroes' diminished cranial capacity had left them unsuited to anything but menial labor were solemnly propounded by southern intellectuals—and sometimes by northerners—then eagerly embraced by planters and politicians; anything to deflect the distasteful truth that slavery was practiced simply as a result of greed and, not to put too fine a point on it, because the world allowed southerners to get away with it.

In the 1840s, a presumption took hold that blacks and whites had developed separately, from different antecedents. This theory, known as polygenism (as opposed to monogenism, or common antecedents), was developed by a Philadelphian, Samuel George Morton. Morton was a physician, geologist, and paleontologist, hailed as "the most famous American anthropologist of his day." He had gained notoriety by analyzing the fossils collected by Lewis and Clark.[1] After studying hundreds of human skulls, he concluded that "the Ethiopian (Negro)"—whom he placed on the bottom rung of his comparative ladder—"is joyous, flexible, and indolent; while the many nations which compose this race present a singular diversity of intellectual character, of which the far extreme is the lowest grade of humanity."[2] Morton died in 1851, but the standard of polygenism was then hoisted by no less a champion than the scientific titan Louis Agassiz, newly arrived at Harvard from across the Atlantic, and thought by many to be the greatest natural scientist in the world.[3]

Polygenism was far too tempting to race theorists not to spread from anthropology to sociology. Here, finally, was the scientific basis on which slave owners and other whites so disposed might deny that blacks were human—or at least human in the same sense as whites. Few northerners, even those who abhorred slavery, saw fit to question the fundamental assertion that Negroes were an intrinsically inferior race.

The year before the United States elected Abraham Lincoln president and set the nation to war, Charles Darwin, the man with whom Lincoln shared a birthday, published his ponderously titled treatise, *On the Origin of Species by Means of Natural Selection, or The Preservation of Favoured Races in the Struggle for Life*, and natural science was changed forever. When the book was released in the United States the following year, the reaction was immediate and compelling. Agassiz, at the height of his fame, condemned it as "a crude and insolent challenge to the eternal verities, objectionable as science and abominable for its religious blasphemies."[4]

Others saw things differently. The *New York Times*, for example, in a full-page review of more than four thousand words, gushed, "It is clear that here is one of the most important contributions ever made to philosophic science . . . Ten times the space given to this article would not suffice for any adequate treatment of this vast and complicated subject."[5]

Whatever one's point of view, few denied that "natural selection" represented so massive an assumptive shift that the full repercussions were impossible to predict. Most theologians understood instantly that their lives had become more complicated. But how many other fields of science would be impacted—or infected—no one knew. The *Times* seemed to recognize that Darwin's theory would soon overflow the bounds of the scientific disciplines for which it had been propounded, positing that Darwin had "laid the foundation of one of the mightiest changes in philosophical thought."[6]

The coming of the Civil War limited the short-term impact of Darwinism in the United States, but even the conflagration did not entirely stifle debate. In 1861, for example, the American Academy of Arts and Sciences published a long dissertation by Agassiz's Harvard colleague Francis Bowen, a professor of "Natural Religion, Moral Philosophy, and Civil Polity." Bowen concluded that "development theory," as it was called, "fails entirely."[7] He asserted that "Mr. Darwin is too imaginative a thinker to be a safe guide in natural science; he has unconsciously left the proper ground of physics and inductive science, and busied himself with questions of cosmogony and metaphysics."[8]

But Agassiz and his acolytes could not dissuade; Darwinism proved inexorable. Agassiz himself died in 1873, and by the mid-1870s polygenism had gone the way of phlogiston theory. (Eight of Agassiz's most prominent students had converted to Darwinism, including Agassiz's own son.)[9] That monogenism had become an ethnological ground point, however, did not mean that acceptance of fundamental racial equality would follow. The Civil War might have ended slavery as a legal entity, but it had little or no impact on the tendency toward racial stratification. If anything, natural selection, precisely because its underpinnings were so much more solid and persuasive, would prove a far greater impediment to African-American equality than polygenism ever had.

Darwin's theory was essentially a five-step process. It began with an individual variation; a mutation. The variation would be inherited and eventually work its way into the species as cumulative variation, in effect a new subspecies. The new and the old would compete for resources, by definition finite, in a "struggle for life." The struggle would culminate in the species more appropriate to its environment winning out over the lesser. Of great significance is that Darwin made no value judgments in the course of this process. More appropriate did not mean "superior." In fact, "superior" and "inferior" were characterizations that had no place in Darwin's construct. He simply asserted that evolution was a phenomenon of adaptability, not quality.

Still, if polygenism had proved too great a temptation not to extend from natural to social science, the implications for racial theorists of Darwinism were nigh unto irresistible. If in civilized society (a definition that could be manipulated to suit) one race or ethnic grouping did "better" (another definition that could be manipulated to suit), did it not then follow that the more successful group was more suited to civilized society? And the less successful, less suited? Darwinism as social science could provide justification to society's winners—the rich, the well placed, and the powerful—and therefore had the potential to create a peculiar assortment of allies. In the United States, two groups that had been at odds for decades and had recently fought one another in the Civil War—southern planters and northern capitalists—each suddenly found themselves with a vested interest in Darwin's theory being proved applicable beyond biology. To both, the notion that prosperity, or even survival, is based not on chance, luck of the draw, or coincidental advantage, but rather on measurable, scientifically verifiable evolutionary advantage, held immense appeal. (In Darwin's actual system, of course, chance and coincidence played quite a vital role, but they chose to overlook this part of the construct.)

Equally appealing in legitimizing racial stratification was the ostensible Darwinist conclusion that tinkering with the social order could have disastrous consequences. Doing so would encourage perpetuation of the less suitable group, thereby corrupting the evolutionary process and humankind in general. If left alone, the inferior groups would—and should—wither away as nature intended. *On the Origin of Species* thus came along at precisely the proper moment for those who saw the paternalism epitomized by Radical Reconstruction as a threat to the fabric of America. "Alarmed conservatives welcomed Darwinism as a fresh substantiation of an old creed. To some of them the Darwinian struggle for existence seemed to provide a new sanction for economic competition, and the survival of the fittest a new argument in opposition to state aid for the weak."[10] If Radical Reconstruction was to be an experiment in social engineering, Darwin's thesis would soon give potent ammunition to those who would allow nature—in this case defined as the status quo—to take its course. "Darwinism was one of the great informing insights . . . of the conservative mind in America."[11]

But before the Darwinian creed could be applied to questions of race, labor, or social welfare, it needed to itself mutate, to wend its way out of natural science, out of biology, and find application in the smokier social sciences. Darwin himself would have had scant interest in such an endeavor; indeed, found it ludicrous. What was needed, then, was some reputable science on which to hang the extension of the theory.

Two men, one English and one American, took up the task. The Englishman came first. His name was Herbert Spencer.

Spencer was born in 1820. His father was a religious dissenter and admirer of empirical science. As a young man, Herbert, prodigiously bright, developed quickly into a freethinking, free-market intellectual, with a deep antipathy to oligarchic authority, which he associated mainly with centralized government. (For a time, he worked as a junior editor for the *Economist*, then, as now, a passionate and articulate advocate of free trade.) Despite his predilections to human interaction uninhibited by law or custom, Spencer did not set out specifically to extend Darwinism to sociology. His goal was to establish what modern-day theoretical physicists call a "unified theory," in this case, however, creating a penumbra that would encompass both the laws of nature and those of human behavior. Spencer's work, therefore, although itself social science, is replete with analogies to natural science. Darwin was not so much his starting point—Spencer began writing of this conception almost a decade before *On the Origin of Species* was published—but rather a natural bridge, one of many, between the two.

Spencer's theories began not with natural selection, but rather by importing the First Law of Thermodynamics, also known as the Law of Conservation of Energy, an exciting subject for nineteenth-century physicists. In his social science application, the notion was termed "persistence of force."[12] Just as physical energy is never destroyed, but merely changes form, human "energy" never disappears, but evolves under pressure of the need for subsistence from lower to higher organisms.* To achieve this effect, Spencer employed the Second Law of Thermodynamics, the Law of Increasing Entropy, another concept new to the nineteenth century. Life, according to Spencer, had been traveling the path of increasing differentiation—"an advance from homogeneity of structure to heterogeneity of structure"—beginning with simple organisms, such as protozoa and amoebas, progressing toward increasing uniqueness, until, finally, the process had created Man, the most unique organism of all.[13] But even the appearance of *Homo sapiens* had not ended the progression. Man himself was evolving from lower to higher forms. "During the period in which the Earth has been peopled," Spencer wrote, "the human organism has become more heterogeneous among the civilized divisions of the species and the species, as a whole, has been growing more heterogeneous in virtue of the multiplication of races and the differentiation of these races from each other."[14] Not only had Man evolved to a higher state than the animal life he supplanted, then, but Man himself, if unencumbered by false notions of do-gooderism, would constantly tend toward higher and higher planes of existence.

Spencer also left no doubt of those attributes that would move Man on his ethereal path. "A premium on skill, intelligence, self-control, and the power to adapt through technological innovation . . . had stimulated human advancement and selected the best of each generation for survival."[15] Spencer, not Darwin, initiated the phrase "survival of the fittest."[16]

Opponents of social engineering—or of the government-sponsored elevation of blacks in the South—could not have found a more perfect ally.

---

* Spencer's theory was actually closer to Lamarck than Darwin. At the end of the eighteenth century, Jean-Baptiste Lamarck, a French biologist, proposed that nonphysical alterations to an organism acquired during its life span from, say, hard work or intense study would then be passed to its offspring. Lamarck had a devoted following until Darwinism eventually overwhelmed his hypothesis.

"Spencer deplored not only poor laws, but also state-supported education, sanitary supervision . . . regulation of housing conditions, and even state protection of the ignorant against medical quacks."[17] Nothing could be more anathema, then, than a concentrated program that aimed to artificially prop up millions of people so inferior—so unfit—that nature had selected them to be slaves.

Spencer's theories were not specific to race—he would differentiate between poor and rich as readily as between black and white—but for Americans so disposed, the leap could not have been easier. In fact, Spencer's divisions were sufficiently ambiguous to apply equally to race or class. "Beginning with a barbarous tribe," he wrote, "almost if not quite homogeneous in the functions of its members, the progress has been, and still is, towards an economic aggregation of the whole human race, growing ever more heterogeneous in respect of the separate functions assumed by separate nations, the separate functions assumed by the local sections of each nation, the separate functions assumed by the many kinds of makers and traders in each town, and the separate functions assumed by the workers united in producing each commodity." Those races or classes which seemed to thrive in modern society, even on a relative basis, could be seen as more suited to modernity than those that did not. "Not only is the law thus clearly exemplified in the evolution of the social organism, but it is exemplified with equal clearness in the evolution of all products of human thought and action."[18] Samuel George Morton's joyous, flexible, indolent black man of the lowest-level intellect could therefore exist just as easily in Spencer's evolutionary model as in the recently discredited polygenism.

As America emerged from war, this belief that wealth and power were not only justified, but were, in fact, expressions of virtue and progress, was received with enthusiasm by segments of a shattered nation eager to enhance both. The wealthier, the more powerful one became, even at the expense of his fellows—perhaps *especially* at the expense of his fellows—the more he was contributing to the advancement of the human race. As a result, Spencer acquired converts among the rich and successful and achieved greater popularity on this side of the Atlantic than his own.

Late nineteenth-century America became the perfect laboratory to test Spencerian theories, "a vast human caricature of the Darwinian struggle for existence and survival of the fittest."[19] When he visited the United States for the first time in 1882, Spencer was feted as a hero by no less than Andrew

Carnegie, who "became his intimate friend and showered him with favors."[20] Carnegie, who would later produce a paean to the very values Spencer promoted, *The Gospel of Wealth*, extolled his first exposure to Darwinism and Spencerism as if, as the above title suggests, describing a religious conversion.[21] "I remember that light came as in a flood and all was clear. Not only had I got rid of theology and the supernatural, but I had found the truth of evolution. 'All is well since all grows better,' became my motto, my true source of comfort."[22]

Carnegie's inner conflict between religion and business practices epitomized the odd dichotomy of Social Darwinism as a whole. For all that the philosophy was conservative, it was also secular, placing theologians on the horns of a dilemma that, historically, they rarely had been forced to face. How could men whose job it was to uphold "religious sanction for morals" square the "ruthless methods in business and politics" that Social Darwinism encouraged? To oppose evolution seemed also to oppose progress and the betterment of the human condition. "'The survival of the fittest' became the rationale of those who shed moral scruples, in the business field at least, in their climb to wealth and economic power."[23]

After Carnegie, the most faithful Spencer admirer was John D. Rockefeller. As Rockefeller declared to his Sunday school class, "The growth of a large business is merely a survival of the fittest . . . The American Beauty rose can be produced in the splendor and fragrance which bring cheer to its beholder only by sacrificing the early buds which grow up around it. This is not an evil tendency in business. It is merely the working-out of a law of nature and a law of God."[24]

That the great American entrepreneurs of the nineteenth century would seize upon a scientific construct that extolled both their virtues and values is no surprise, but rarely has theory and practice found a more perfect match. Although the business titans were "distinctive individuals with widely varying personalities," in addition to persistence and determination, all seemed to share "a fierce drive to succeed" in which they "let no obstacle stand in their way." These men already considered themselves superior; how pleasant, then, to have their opinion confirmed by science.

Ironically, considering the manner in which his theories would be applied, Spencer always saw himself as contributing to rather than detracting from an ethical and even a charitable existence. He merely believed, as had Adam Smith before him, that the unfettered pursuit of individual wealth, and therefore power, led to a society with better conditions for all, the poor and powerless being dragged along in the wake of the ambitious and successful. Some dregs would drop away, it was true, but only to allow the more fit to gain a share of resources that, regardless of how prosperous a society might become, would never be sufficient for all.[25]

The endorsement of Carnegie, Rockefeller, and other industrialists notwithstanding, and regardless of how popular was the man himself, Spencer's notions needed American champions—intellectuals, not businessmen—to take genuine root in the United States. By the early 1870s, a number of prominent thinkers had made clear that they were eager to make themselves available for the role. The man who eventually emerged from a crowded field was a Yale professor of political and social science named William Graham Sumner.* During his tenure at Yale from 1872 to 1910, Sumner was one of the most influential academicians in the nation, a founder of modern sociology. For most of that period, although known for his dour personality and glum outlook, Sumner was called "probably the most popular and inspiring teacher that Yale University or American social science has produced."[26]

Sumner was a product of the hardworking Protestant middle class whose virtues he would later extol in a series of essays featuring "The Forgotten Man." He trained for the Episcopal ministry but turned to academia because "he wanted to be able to turn his attention to political, economic, and social questions rather than to the preparation of sermons on theological subjects."[27] He was, however, described as creating "an intellectual ministry" among his students.

His writing is terse, incisive, and dogmatic. It is difficult to imagine a man less sentimental. Sumner, at various times, expressed antipathy for "gushers," "smart Alecks," "ignorant uplifters," "false sentimentalists," "pseudo research workers," "adjusters," "incompetent social engineers," "noise-makers," and "publicity seekers," who formed a "Mutual Back-patting Insurance Co."[28] His essential philosophy as noted by one of his students was "Don't be a damn fool!"

Still, Sumner's adopted virtues were those of white America. In a treatise titled "What the Classes Owe Each Other," Sumner utilized Darwin's notion of the struggle for existence as his starting point, his "first fact of life." He then asserted that "the greatest step forward in this struggle is the production of capital, which increases the fruitfulness of labor and provides the

---

* No relation to Charles Sumner, the Radical senator.

necessary means for an advancement of civilization." Here was the most direct link of Darwin to the laissez-faire capitalism of which Sumner would be a ferocious defender his entire life. "If the fittest are to be allowed to survive," Sumner insisted, "if the benefits of efficient management are to be made available to society, the captains of industry must be rewarded for their unique organizing talent."[29] Wealth therefore became not simply the means by which the fittest survive, but the proof of such fitness itself.

Then, in true Darwinian fashion, fitness should be passed on. Sumner believed fervently that society would advance only if wealth was perpetuated from one generation to the next, that "hereditary wealth assures the enterprising and industrious man that he may preserve in his children the virtues which have enabled him to enrich the community." An attempt to limit inheritance was an attack on the family, the single bedrock institution of any successful society. To Sumner, such an act reduced men to "swine." The notion of the sanctity of family is all well and good, of course, assuming that a family unit was allowed to exist and not, as had been true for most slaves, been either ignored or forcibly torn asunder.

If capitalism was to be the vehicle to the ennobling of humankind, contract would be the instrument. Sumner separated "rule by contract" from "rule by sentiment," with the latter surely more backward than the former. "Contract is rational . . . It is also realistic, cold, and matter-of-fact. A contract is based on sufficient reason, not on custom or prescription . . . It endures only so long as the reason for it endures . . . It seems impossible that any one who has studied the matter should doubt that we have gained immeasurably, and that our further gains lie in going forward, not in going backward."[30]

But Sumner, his middle-class roots deep and strong, could never reconcile the relation of the accomplishments of these captains of industry to crass power politics. He, like Spencer, considered himself a moralist and in his "Forgotten Man" essays, he exalted the diligent, selfless members of the middle class who toiled honestly, lived ethically, and strove virtuously but were often destroyed by greed or the power of interest groups. Despite being accused by both progressives and socialists as a tool of the rich, Sumner despised "plutocrats," which of course took in some of the very men he had extolled as society's beacons, men who revered Herbert Spencer. As a result, Sumner, although his defense of laissez-faire capitalism was more unashamed than Spencer's, never received the acclaim in the business community as had his British colleague.[31]

Sumner did not see much hope for individuals or groups that had not in the past measured up. "Social mores," which determined the groups that might potentially thrive and those that would fail, were something of a stacked deck. These values, Sumner wrote, "have a model of the man-as-he-should-be to which they mould him, in spite of himself and without his knowledge. If he submits and consents, he is taken up and may attain great social success. If he resists and dissents, he is thrown out and may be trodden under foot. The mores are therefore an engine of social selection . . . It is vain to imagine that a 'scientific man' can divest himself of prejudice or previous opinion, and put himself in an attitude of neutral independence towards the mores. He might as well try to get gravity or pressure out of the atmosphere."[32] Black Americans, then, with their lack of appropriate grounding in those skills and attributes that lead to "social success," were victims of inferior mores and seemed doomed to be among those "trodden under foot."

On first blush, Spencer and Sumner seemed to be well within Darwinian boundaries. If the fittest will survive biologically, why not socially? Does it not follow that the superior will thrive and the inferior fall away? But Darwin's theory is based on *individual* mutations slowly but inexorably altering a species' makeup to allow it to survive in an inhospitable climate. Spencer and Sumner presupposed either a lack of mutation, or that an entire substratum would be altered virtually at once to adapt to a change in socioeconomic environment. Spencer and Sumner were not describing evolution as much as war; absent total incompetence in command, the superior force will generally win a battle, but that victory hardly extrapolates to an advancement of the species. In fact, since often it is the brutish and barbarous who triumph in war at the expense of the enlightened and the virtuous, survival of the propertied classes might as easily be seen as a step downward rather than a step up.

This is not to say that the doctrine that came to be known as "Social Darwinism" near the turn of the century was universally accepted. Spencer and Sumner had many opponents among intellectuals.[33] But their theories were far too appealing to political and financial elites to fail to be embraced. Social Darwinism had given the capitalist class a great gift: the ability to consider itself virtuous while acting in blatant self-interest. In the 1780s, slaveholders brandished their Bibles; in the 1880s, Andrew Carnegie brandished *Social Statics*. Although most who espoused the work of Spencer and Sumner believed in the inherent inferiority of the black race—most Americans, after all, did—many others were not racist per se, but merely concluded that blacks' inferior position had made them "less fit" to thrive in a white, modern society. For those who would advance the cause of the newly freed slaves, this ambiguity created a far more elusive target. How could one assert the equality of African-Americans without, in the process, denouncing what was rapidly becoming acknowledged as one of the greatest scientific advances in history? Arguing that Darwinism, while perfectly sound natural science, was shoddy social science was unlikely to gain much support in society at large.

But, Andrew Carnegie notwithstanding, plutocrats like Pierpont Morgan, John Jacob Astor, and Philip Armour did not parade about waving Spencer's work like a Maoist proffering the Little Red Book during the Cultural Revolution. For most, Social Darwinism was mood, not mantra. The propertied classes didn't really need scientific justification for their behavior; but it was nice to have, particularly among the more intellectual.[34]

Call it Social Darwinism or another name, but the pseudoscience of the nineteenth century justified both the amassing of great wealth by any means necessary and artificially maintaining a position in society by repressing potential competition as more than acts of greed or selfishness. They acquired the mantle of a "higher calling," an improvement of the human condition, which only coincidentally provided gratification or advantage to the perpetrator.

Also easy to overlook is the admiration the new entrepreneur class inspired among ordinary Americans in the 1870s and 1880s. Denunciations of greed and profiteering, for all their passion, tended to be centered in small but vocal segments of society. For the most part, Carnegie, Rockefeller, Morgan, Marshall Field, Gustavus Swift, and Frederick Pabst were heroes, what other Americans aspired to become. That these men, smart, innovative, ruthlessly efficient, and financially astute, epitomized a higher order of human being engendered envy in most and surprised few.

Even if a man could not be a railroad magnate or a steel baron, he could still function in the orbit of industry, gaining wealth for himself while helping America and the human race hurtle forward to previously unimagined glories. Those who toiled in support of capitalists, then—lawyers, for example—could only feel a rush of pride in the knowledge that while they enriched themselves, they were also enriching society. Some of those lawyers found their way to the Supreme Court.

By linking the industrialists of the North with the planter class of the South, Social Darwinism also helped solidify a national socioeconomic elite. The planters had been disemboweled by war and disenfranchised by Reconstruction, but those who survived still represented the most sophisticated, educated, politically experienced, and socially astute segment of southern society. To imagine that they would simply cede power and the remains of their wealth to some new order imposed by men they considered foreigners was fanciful. And while the northern industrialists might be contemptuous of the plantation system, they had more in common with men who had been on a similar economic plane than with a group of newly freed blacks or white liberal do-gooders. The planters were aware that if they could survive the war's aftermath, they and their offspring stood a fair chance of regaining prosperity, if only the efforts of those social engineers in Washington could be turned aside. This confluence of interests could, and eventually would, set a base value system in America that would hardly favor the freedmen.

SIX

Corporate Presidency: Ulysses Grant and the Court

L ITTLE DEBATE EXISTS among historians as to Ulysses Grant's over-all presidential fitness. The Grant presidency was infamous for cronyism, the appointment of unknown mediocrities, and widespread corruption; but the years from 1868 to 1876 were, ironically, also a high-water mark for African-American liberty and equality of civil access in the United States. Under Grant, the Reconstruction Acts were enforced by military authority, and the South, to the intense displeasure of the vast majority of its residents, showed glimmers of becoming a society based on a different set of parameters than ever before in its history.

In recent decades, some historians have posited that the Reconstruction experiment, although flawed and uneven, achieved some very real gains, which, if the program had been allowed to continue, might have permanently transformed the old Confederacy. For a century following the Civil War, however, Sumner's and Stevens's creation was considered by traditionalist historians as a blight on the democratic process. Articles, cartoons, and even a classic motion picture, Birth of a Nation, perpetuated images of lazy, brutish, illiterate black men, manipulated by greedy, venal carpetbaggers or scalawags. Conniving whites and bestial blacks made a mockery of government and drove the South toward chaos and anarchy, while "proper" white, Christian society was forced to stand helplessly by, prohibited by Yankee soldiers from interfering in their own destruction. Southern women were often prominently featured in these caricatures as threatened or defiled victims, the perpetrators of this myth conveniently forgetting that black women had been regularly, systematically, and legally raped for the two centuries in which slavery had flourished.[1] Stevens in particular was vilified as a despot, a borderline fascist. At best, the Negro was portrayed as childlike and innocent, not inherently evil but certainly not up to the task of self-government.

After a time, traditionalists wrote with relief of "Redeemers," right-thinking southerners (all of whom were white) rose up against these injustices and returned democracy, the Constitution, and good government to the southern states. The Negro, although free, was returned to the subservient position that he deserved, allowed to thrive in those simple tasks for which he was suited. Andrew Johnson, according to this legend, was a moderate and fair-minded man, but his plans to continue the policies of Abraham Lincoln were thwarted by Stevens, Sumner, and other fire-breathing Radicals.*

Nowhere was the traditionalist view of the Reconstruction black man painted more persuasively than in an article in the January 1901 edition of the *Atlantic Monthly*, penned by one of the nation's most prominent historians. He accused Radical Republicans of using "their restored power [to bring] absolute shipwreck upon the President's [Johnson's] plans." He added:

> An extraordinary and very perilous state of affairs had been created in the South by the sudden and absolute emancipation of the negroes, and it was not strange that the southern legislatures should deem it necessary to take extraordinary steps to guard against the manifest and pressing dangers which it entailed. Here was a vast laboring, landless, homeless class, once slaves, now free; unpracticed in liberty, unschooled in self-control; never sobered by the discipline of self-support, never established in any habit of prudence; excited by a freedom they did not understand, exalted by false hopes; bewildered and without leaders, and yet insolent and aggressive; sick of work, covetous of pleasure, a host of dusky children untimely put out of school.

The historian went on to defend the laws restricting Negro freedom and establishing severe limits on the movement and exercise of fundamental

---

* A particularly dreadful 1942 film, *Tennessee Johnson*, in which Van Heflin plays Andrew Johnson and a sneering Lionel Barrymore oils his way through as Thaddeus Stevens, might well have marked the low point of the traditionalist treatment. A Hollywood movie is just that, of course, but the portrayals of Johnson and Stevens were widely accepted as essentially accurate. Sumner was luckier; he was not portrayed in the film at all.

rights and even of vagrancy laws that reestablished slavery in all but name. He denounced the Freedmen's Bureau and the wresting of Reconstruction away from Andrew Johnson by Stevens and Sumner, claiming that the Johnson Reconstruction governments were precisely as they would have looked if Abraham Lincoln had lived.

The author of this piece was no rabid racist, no devotee of pseudoscience, but rather a respected faculty member of one of America's preeminent institutions of higher learning and the following year would become its president. Ten years after that, he would be elected president of the United States. The institution was Princeton, and the historian was Woodrow Wilson.[2]

The most glaring mischaracterization in the traditionalist construct was the notion of a government dominated by illiterate blacks. In fact, the first African-Americans were not seated in Congress until 1870, when Joseph H. Rainey of South Carolina entered the House of Representatives, and Hiram R. Revels of Mississippi became the first black senator. (Revels was later referred to, probably by Wendell Phillips, as "the Fifteenth Amendment in flesh and blood.")

During Reconstruction, only sixteen African-Americans served in Congress; one, P. B. S. Pinchback, as governor, in Louisiana; six as lieutenant governors; two as state treasurers; four as superintendents of education; and eight in the largely ceremonial position of secretary of state. In national office, the number split roughly equally between freedmen and freeborn. Larger numbers of African-Americans served in lower-level state offices, particularly as postmasters and justices of the peace, but only in a few isolated cases represented a significant force in state or local governments. The vast majority of political decisions during Reconstruction were made by whites, and the vast majority of these whites were southern born. Forgotten in the rush of propaganda was that a hefty white minority in the South had opposed secession, either actively or passively, and were thus waiting in the wings when the war ended. Upon ratification of the Fifteenth Amendment, although blacks were free to elect a member of their own race regardless of qualifications, they often chose to vote for whites. In fact, evidence indicates that newly enfranchised African-American voters followed President Grant's advice and took their responsibilities quite seriously.[3]

Ironically, the relative paucity of African-Americans in government has often been seized on to demonstrate that, in the end, Reconstruction changed the South, and America as a whole, very little. While from the standpoint of practical politics that may well be true, it misses the point. Certainly, while the numbers of black legislators were not nearly proportionate to black residents, or even black voters in the Reconstruction South, that an African-American could enter the United States Congress as a duly elected representative of any state would have been considered laughable just a decade earlier. Moreover, the local positions, while lacking in the prestige of the more glamorous state and national offices, afforded African-Americans, for the first time, a significant degree of control over their daily lives. That the experiment would end before its full effects could be felt is undeniable, but one need only to view the vitriol of its opponents to appreciate its impact.[4]

The claim that a number of the new legislators or administrators had never learned to read and write is true, but more thorough scholarship has found ample evidence that most of these, like black voters, were by and large serious men who, during a period of immense economic hardship, achieved some major successes, particularly in advancing public education.

Another reason that more African-Americans were not represented in government was that, like many whites, they saw public service as a thankless endeavor in which one generally ended up poorer than when one began.[5] More than a few African-Americans, most but not all freeborn with at least a smattering of education, chose to amass wealth rather than political power. Contract rights being ensured by both legislation and constitutional amendment, unique business opportunities existed for black Americans.

To whichever interpretation of Reconstruction one subscribes, that progress in integrating freedmen and freeborn blacks into the political mainstream is impossible to deny. The debate, rather, seems to center on whether or not this was a positive development. But all of this advancement, if indeed that is what it was, did not take place in an atmosphere of acquiescence and cooperation from the white South. The "Redeemers," resistance movements that ran the gamut from the oratorical to the violent, worked tirelessly both in the legitimate political arena and in more disagreeable incarnations (of which the Ku Klux Klan was the most notorious, but hardly unique) to undermine both the letter and the spirit of the Reconstruction Acts. In order to make any of the Reconstruction gains permanent, then, once the coercive force of the army was gone, an equally potent local constabulary would have to replace it, and that, in turn, could not be achieved without the support of the courts.

That Ulysses Grant presided over a nation edging toward equal rights, no matter how stutteringly, in no way meant that the president himself felt a personal commitment to the cause. His administration, corruption-ridden as it was, epitomized the shift from the party of equal rights to the party of business rights. Grant's appointments to the Supreme Court turned out to be instrumental in undoing the very growth of equal opportunity that might have permanently altered history's view of his administration.

After Andrew Johnson was safely out of the White House, a relieved Congress almost immediately undertook to free the Court from some of the strictures it had instituted to hamstring the reviled Tennesseean. On April 10, 1869, only one month after Grant took office, "An Act to Amend the Judicial System of the United States" was passed into law. The legislation contained three major alterations to the federal court system, each of which would bear significantly on the coming battles over civil rights. Most significantly, the number of Supreme Court justices was set at nine, thus rescinding the reductions made in 1866. As eight justices were then impaneled, Grant would have one vacancy to fill immediately. The law also, for the first time, established pensions for the federal judges. Any judge who had served for ten years and was at least seventy years old could retire on whatever salary he was receiving at the time he left the bench. Justice Grier, who was ill and approaching senility, immediately took advantage of that provision, leaving the new president a second seat to fill. Finally, the law created nine federal circuits, each to be manned by a circuit court judge, reducing the frequency with which Supreme Court justices were required to ride circuit from every year to every two. This last measure allowed Grant additional senior appointments.[6]

The circuit court nominations were announced on December 8, 1869, at much the same time as Radical Republicans had initiated their final, failed, post-*Yerger* attempts to restrict the Court's jurisdiction. That these circuit court judges were confirmed largely without incident was primarily the work of Grant's attorney general, Ebenezer Rockwood Hoar. An atypically competent member of Grant's cabinet, a flinty, plainspoken Yankee from Massachusetts, the grandson of Roger Sherman, another flinty, plainspoken

Yankee who had been a key member of the Constitutional Convention of 1787, Hoar valued honesty, the rule of law, and individual industry. Although he was no Radical, he abhorred slavery. He had also volubly opposed Andrew Johnson's impeachment and was a strong advocate of transition to a meritocracy through civil service reform, neither of which endeared him to his fellow Republicans in the Senate. (Meritocracy was not a concept that would become synonymous with the Grant administration.) Still, while both Hoar's abilities and his integrity might be unquestioned, he was widely considered one of the most personally offensive men in Washington. (As a Massachusetts judge, Hoar had once dismissed, on a technicality, a libel suit brought by Benjamin Butler against a detractor who insisted Butler looked precisely like "a Borneo ape"—no small slight in those post-Darwin years— earning Butler's undying enmity.)

With the circuit courts manned, Grant turned his attention to the Supreme Court. To fill one vacant seat, on December 14, 1869, the president nominated the very same Ebenezer Hoar. From a quality standpoint, at least, the appointment seemed a good one. "His elevation to the Supreme bench is received with profound satisfaction by all," reported the *New York Times* rosily, "and by none more than those who have business with the Attorney general's office."[7] "It is gratifying proof of the increased respect in which the Supreme Court is held that we do not hear of any attempt to foist upon it . . . a partisan Judge," reported the *Nation*. "The present Chief Justice [Chase] has been 'in politics' enough . . . If Judge Hoar is appointed, the appointment will be an admirable one."[8]

Unfortunately, a number of senators who had experienced Hoar's inflexible morality, his sharp tongue, and his dismissive self-righteousness did not agree. In fact, at least two influential senators from Hoar's New England were spoiling to torpedo his nomination, one of them being the Borneo ape himself, Benjamin Butler.[9] Within weeks, the *Times* changed its tune. "The chief opposition [to his confirmation] has unquestionably been inspired by a sense of the affronts which Senators and Representatives have received at his hands," the newspaper wrote.[10] Hoar's nomination was also questionable on sectional grounds. The circuit over which he would preside included a number of southern states, and legislators from those states, even under Reconstruction governments, objected to not having one of their own fill the seat. Before long, that the nomination might not even make it out of committee became apparent. Grant was urged to withdraw the nomination, but he refused. Ultimately, Hoar's appointment was not approved. On February 3, 1870, he was rejected by a vote of 33–24.

The other seat seemed to promise no similar difficulty. To replace Grier, Grant nominated Edwin Stanton, Lincoln's secretary of war, "Mars," as the martyred president had referred to him. Stanton was none too popular personally either, but had none of Hoar's political baggage. He had, in fact, been recommended to President Grant in a petition signed by a number of key senators. He was nominated on December 20, 1869, and was, as promised, confirmed the same day. The appointment was to take effect at the beginning of the February 1, 1870, term. Unfortunately for Grant, Stanton died four days later under questionable circumstances, having never taken his oath of office.[11] By early February, when Hoar's rejection was certain, Grant once more had two vacancies to fill.

Hoar's rejection and Stanton's death would have immense impact, not simply for the Court but for the struggle for African-American equality as well. Instead of the independent Stanton, the nation got William Strong; instead of the indomitable Hoar, Joseph P. Bradley. These two justices, perhaps the first "corporate appointments" in Court history, marked a dramatic change in Court politics and the beginning of the end of the quest for equal rights.

It all came down to a question of money. Paper money, to be precise.

On February 25, 1862, Congress passed the first Legal Tender Act, an authorization for the Treasury to issue "greenbacks," paper money not backed by gold. The law stated that greenbacks "shall be receivable in payment of all taxes, internal duties, excises, debts and demands of every kind due to the United States, except duties on imports, and of all claims and demands against the United States, of every kind whatsoever, except for interest upon bonds and notes, which shall be paid in coin: and shall also be lawful money and a legal tender in payment of all debts, public and private, within the United States, except duties on imports and interest as aforesaid."[12]

Although paper money had been employed in certain states, never before had an unbacked national paper currency been in circulation. But President Lincoln and then-Secretary of the Treasury Salmon P. Chase, needing to finance a costly war, felt they had little choice. Gold reserves were at such critically low levels that first the government and then banks had been forced to suspend specie payments. There simply wasn't enough gold to pay on demand in exchange for the government bills and state bank bills that were in general circulation as money. The Treasury was unable to persuade bankers to lend to the United States, even at an interest rate of over 7 percent. The United States was $60 million in debt and running expenses of $2 million per day.

Two alternatives were available: issue bonds and sell them in the open market, or print paper money. (Raising taxes, which would have solved the problem if initiated when the war began, would, by 1862, have brought in funds at far too slow a pace.) Bonds could only have been sold at disastrous discounts and would have highlighted the weakness of the federal government, further undermining confidence in a war none too popular to begin with. Chase convinced Congress that printing paper money would grease the wheels of commerce, keep goods flowing through the economy, and thereby bring in revenues necessary to keep the government functioning. (In this case, North emulated South; the Confederacy had issued paper money from the war's inception.) Exempting "interest on bonds and notes," Chase believed, was necessary for a nation whose need to borrow might remain acute for the foreseeable future. The exemption on import duties meant the Treasury could continue to bank, in gold, the revenues generated from international trade.

Printing money was, and still is, inflationary. The more actual money in circulation, the less each unit is worth, and the more units it takes to buy a commodity. Also then as now, inflation favors debtors over creditors, as long as the debts were initiated before inflation set in. Paying back a fixed amount is easier when that fixed amount is worth less and therefore easier to come by. Bankers, the classic creditor class, will react to inflation by charging higher rates of interest; new debtors, such as governments issuing bonds, are therefore forced to offer a higher rate of interest in order to make their issuance attractive to investors.

Although the Lincoln administration had attempted to cool resulting inflation by the imposition of new taxes, the shock engendered by the sudden infusion of $450 million into an economy that had always seen a money supply limited to what could be backed by gold could not be planned for.[13] Paper money had never been allowed as payment of private obligations before. With its issuance, gold immediately began trading at a premium, or conversely, paper traded at a discount. In an instant, then, debtors found themselves able to pay back loans at much less in real terms than that which they had borrowed. Not surprisingly, the Legal Tender Acts engendered an instant round of lawsuits.

The Court had dodged the paper money issue in 1863, using its standard wartime ploy of denying jurisdiction.[14] But with the war over and the currency still diluted, little choice remained but to adjudicate the question. The legality of paper money was not a transitory issue, like war powers or habeas corpus. The nation, for better or worse, had been operating for a number of years under the Legal Tender Acts, and a formal decision as to their constitutionality would be necessary to maintain long-term economic growth. Much of the industrial boom, particularly in railroads, had been created by debt financing.[15] Creditors would, of course, be thrilled to see the money they received in repayment of those debts be worth a good deal more than when they had loaned it out, but rescinding the Legal Tender Acts might constrict further expansion.

In a number of cases the Court, although ruling narrowly, had given indications that the justices might well decide against paper money.[16] There seemed to be a clear division among the justices; Democrats Field, Grier, Nelson, and Clifford, joined by the chief justice, took a narrow view of the "necessary and proper" authorization in the Constitution (although Chase, as treasury secretary, had seen the matter differently), while Republicans Davis, Swayne, and Miller took a broader view. Nothing definitive, however, was announced. Finally, on February 7, 1870, in *Hepburn v. Griswold*, the Court gave clear indications of its overall intentions.

In June 1860, Susan P. Hepburn had given a promissory note to Henry A. Griswold for $11,250 to be paid on or before February 20, 1862, five days before the first Legal Tender Act had been enacted. Thus, the entire term of the debt fell within a period where payment of private debts could "lawfully be tendered [only in] gold and silver coin."[17] Susan Hepburn did not pay the debt, which began to accrue interest. Henry Griswold sued in chancery court in Kentucky, and in March 1864, Mrs. Hepburn paid $12,720 to settle the claim. She paid in greenbacks. Griswold refused to accept the paper, so Mrs. Hepburn paid the money to the court, which then declared the debt satisfied. The ruling was then reversed in Kentucky, and Susan Hepburn appealed to the Supreme Court.

The decision was 4–3 for Griswold, once again, Chase excepted, breaking along Democrat/Republican lines. (The doddering Justice Grier was too ill to take part, although Chase took pains to note that he favored the ruling.) The chief justice wrote for the majority.

He first noted the economics of the situation.

> There is a well known law of currency that notes or promises to pay, unless made conveniently and promptly convertible into coin at the will of the holder, can never, except under unusual and abnormal conditions, be at par in circulation with coin. It is an equally well known law that depreciation of notes must increase with the increase of the quantity put in circulation and the diminution of confidence in the ability or disposition to redeem. Their appreciation follows the reversal of these conditions. No act making them a legal tender can change materially the operation of these laws. Their force has been strikingly exemplified in the history of the United States notes. Beginning with a very slight depreciation when first issued, in March, 1862, they sank in July, 1864, to the rate of two dollars and eighty-five cents for a dollar in gold, and then rose until recently a dollar and twenty cents in paper became equal to a gold dollar.[18]

Significant in this exposition is the appreciation of greenbacks to eighty-three cents on the dollar from thirty-five cents during the war. What Chase, who certainly understood finance, neglected to add was that, with increased demand for paper against gold, the currency was becoming a more accepted means of exchange.

For the purposes of the case at hand, of course, Griswold, who was paid in 1864, had only received one third the value to which he was entitled. This, Chase insisted, was an arbitrary alteration by the federal government of constitutional guarantees of contract. While the chief justice conceded that, on occasion, contract rights must be subordinated to the necessities of governance, as during time of war, the power was essentially an emergency one and could not, under the necessary and proper clause, extend to quotidian administration of government. The United States must, in the ordinary course of things, protect, not arbitrarily abrogate, rights conferred by grant or contract. In other words, the definitions of what the federal government could and could not do were a good deal narrower than the paper money advocates would have them.

The impact, in this case, was plain. "To compel the creditor to accept less than the amount of the debt, or to compel him to accept something which might bear the same name but was in reality less valuable, was in effect to take private property without compensation, and not in the due course of law."[19] Any act of Congress that purported to such an end was thus unconstitutional.

While Chase took pains to apply the *Hepburn* decision specifically to contracts entered into before the Legal Tender Acts were enacted, the wording left no doubt among Republicans (and railroad men) that the Legal Tender Acts were living on borrowed time.

The same day *Hepburn* was announced, Ulysses Grant nominated Strong and Bradley to the Court. If both were confirmed, what had been a 4–3 majority against paper money—Grier being no longer in the equation—would be transformed into a 5–4 majority in favor. For whatever other views the two men held, each, as an attorney, had garnered some significant portion of their income representing railroads.[20] Ebenezer Hoar, who had himself been rejected for a seat on the Court, became determined to identify nominees who would reverse the decision of the Chase Court. Whether he did so for retribution or simply on philosophical grounds is not known, but Hoar had written of *Hepburn*, "Chase's decision on legal tender is not constitution, nor right reason, nor safe doctrine for the country in its time of peril, in my opinion, and I shall not stand it if I can help it."[21] Grant, for his part, later admitted that he knew Strong "had given a decision sustaining the constitutionality" of the Legal Tender Acts as a Pennsylvania judge, and "he had reason to believe Judge Bradley's opinion tended in the same direction."

Both Bradley and Strong were confirmed without delay. William Strong would serve on the Court for ten years; Joseph Bradley would serve for more than two decades and become one of the most important men in American history, with a unique distinction that almost certainly will never be matched.

As soon as they were seated, Strong and Bradley joined with the three dissenters in *Hepburn* to petition the chief justice to rehear the issue. Chase was furious, but, with a number of cases on the docket bearing on the paper money issue, there was little he could do. Within one year, the *Hepburn* decision had been overruled, and both overheated industrialization and financial speculation (which more often than not go hand in hand) had received the imprimatur of the high court.

But Grant was not done with the judiciary. Late in 1872, Justice Nelson, who had sat on the Court since the Tyler administration, resigned. To replace Nelson, Roscoe Conkling, a New York senator and powerful political boss, "the champion of partisanship," persuaded Grant to appoint his crony, Ward Hunt.[22] Hunt, by all accounts a lackluster mediocrity, arrived just in time to sit on a rehearing of a pivotal case involving New Orleans butchers.[23]

Dubbed the *Slaughterhouse Cases*, the action stemmed from an effort by the city of New Orleans to prevent animal wastes from contaminating the city's drinking water. The slaughterhouses in question were along the Mississippi River, north of the city, and the butchers who worked in the facilities blithely tossed animal intestines, kidneys, urine, dung, and other unwanted by-products into the river. The result was regular cholera and yellow fever epidemics within the city's border.

At the city's request, the Louisiana legislature enacted a law relocating the butchers south of the city at a facility run by a private corporation to be established under state auspices from which the butchers would obtain licenses. The licenses would be granted without favoritism or prejudice, and, in fact, none was ever alleged. This centralized facility would not only protect the city's water supply but also set a means by which animals for slaughter could be inspected for disease. The notion was not new. A number of other major cities, including New York and Boston (but not Chicago), had enacted similar legislation, engendering little more than grumbling from the affected butchers.

The New Orleans butchers, however, brought suit. The Crescent City Live-Stock Landing and Slaughter-House Company, they claimed, was a monopoly that would provide advantage to a few "at the expense of the great body of the community of New Orleans," although who would actually be harmed by the legislation was never made precise. The suit also claimed that butchers would be prevented from plying their trade, a claim that seemed to have little basis in fact. What made this suit noteworthy, however, were not the particulars of the case, but rather the provision on which it was based. For the butchers sued not under the commerce clause of the Constitution or some other piece of legislation relating to business, but under the "due process," "privileges and immunities," and "equal protection clauses" of the Fourteenth Amendment.

The butchers' lawyer was none other than former Supreme Court associate justice John Campbell, whose resignation had allowed President Lincoln to appoint David Davis. Campbell had become an indefatigable advocate in cases testing the Reconstruction Acts. His avenue of attack for the butchers, to apply the Fourteenth Amendment not as race-based but universally, would have immense consequences in the future.

But not, however, for his clients. Campbell lost all the way up the line and fared no better in the Supreme Court. He did manage to persuade four justices of his argument, including the newly seated Joseph Bradley and Lincoln appointees Chase, Field, and Swayne. The other five justices, however, including Campbell's replacement, David Davis, took a narrower view of the amendment. First of all, the majority agreed, it was common knowledge that the postwar amendments had been inserted in the Constitution specifically and solely for the protection of the freedmen. Justice Miller wrote, "We doubt very much whether any action of a State not directed by way of discrimination against the negroes as a class, or on account of their race, will ever be held to come within the purview of [the fifth section of the Fourteenth Amendment].* It is so clearly a provision for that race and that emergency that a strong case would be necessary for its application to any other."[24] Miller took an equally narrow, race-based view of the remainder of the amendment, as well as of the Thirteenth and Fourteenth. Of course, to insist that the postwar amendments had been incorporated into the Constitution for the sole purpose of ensuring equal rights for black Americans was not difficult in a case where black Americans' rights were not at issue. As will be seen, the Court pivoted smartly from its *Slaughterhouse Cases* opinion when black Americans eventually did seek protection under the very amendments Justice Miller insisted had been enacted solely for their benefit.

But even if the amendments were broadly interpreted, Justice Miller went on, their provisions could not be applied to the butchers' case. There were, in fact, two classes of citizenship, national and state, and the power of the state of Louisiana to regulate the health and safety of its citizens could not be impeded by federal action. One holding of the *Slaughterhouse Cases* that would survive was a narrow view of the Fourteenth Amendment with respect to the Tenth.[25]

In their dissents, Bradley, and particularly Field, were incensed in condemnation. Field, in a passage reeking with irony considering the views he would later put forth on the Fourteenth Amendment and race, wrote, "The question presented is, therefore, one of the gravest importance not merely to

---

* "The Congress shall have power to enforce, by appropriate legislation, the provisions of this article."

the parties here, but to the whole country. It is nothing less than the question whether the recent amendments to the Federal Constitution protect the citizens of the United States against the deprivation of their common rights by State legislation. In my judgment, the fourteenth amendment does afford such protection, and was so intended by the Congress which framed and the States which adopted it."

Lest there be misunderstanding, Field added later, "If [the Fourteenth Amendment restrictions] only refer, as held by the majority of the court in their opinion, to such privileges and immunities as were before its adoption specially designated in the Constitution or necessarily implied as belonging to citizens of the United States, it was a vain and idle enactment, which accomplished nothing and most unnecessarily excited Congress and the people on its passage. With privileges and immunities thus designated or implied no State could ever have interfered by its laws, and no new constitutional provision was required to inhibit such interference. *The supremacy of the Constitution and the laws of the United States always controlled any State legislation of that character.*"[26]

The expansive, race-based view of Fourteenth Amendment protections embodied in the *Slaughterhouse Cases* would prove a false dawn for equal rights. For the next three decades, the Court would systematically chip away at the guarantees the justices had here insisted were embodied in the postwar amendments. Eventually, the amendments would be stripped of even the most fundamental rights of citizenship for African-Americans. In perhaps a greater irony, the *Slaughterhouse Cases*' position on state police power versus the laissez-faire rights of corporations would also be sent to the judicial trash heap, and the vehicle would be the very same Fourteenth Amendment.

One month after the Court issued its ruling in the *Slaughterhouse Cases*, in May 1873, Chief Justice Chase died. To replace him, Grant nominated Roscoe Conkling himself. Conkling, devious, pragmatic, and a bare-knuckles political infighter, had been characterized as "about as well suited for the bench as for a monastery." He declined the appointment, a move described as "fortunate for the nation."[27] Undaunted, Grant tried another hack, seventy-four year-old Caleb Cushing, who had a first-rate legal mind but, in addition to his age, was known to blow with the political winds and "place political opportunity before principle."[28] He was sunk when a praising letter he had written to Jefferson Davis in 1861 was unearthed by an old political opponent.

Grant then "stunned the nation" by nominating his new attorney general, George H. Williams of Oregon, "a weak if not corrupt politician who would have doubtless been hopeless as Chief Justice." Williams was described by one newspaper as "knowing little of all law and less than that little of the law requisite for the Government cases."[29] Had Williams been confirmed, he might have served until his death in 1910. But Williams was too far down the barrel even for the Grant administration, and congressional outrage forced the president to withdraw the nomination and reload once more.[30] Finally, Grant tried Morrison R. Waite, described by the Nation as being among "the first rank of second rank lawyers." Attorney General Williams, now himself a reject, described the process. "Morrison R. Waite, of Ohio, was supposed to be sufficiently obscure to meet the requirements of the occasion. One can readily imagine the surprise of Mr. Waite when I telegraphed to know if he would accept the office of Chief Justice. He had never dreamed of such a thing . . . Judge Waite at the time of his appointment had never held a federal office, had never argued a case in the Supreme Court, and was comparatively unknown in Washington."[31] Perhaps because Congress was now too fatigued to object, Waite was confirmed and seated in 1874.

With four appointments out of the nine justices, Ulysses Grant became, like Abraham Lincoln, a president who could shape the Supreme Court to conform to his political vision. The problem was that Grant did not really have a vision. He was a pastiche of the visions of those who ingratiated themselves into his administration, and the men whispering in the president's ear were hardly champions of freedmen's rights. The only rights that concerned them were their own. As such, the appointment of Strong, Bradley, Hunt, and Waite began a movement away from not only an emphasis on equality for freedmen but even a willingness to deal with the issue as a serious priority.

SEVEN

EQUALITY FRAYS:
CRUIKSHANK AND *REESE*

O N APRIL 13, 1873, Easter Sunday, upwards of 250 armed white men, most on horseback, some dragging a six-pound cannon, converged on the courthouse of Colfax, seat of Grant Parish, in central Louisiana. In and around the courthouse were approximately 150 freedmen, also armed, awaiting the invasion behind hastily constructed redoubts in front of which they had dug a ditch. Many of the black men were members of the Louisiana militia; many of the white men were members of the Ku Klux Klan or other white supremacist Redeemer groups. Three weeks earlier, the freedmen, with full governmental authority, had evicted a group of whites who had seized the courthouse with the intention of establishing a rump government. The whites had come in force to return the favor.

The confrontation grew out of the bitterly disputed 1872 Louisiana gubernatorial election, in which both Republican William P. Kellogg and Democrat Samuel D. McEnery had claimed victory. Kellogg, a native of Vermont who had first come south when Lincoln appointed him collector of the port of New Orleans, was reviled by the Redeemers. McEnery, on the other hand, was Louisiana born and bred and had served as a battalion commander in the Confederate army. McEnery had been declared the winner by the election board, which then changed its mind, possibly under pressure, and declared for Kellogg. Both men held inauguration parties. The election was finally decided in the courts, with a Republican federal judge supporting Kellogg. The true result would never be determined as the election was marked by egregious fraud on both sides.

After Kellogg had been installed in office, Redeemers embarked on a series of acts of rebellion, one of which was to seize the Colfax courthouse. That they were evicted by blacks was the ultimate humiliation.

After the white men besieged the courthouse, whether they offered ultimata or terms of surrender was never definitively established. Once the shooting started, however, it became apparent that the black militia, outnumbered and outgunned, had no chance. In short order, the freedmen gave up. After their weapons had been confiscated, the white invaders proceeded to slaughter their captives.

That the carnage was vast was bad enough, but worse were the conditions under which the killings took place. The *New York Times* reported in a special dispatch, "It now appears that not a single colored man was killed until all of them had surrendered to the whites who were fighting with them, when over 100 of the unfortunate negroes were brutally shot down in cold blood. It is understood that another lot of negroes was burned to death in the Court-house when it was set on fire." The *Times* then expressed suitable outrage. "The details of the massacre . . . are positively appalling in their atrocity, and would appear to be more like the work of fiends than that of civilized men in a Christian country."[1] Rumors circulated that the bloodshed was a "Ku Klux Klan outrage," although reports from the scene never confirmed to what extent the Klan was specifically involved.[2]

Because Colfax was relatively inaccessible except by boat, federal troops were unable to get to the town until long after the massacre was complete. They arrived in time to bury more than sixty of the victims. Before the troops appeared, two United States marshals telegraphed Attorney General Williams confirming the most horrendous aspects of the incident. Numbers of the dead vary, but at least 105 African-Americans were killed (to three whites), making the incident the bloodiest of the Reconstruction period. Among the white casualties was Captain J. H. Hadnot, one of the leaders of the invasion. Whether he had been shot during the battle or after the surrender by a freedman firing from inside the courthouse remained, significantly, in dispute. The white attackers and their supporters later claimed that it was the shooting of Hadnot after the surrender that precipitated the carnage. Not in dispute is that the killing went on for hours and took place not only in the town but also in the surrounding woods, where freedmen trying to flee were shot down on sight.

Despite the slaughter, not everyone saw events the same way as the *New*

York Times. Across the bay, the *Brooklyn Daily Eagle*, in a lengthy editorial, acknowledged that many blacks had been shot, but insisted virtually all the killing had occurred during the battle. Those who were killed afterward, the *Daily Eagle* observed, had been in the courthouse when Captain Hadnot was gunned down approaching the barricades under a flag of truce.

Of the armed resistance the freedmen had organized to repel the coming assault, the newspaper noted, "No community worthily peopled by representatives of the Saxon race relish an incursion of one hundred colored men armed with shot guns," neglecting to add that many of the armed colored men were members of the duly recognized state militia. In summation, the *Daily Eagle*, while abhorring the loss of life, saw the devastation as inevitable. "The people of Louisiana won't submit to a usurpation," the editorial concluded. "The Government of the United States can do many things . . . but it cannot keep up a State Government on a people who never elected it, who won't live under it, and who manifest no disinclination to die in resisting it, and to kill those who endeavor to impose it on them."[3]

In Louisiana, the *New Orleans Picayune* asserted that "the negroes of Grant Parish, having had their minds poisoned against the white people by the industrious inculcations of a few scalawags and carpet-baggers, malignant and bad men," had precipitated the confrontation by "threatening the lives of their political opponents, giving some of them a short time to leave the place on pain of death, shooting at others, breaking open and gutting dwelling houses, driving women out, robbing a female school teacher of her jewels and effects, even rifling the coffin of Judge Rutland's dead babe, and flinging its body in the middle of the highway." That not one of these charges was ever in any way substantiated did not prevent the *Chicago Daily Tribune* from running the dispatch verbatim as "a service to its readers."[4]

The *Daily Eagle* and the *Daily Tribune* were Democratic newspapers to be sure, but even so, for such articles to appear in northern newspapers even three years earlier would have been extraordinary. Both newspapers' willingness to openly voice such sentiments is powerful testimony to the change in mood in the nation.

If the Colfax affair (called either a "massacre" or a "riot" depending on the political point of view of the speaker) did nothing else, it reminded anyone who was considering removing federal troops from the South what the consequences might be.

Aware that Louisiana, even under a Republican governor, might not respond energetically to the killings, the federal government moved to indict members of the Redeemer band for conspiracy under the Enforcement Act of 1870.

The 1870 law was one of three enforcement acts (the others were passed in 1866 and 1871) designed to give teeth to the Fourteenth and Fifteenth amendments. They applied criminal penalties to a wide variety of activities that could be seen as interfering with the exercise of civil rights guaranteed both implicitly and explicitly in both amendments. Most significantly, they transferred jurisdiction away from state government to federal court. All three acts were drawn broadly so as to provide maximum latitude, which also rendered them constitutionally questionable. The 1870 law, for example, was enacted primarily to ensure compliance with the Fifteenth Amendment but in the Colfax affair was applied to the Fourteenth.

Specifically, the Colfax defendants, almost one hundred in all, were charged by United States Attorney J. R. Beckwith with "unlawfully and feloniously [banding] together with the unlawful and felonious intent and purpose to injure, oppress, threaten and intimidate one Levi Nelson and one Alexander Tillman, being citizens of the United States of African descent, and persons of color, and in the peace of the state and the United States, with the unlawful and felonious intent thereby to hinder and prevent them in their free exercise and enjoyment of their lawful right and privilege to peaceably assemble together with each other and with other citizens of the United States for a peaceable and lawful purpose."[5] Those indicted were not charged with murder, since jurisdiction for that crime lay specifically with the states. Among the defendants was one William J. Cruikshank. What precisely was Cruikshank's role in the affair was never made clear, but he was one of only three defendants found guilty. Those three immediately appealed the decison to United States Circuit Court, arguing that the conviction should be thrown out since the federal government had no power to restrict the actions of individuals in the manner prescribed by both the enforcement acts and the Fourteenth Amendment. That responsibility, they claimed, was reserved to the states. Among the judges hearing the appeal in circuit court was the newly appointed Supreme Court justice Joseph P. Bradley.

A dour, meticulous man with a love of mathematics and an obsession with order, detail, and punctuality, Joseph Bradley had "an extreme interest in control over his environment" and was "unconcerned with people, social life, or material rewards. His views tended to be rigid and at times narrow."[6] Bradley described himself as "cold; stoical; willing to do favors without caring for the objects of them, and willing to receive them without making very intemperate demonstrations of gratitude."[7] Taken as a whole, Joseph Bradley might easily fit the general characterization of what in contemporary terms would be referred to as a "technocrat."

In *Cruikshank*, Bradley would be thrust into a pivotal crisis of American constitutionalism. He would face an even more crucial crossroads two years later. In these most vulnerable moments for American democracy, as is often the case at a time when greatness is required, the person charged with rising to meet the challenge is drawn by chance, from humble origins, having given no previous indication whether or not he or she would be up to the task.

Bradley was from a poor family, his parents having little formal education. Unable to provide their son "even a common school education," young Joseph attended a "winter school" but showed such aptitude in mathematics that he came to the attention of the headmaster.[8]

Eventually, he was sent to Rutgers University, a Dutch Reformed institution, to study for the ministry. At the urging of Frederick Frelinghuysen, who would become one of Bradley's few lifelong friends, Bradley switched to law and, after graduation, joined Frelinghuysen's legal firm. Bradley specialized in railroad and patent law.[9] His temperament and intelligence were ideal for his profession, and he became wealthy and well known both in New Jersey and in Washington. It is a testament to the metamorphosis of the Republican Party that Bradley, with no previous experience on the bench, was nominated by President Grant to serve on the Supreme Court strictly on the basis of his notoriety as a corporate lawyer.

Bradley's circuit court opinion was characteristically thorough and meticulous, and its early sections promised a favorable view of the enforcement acts and, therefore, freedmen's rights. The key to the case, as Bradley correctly noted, was the notion of state versus private action. Put another way, Bradley was being asked to determine what limits existed on the United States government's authority to pass laws controlling the behavior of its citizens, even if those citizens were acting in a manner that contravened the Constitution. This, of course, cut to the very heart of Radical Reconstruction, where the guiding ethos was the responsibility of the national government to guarantee fundamental rights when state governments could not be trusted to do so. Beyond the philosophical questions was the very practical issue of whether or not private individuals could be compelled by federal law to adhere to the Bill of Rights.[10]

To answer that question, Bradley immediately created a distinction, separating the Constitution from what might be termed "natural law." He wrote, "Where rights of individual citizens are not derived originally from the Constitution, but are part of the political inheritance from the mother country, the power of Congress does not extend to the enactment of positive laws for the protection of such rights, but only to the prevention of the states from violation of them. But where a right is derived from the Constitution and affirmative legislation is necessary to secure it to the citizen, then Congress may pass positive laws for the enforcement of the right and for the punishment of individuals who interfere with it."[11]

To illustrate this distinction, Bradley observed, "The Fifteenth Amendment confers no right to vote. That is the exclusive prerogative of the states. It does confer a right not to be excluded from voting by reason of race, color or previous condition of servitude, and this is all the right that Congress can enforce." Although Bradley took a far less expansive view of the Fourteenth Amendment than of either the Fifteenth or the Thirteenth, his narrow interpretation of federal prerogative held steady throughout.

As precedent, Bradley cited the 1842 Supreme Court decision in *Prigg v. Pennsylvania*, in which the Court determined that the fugitive slave clauses of the Constitution and the 1793 fugitive slave law passed by Congress superseded two Pennsylvania laws that protected from deportation any fugitive slaves who had successfully escaped to the commonwealth. *Prigg*, while lacking the notoriety of *Dred Scott*, was nonetheless roundly condemned by abolitionists and resulted in an additional stain on the Taney Court (although Taney himself had dissented).

Obviously, even this limited power of the federal government to intrude on state and individual privilege had proved controversial. Southern states were pleased to have their fugitive slave rights upheld but were all too aware that federal law was a sword with two quite distinct blades. Northerners decried *Prigg* but understood that the power to bulldoze a state law that might be found offensive had just been transferred to the federal government.

Thus, by extending *Prigg* to an instance in which African-Americans were victims, Bradley not only justified southern fears but had staked out—or seemed to have staked out—radical territory. Congress, he asserted, could indeed legislate against the action of individuals in the pursuit of civil rights, albeit only under the narrow circumstances he had defined. That Joseph Bradley would use a case that validated fugitive slave legislation to uphold Congress's authority to ensure the constitutional rights of freedmen might have been ironic if Bradley had stopped there. But Bradley had asserted a definition of which United States Attorney Beckwith had been unaware when preparing his case. And, in being unaware of the rules, Beckwith had violated them.

The first section of the Enforcement Act of 1870, Bradley noted, "provides that all citizens of the United States, otherwise qualified, shall be allowed to vote at all elections in any state, county, city, township, etc., without distinction of race, color or previous condition of servitude, any constitution, law, custom or usage of any state or territory to the contrary notwithstanding." But this, he insisted, "is not quite the converse of the Fifteenth amendment." The Constitution, Bradley repeated, "does not establish the right of any citizens to vote; it merely declares that race, color or previous condition of servitude shall not exclude them."[12]

Bradley turned his gaze to the fourth section of the Enforcement Act, which made it "a penal offense for any person, by force, bribery, threats, etc., to hinder or prevent, or to conspire with others to hinder or prevent, any citizen from performing any preparatory act requisite to qualify him to vote, or from voting, at any election." To Bradley, in this, Congress went over the line. "This section does not seem to be based on the Fifteenth amendment, nor to relate to the specific right secured thereby. It extends far beyond the scope of the amendment."[13]

The right of the federal government, Bradley insisted, citing any number of examples, only extends to providing remedies to those actions by states that violate *specific* rights guaranteed in the Constitution and not one inch farther. "One method of enforcement may be applicable to one fundamental right, and not applicable to another." And, in this case, "this power does not authorize congress to pass laws for the punishment of ordinary crimes and offenses against persons of the colored race or any other race. That belongs to the state government alone."

So the case rested on whether the actions of the Colfax defendants were a violation of a constitutionally guaranteed right or an ordinary crime. And the former was restricted to actions by the defendants that were based explicitly on racial grounds. Lacking that absolute determination, federal authorities had no right to intervene in what was then simply a state matter.

Bradley then came to the crux of his argument.

> The conspiracy charged in the fourth count . . . does not contain *any allegation that the defendants committed the acts complained of with a design to deprive the injured persons of their rights on account of their race, color, or previous condition of servitude.* This, as we have seen, is an essential ingredient in the crime to bring it within the cognizance of the United States authorities. *Perhaps such a design may be inferred from the allegation that the persons injured were of the African race,* and that the intent was to deprive them of the exercise and enjoyment of the rights enjoyed by white citizens. *But it ought not to have been left to inference; it should have been alleged.* On this ground, therefore, I think this count is defective and cannot be sustained.[14]

Not surprisingly, United States Attorney Beckwith would not have considered in preparing his indictments that the summary execution of more than 100 black Americans by a mob of at least 250 whites would not be prima facie a racially motivated act. But then, neither could he anticipate he would be facing a judge as obsessively punctilious as Joseph Bradley. (This assumes, of course, that Bradley had not made up his mind to rule for the defendants in advance.) In any case, that Bradley would throw out the convictions on such shaky technical grounds, which even he acknowledged in the admission that racial motivation "may be inferred," had vast implications for future prosecutions. Since intent is generally nigh unto impossible to demonstrate, the Colfax defendants would have had to *announce* their plan to violate their victims' rights on account of the color of their skin in order to be culpable. Justice Bradley had thus communicated to any Redeemer with violent intent that to avoid federal prosecution one need simply to keep one's mouth shut before committing murder.

On a broader scale, Bradley had provided Redeemers, even those not disposed to violence, a temporary road map to bypassing national sanction. Further, Bradley's opinion took a much more restrictive view of the Fourteenth Amendment than the Fifteenth. Bradley was loath to create a federal "municipal" power to enforce sanctions against "ordinary" crimes, such as murder or robbery, or provide the basis for federalizing protection of "fundamental rights," such as the right of assembly. The scope of *Prigg* had thus been narrowed considerably, perhaps fatally. Federal action against private individuals, it seemed, was to receive far more latitude when it protected whites than when it attempted to do so for African-Americans.

The circuit court decision, of course, did not put an end to the matter, but rather merely passed the case up the line.[15] When the case reached the Supreme Court, the Redeemers' path to power would become even more accessible, ultimately affording them a clear and simple blueprint to implement Jim Crow laws with impunity.

Cruikshank was to be Morrison Waite's first major case on the Court, and he wrote the majority opinion himself. Although to set aside the convictions, he would, as had Bradley, use flaws in the indictment, the larger issue was the enforcement acts themselves, which assumed, inappropriately to the new chief justice, that the Fourteenth Amendment applied the Bill of Rights to states as well as the federal government. "The first amendment to the Constitution," he wrote, "prohibits Congress from abridging 'the right of the people to assemble and to petition the government for a redress of grievances.' This, like the other amendments proposed and adopted at the same time, was not intended to limit the powers of the State governments in respect to their own citizens, but to operate upon the National Government alone."[16]

Extending Bradley's reasoning, Waite asserted that such a transference could only exist if the "new rights" had been created. A mere prohibition against encroachment of "old rights" was insufficient to bring state action under federal law. Waite added, "The particular amendment now under consideration assumes the existence of the right of the people to assemble for lawful purposes, and protects it against encroachment by Congress. The right was not created by the amendment; neither was its continuance guaranteed, except as against congressional interference. For their protection in its enjoyment, therefore, the people must look to the States. The power for that purpose was originally placed there, and it has never been surrendered to the United States."

The chief justice did acknowledge that the Fifteenth Amendment created a "new right," that of "exemption from discrimination in the exercise of the elective franchise on account of race, color or previous condition of servitude." Waite thus endorsed Bradley's view that Congress could indeed enforce the Fifteenth Amendment against the actions of private individuals, although only when specifically and explicitly stemming from racial discrimination. Having subscribed to the same absurd test, Waite then proceeded to agree with Bradley that, in *Cruikshank*, the standard had not been met and dismissed the indictments.[17]

Neither *Cruikshank* nor its companion case, *United States v. Reese*, in which Chief Justice Waite, again writing for the Court, upheld such obvious ploys to limit black suffrage as a poll tax or arbitrarily administered literacy tests, was a true watershed. By March 1876, when these opinions were delivered, Congress, the Court, and the American citizenry had grown fatigued at the degree to which national resources were being spent to elevate a group of people most of them thought were inferior to begin with. But *Cruikshank* did represent the most blatant attempt since the Reconstruction Acts had been signed into law to contort the spirit, and sometimes the letter, of both congressional prerogative and the United States Constitution.

The bitter debate over the Fourteenth Amendment, after all, had been engendered because no doubt existed among proponents and opponents alike that the intent was to apply federal guarantees of citizenship to the states. And where a case could have been made during the drafting of the amendment that Congress, under the Tenth Amendment, lacked the power to expand federal jurisdiction, once the Fourteenth Amendment was ratified, that argument became moot. In *Cruikshank*, then, the Court was, in fact, overruling a constitutional amendment. As in the *Slaughterhouse Cases*, the Court, an unelected body of lifetime appointees, did not so much follow the Constitution as impose its own definition on Congress and the president, and thus on the people of the nation as well.

Despite this encroachment on the Constitution by the very body charged with protecting it, public reaction to *Cruikshank* and *Reese* was overwhelmingly favorable. One newspaper claimed that "to assume State powers as the method of punishing and preventing wrongs in the State would be an experiment with our political system that had better be omitted. Southern questions, so far as they are State questions, must be left to the States themselves, and to those moral influences that finally shape the course of legislation. The General Government cannot authoritatively deal with them, without producing more evils than it will remedy."[18] What was more, Morrison Waite, the object of jibes upon his nomination, received unmitigated praise for his courageous stand. "Chief Justice Waite, in this decision and in the terms of its utterance has vindicated his disposition and his capacity to emulate the fame of Jay, Marshall, and Taney," one newspaper crowed. The

Supreme Court historian Charles Warren concluded that the *Cruikshank* and *Reese* decisions were "most fortunate," in that they "eliminated from politics the negro question which had so long embittered Congressional debates; they relegated the burden and duty of protecting the negro to the States, to whom they properly belonged."[19]

Once the Court had erected these virtually insurmountable barriers to the protection of even the most fundamental constitutional rights of African-Americans, the only obstacle then remaining, it seemed, to full restoration of white domination in the South was the dwindling contingent of Radical Republicans in Congress and the army of occupation.

EIGHT

1876: JUSTICE BRADLEY DISPOSES

FOR PRACTICAL PURPOSES, the end of the Reconstruction experiment coincided with its greatest triumph: passage of the most sweeping and comprehensive civil rights law in the nation's history.

On March 1, 1875, President Ulysses Grant signed into law "an act to protect all citizens in the civil and legal rights," a law that became known as the Civil Rights Act of 1875. This legislation had finally been passed by a lame-duck session of the overwhelmingly Republican Forty-third Congress.

A more aggressive enhancement to the Civil Rights Act of 1866 had been on the table for years. On May 13, 1870, Charles Sumner had introduced a "supplementary" to the 1866 law, in which the federal government would specifically guarantee "equal rights in railroads, steamboats, public conveyances, hotels, licensed theaters, houses of public entertainment, common schools and institutions of learning authorized by law, church institutions, and cemetery associations incorporated by national or State authority; also in jury duties, national and state."[1] The notion of enforced integration in schools and churches—in the North as well as the South—made even most Republicans blanch. Sumner got nowhere. A number of prominent Republicans, such as Lyman Trumbull from Illinois, even took the position that both the Civil Rights Act of 1866 and the Fourteenth Amendment demanded only that facilities available to the races be "equal." Freedom of association or, in the case of churches, free exercise of religion would bar the federal government from requiring that the races actually mix. "If the facilities for education are the same nobody has a right to complain," Trumbull asserted.[2] Undaunted, Sumner reintroduced his supplementary the following year with the same lack of results.

Even as the Republican Party quite publicly began to drift away from the Radical vision, Sumner refused to abandon the specifics of his proposal; he hung tenaciously to the church provision until December 1873. A willingness to settle for a more general guarantee of equal access to public facilities might have gained him support, but Sumner had grown unused to compromise. He pushed on, expecting that, in the end, the Senate could not help but "crown and complete the great work of Reconstruction."[3]

But Sumner's influence had all but disappeared, and, as is often the case, he was the last person to realize it. As 1874 dawned, Sumner, ill and dispirited, finally demonstrated a willingness to accept a less stringent version of the bill, but the time had passed even for that. Most Republicans were loath to revisit an ideology repugnant to so many voters. Twice Sumner attempted to have a watered-down bill reported out of the Republican-dominated judiciary committee, and twice he failed.

Then, in March 1874, Charles Sumner died. The second lion of Radical Reconstruction was gone. When Thaddeus Stevens had passed from the scene in August 1868, the Radical program was intact in the South and Andrew Johnson had been acquitted but politically neutered. Charles Sumner had survived to see the America of higher purpose that he and Stevens had built degenerate into a nation of what he considered to be crass commercial pragmatism. Sumner was buried with his most treasured ambition, full equality under the law, unfulfilled.

Ironically, the bill to which Sumner was so passionately attached acquired a momentum after his death that had been impossible to generate when he was alive. Benjamin Butler, Sumner's fellow senator from Massachusetts, picked up the standard, determined to enact some version of the supplement as Sumner's valediction. Stunningly, in a chamber where sentiment was often evoked publicly but sneered at in private, the tactic seemed to work. "Champions of equal rights seldom heard from before sprang up to defend the bill's constitutionality and its reasonableness."[4] After a good deal of debate, the Senate passed the bill in May 1874. But then the House refused to follow along. The bill was tabled in the lower chamber without being brought to a vote while the congressmen returned home to campaign for reelection.

When the Forty-third Congress reconvened for its lame-duck session in December 1874, the supplementary still pending, pressure on its advocates to enact the legislation became acute. The elections of 1874 had been a disaster for Republicans. When the Forty-fourth Congress was sworn in on March 4,

1875, the House of Representatives would shift from a 199–88 Republican majority to a 182–103 edge for the Democrats. Since only a third of the Senate had been up for reelection, Republicans would keep control of the upper chamber, but a 54–19 majority would shrink to 47–28.[5] At the next round of senatorial elections in 1876, the Republican majority was certain to erode further, if not disappear altogether. President Grant would complete his second term in 1876 as well, and, for the first time since the Civil War, a Democrat was favored to succeed to the presidency. Even with the new law, African-American equality in the United States was problematic; without it, the future appeared grim.

Butler renewed the fight. Despite party infighting and a Democratic filibuster that reduced senators to "whiling away the hours by tearing newspapers to shreds [as] stale cigar smoke choked the air, and members sprawled on the unswept carpet," Butler got the bill passed by both houses of Congress, although the schools and cemeteries provisions had to be dropped.[6] Section 1 of the final bill read, "All persons within the jurisdiction of the United States shall be entitled to the full and equal enjoyment of the accommodations, advantages, facilities, and privileges of inns, public conveyances on land or water, theaters, and other places of public amusement; subject only to the conditions and limitations established by law, and applicable alike to citizens of every race and color, regardless of any previous condition of servitude."[7] An unenthusiastic President Grant signed the bill into law on March 1, three days before the new Congress would take office.

The public reaction to *Cruikshank* had left little doubt that the electoral shift that had manifested itself in the Democratic ascendancy of 1874 was the result of the nation losing its taste for Reconstruction. Democrats, who had been attempting to exploit growing disaffection with the obsession for Negro rights for years, were finally meeting with significant success in the North. Even states that had enthusiastically supported equal rights initiatives in the past were now amenable to, if not abandonment, at least severe dilution of the Reconstruction program. With the passing of the Radicals, not only did the zeal for freedmen's equality wane, but Andrew Johnson's view of Reconstruction and even the infamous Black Codes began to be viewed with sympathy by northern whites. As Woodrow Wilson so persuasively demonstrated in his 1901 article, this perverse interpretation was to dominate American political and historical thought until well into the twentieth century.[8]

By the mid-1870s, Republicans had gotten the message as well. Running on Negro rights was, with few exceptions, hardly the path to electoral success. The party was fast shifting its emphasis from fashioning a post–Civil War social structure based on full citizenship for newly freed slaves to hitching its fortunes to the new, burgeoning capitalist class. For these "new Republicans," Negro rights had become at best a distraction and at worst an impediment. As a result, for the rapidly disappearing Reconstruction Republicans, the Civil Rights Act of 1875 seemed an unmitigated triumph, a final, unlikely victory just moments before the window of opportunity slammed shut.

The law President Grant signed on March 1, 1875, ensured that, for the first time, the promise of Thomas Jefferson's famous passage in the Declaration of Independence asserting that "all men were created equal" would be kept.[9] The preamble of the new law proclaimed it "the duty of the government in its dealings with the people to mete out equal and exact justice to all, of whatever nativity, race, color, or persuasion, religious or political."

For those freedoms guaranteed in Section 1 of the law, Section 2 enumerated penalties for those who would deny to any American fundamental rights of citizenship. Transgressors were liable for civil penalty, up to $500 for each offense, payable to the aggrieved; and if convicted in criminal court, subject to a fine of between $500 and $1,000 and up to one year in jail.

Section 3 gave federal rather than state courts jurisdiction over suits arising from "offenses against, or violations of, this act," specifically granting federal officials powers of arrest over state officials who were in violation. Section 4 guaranteed that "no citizen possessing all other qualifications which are or may be prescribed by law shall be disqualified for service as grand or petit juror in court in the United States, or of any State, on account of race, color or previous condition of servitude." Section 5 ensured that any case brought to federal district court or circuit court under this act be reviewable in the Supreme Court, regardless of how much in damages was at stake.

Taken in total, this new law could be thought of as laying out in specifics the rights and protections that the Fourteenth Amendment had asserted in general. By removing any suits brought under the auspices of this law (and the changes to legal codes it engendered) to federal court, Congress ensured that to challenge the law would be to challenge the Constitution.

The wording was very much both a response and a challenge to *Cruikshank* and *Reese*. Congress was, in effect, initiating a confrontation with the justices as to who had the power to make law. Would the Court be willing to disembowel, perhaps even nullify, a constitutional amendment? This was a high-risk strategy by the Radicals, albeit one in which they had little alternative, because the American public had shown great antipathy to the enforced equality of black Americans.

Passage of the Civil Rights Act stoked passionate response, although the direction of those passions was quite different depending on the social stratum in which one resided. Black Americans rejoiced and moved immediately to exercise their new freedoms. Hoteliers, theater managers, restaurateurs, tavern owners, and railroad agents were suddenly awash in requests for first-class tickets, dress-circle seats, front tables, or a beer at the bar. Most whites, however, were equally determined to continue to exclude African-Americans from public accommodations whenever they so chose. Across the Potomac from the nation's capital, the two principal hotels in Alexandria, Virginia, closed rather than be forced to rent rooms to Negroes. (Both subsequently reopened when their owners realized that refusing blacks would not land them in any legal difficulty.) In Memphis, four African-Americans demanded to be seated in the dress circle at a local theater. When the management grudgingly acceded, most of the white patrons walked out. In Richmond, African-Americans demanded service in restaurants, a tavern, and a barbershop, but in each case were refused.

The *New York Times*, which had praised passage of the Fourteenth Amendment in 1868 as "settling the matter of suffrage in the Southern States beyond the power of the rebels to change it, even if they had control of the government," denounced the law in an editorial. "It has put us back in the art of governing men more than two hundred years . . . startling proof how far and fast we are wandering from the principles of 1787, once so loudly extolled and so fondly cherished."

But the *Times*, despite its despair, knew where to look for relief. "The Supreme Court, in instances such as this, is the last hope of all who attach any value to that somewhat despised instrument, the Constitution of the United States," the editorial asserted with Confederacy-era sarcasm.[10]

Not every newspaper felt the need to be so shrill. The *Chicago Daily Tribune* soberly, and correctly as it turned out, predicted the law would have little practical impact. "At present, its effect will be mainly political. It will be used on the one side to retain the hold of the Republican party on the negroes of the South; on the other, to excite new opposition to the Republican party among the whites." The *Daily Tribune* added, "After the provision for enforced mixed schools had been eliminated from the bill, it became a comparatively insignificant measure." The newspaper also agreed that the constitutionality of the bill would be settled in the Supreme Court and foresaw, again correctly, that the first challenges to enforcement would come from the North.[11]

As most observers had assumed, whites dug in their heels, determined to restrict access to public institutions to blacks regardless of federal law. A commitment by whites to enforce the law was minimal. The notion of black mixing with white was sufficiently repugnant that tacit nullification by the white population enjoyed the almost total support of police, politicians, and the courts. Even United States attorneys, specifically charged with enforcing Section 2 in federal district court, took to steering aggrieved blacks to civil court rather than press the claims themselves. As a result, "with the uncertainty of a positive verdict, and the cost of court litigation, the number of cases sharply decreased."[12] African-Americans thus were rarely successful in expanding their access to mainstream American life. A law on the books, black Americans had learned, meant little if those to whom it was meant to apply refused to obey it.

Despite the obstacles, some African-American petitioners would not be turned aside. A number of lawsuits were initiated in district court in the hope that at least some federal judges would be unwilling to ignore a law whose provisions were so specific. In this, the plaintiffs were once again mistaken. While in some rare instances the suits were successful, the vast majority were not. In any event, that the Supreme Court would be the ultimate arbiter was almost universally assumed. Any number of federal judges simply shunted their cases up the line, and some refused to rule on civil rights cases entirely, citing "an impending decision by the Supreme Court," even before the Court had agreed to hear an appeal of the law.[13]

Before any of these cases reached the Court, two significant changes had occurred in Washington, one on the Court itself and another in the White House.

The 1876 presidential election between the Republican Rutherford B. Hayes and Democrat Samuel Tilden swung on two main issues: the widespread corruption in the Grant administration—Governor Tilden touted his reputation as the man who had taken on New York's Tammany Hall and Boss Tweed—and whether the Reconstruction state governments in the old Confederacy would be perpetuated or fall to white rule.

Hayes, ironically considering what was to come, ran as a friend to recently enfranchised black Americans, pledging to maintain the social advances of Reconstruction against Redeemer movements. He was not above evoking old wounds from the Civil War to do so. Former chief justice William Rehnquist observed that Hayes's tactic was "to impress on the electorate that while every Democrat had not been a rebel, every rebel had been a Democrat."[14] Tilden, on the other hand, "appealed to those throughout the country who were fed up with the corrupt mess in Washington and to white Southerners who sought to recapture the control of their state governments from Republican carpetbaggers and from newly free African Americans."[15]

Left unspoken by both campaigns was the need to stem the rising tide of violence in the southern states. Even with the constant protection of the army, the possibility that a Reconstruction state government might be overthrown by armed rebellion had become not at all unlikely. The Colfax incident might have been the most egregious, but it was hardly isolated. The only alternatives seemed to have been escalation, toughening the military presence and perpetuating Reconstruction by martial law, or withdrawal, pulling the troops out, ceding the South to Redeemers, and leaving blacks and their supporters to their fates. Despite Tilden's self-proclaimed purity, Republicans feared that Democrats would cement their advantage by carrying the South through the intimidation of black voters and other Republicans by tacitly backing militant white supremacist organizations.[16]

When the ballots were counted, Tilden had won the popular vote handily and could solidly claim 184 electoral votes, one short of the number needed for election. Hayes could claim only 165. Twenty electoral votes were in dispute, nineteen of which were in the three Reconstruction states still titularly under Republican control: Florida, Louisiana, and South Carolina. In each of those, Tilden seemed to have won the popular vote, but reports of voter intimidation and fraud were widespread.* If even one of these disputed electoral votes went to Tilden—and he certainly seemed entitled to some of them—he would win the presidency.

Virtually every newspaper in America reported Tilden as the winner, except the *New York Times*, which on November 6, the day before the election, had proclaimed, "Republican Success Certain."[17] The *Times'* managing editor, John

---

* The twentieth was for a disputed Republican elector in Oregon who was eventually allowed to cast his vote for Hayes.

C. Reid, had been held as a prisoner of war at the infamous Andersonville Prison during the Civil War, and loathed Democrats. Reid "was instrumental in convincing Republican leaders on election night that Tilden may not have won the election despite the initial returns suggesting as much."[18] Energized New York Republicans wired partisans in the disputed states to hold out, to challenge the results. The *Times* did its bit by announcing, RESULT STILL UNCERTAIN, on November 8, and then running a page-one headline on November 9, two days after Election Day, "THE BATTLE WON. GOVERNOR HAYES ELECTED—THE REPUBLICANS CARRY TWENTY-ONE STATES, CASTING 185 ELECTORAL VOTES."[19] To get to 185, the *Times* had awarded the Louisiana, Florida, and South Carolina electors to Hayes. The article claimed to be based on canvasses in the disputed states, although the *Times* was vague on just who had done the canvassing.

Canvassing boards were indeed appointed in each state by the sitting Republican governments, backed, of course, by the army, although not until after the *Times* ran its piece. Not surprisingly, the canvassing board in each state, ignoring the reported vote totals, confirmed the *Times* assertion and also declared Hayes the winner. Fraud and chicanery were certainly rampant on both sides, but "Tilden was almost certainly the rightful winner in Louisiana, probably the victor in Florida by an even closer vote than occurred in [the] 2000 [presidential election], and perhaps the winner in South Carolina, too."[20]

Democrats howled fraud. Threats of armed insurrection spread throughout Washington. Calls for secession were heard for the first time since the war. A shot was fired at Hayes's home in Ohio while the candidate was having dinner inside.

No constitutional provision existed to handle such an eventuality, but the necessity to devise some solution was apparent to both sides. Eventually, the decision was reached to appoint a fifteen-man electoral commission: five senators; five representatives; and five Supreme Court justices. Fourteen would be members of the two parties, divided equally, and the fifteenth nonpartisan. Little knowledge of politics and even less of arithmetic is necessary to discern that, in effect, one man, hopefully worthy of Diogenes, would choose the president.

Incredibly, such a man seemed to both exist and be available. Associate Justice David Davis, a Lincoln appointee, was deemed acceptable to both sides. In what was certain to be an 8–7 vote, he would be the ideal eight. So trusted as an independent was the justice that it was said, "No one, perhaps not even Davis himself, knew which presidential candidate he preferred."[21]

But before the commission could meet, the Democratic-controlled state legislature in Illinois appointed Davis to a vacant seat in the United States Senate. Republican newspapers decried the bald-faced attempt at flattery. Both sides assumed Davis would decline the seat and remain on the Court, but that the honor of being named might tip his vote toward Tilden. But Davis flummoxed the Democrats by immediately resigning from the bench to accept the appointment. He never stated his reasons for leaving both the Court and the commission, but perhaps the enormity of the responsibility got the better of him.

With Davis, perhaps the only acceptable independent in the entire nation, now ineligible, one of the remaining four justices would be forced to sit in his place. Each was associated with one of the political parties. Eventually, also for reasons never made public, recently appointed associate justice Joseph Philo Bradley was chosen to take Davis's place. Democrats denounced the choice as a fix, but after the Davis fiasco, their credibility was somewhat strained. Bradley accepted the appointment and thus became the only man in American history empowered to choose a president essentially on his own.[22]

Before deciding which man would sit as the next president of the United States, Bradley, ever meticulous, drew up a written opinion for each man. His few friends claimed that he weighed the facts carefully, although no one recalls him expressing any hesitancy or demonstrating indecision. Then, after all of this supposed soul-searching, surprising no one but infuriating many, Joseph Bradley, using arguments precisely along the party line, chose Hayes. Some Democrats once more threatened rebellion. Rumors circulated that an army of one hundred thousand men was prepared to march on the capital to prevent "Rutherfraud" or "His Fraudulency" from being sworn in. In the House of Representatives, Democrats began a filibuster to prevent Hayes's inauguration.

What happened next has been a subject of debate among historians ever since. For decades, a simple explanation was put forth. "Reasonable men in both parties struck a bargain at Wormley's Hotel. There, in the traditional smoke-filled room, emissaries of Hayes agreed to abandon the Republican state governments in Louisiana and South Carolina while southern Democrats agreed to abandon the filibuster and thus trade off the presidency in exchange for the end of reconstruction."[23] The "Compromise of 1877," as it came to be known, made Rutherford B. Hayes the nineteenth president of the United States. As one of his first orders of business, this erstwhile defender of Negro rights ordered federal troops withdrawn from the South.[24] When the soldiers marched out, they took Reconstruction with them.

As another of his early orders of business, President Hayes appointed a former slaveholder and failed gubernatorial candidate from Kentucky named John Marshall Harlan to fill David Davis's Supreme Court seat.

Harlan's was a payoff appointment. He had almost single-handedly delivered the Kentucky delegation to Hayes in the 1876 Republican Convention. Still, Harlan seemed an odd choice for a Republican president. He had been raised in a family of slaveholders, had opposed the Emancipation Proclamation, and had spoken out passionately against the postwar amendments.

Below the surface, however, Harlan was a study in contradictions, much more difficult to pigeon-hole into any particular philosophy. At age twenty-one, he joined the xenophobic, semisecret "Know-Nothing" society, whose motto was "Put none but Americans on Guard." Catholics were also anathema. "On the evening of my initiation," Harlan wrote later, "an oath was administered to me which bound me to vote only for native Americans, and, in effect, only for Protestants."[25] Harlan, at six foot two inches, 240 pounds, with a shock of red hair and stentorian delivery, soon became all the rage on the Kentucky oratorical circuit. "He was billed as the 'young giant of the American Party,' and his speeches were described, approvingly, as 'orthodox Know-Nothing scripture'—anti-foreign, pro-slavery and anti-Catholic in just the right proportions."[26]

But Harlan's was a benign view of slavery. His own family's slaves were treated as part of the family. In a famous incident, Harlan recalled a Sunday morning when, as a boy walking to church with his father, they came upon an overseer physically abusing a line of chained slaves. Harlan's father was incensed. He strode up to the overseer, shook his finger in the man's face, and exclaimed, "You are a damned scoundrel. Good morning, Sir." But the Harlans, father and son, opposed abolition both on practical grounds and because it would constitute a violation of the property rights of the owners. The younger Harlan defended *Dred Scott.* "Congress," he asserted, "had the power, and it was its bounded duty, to pass such laws as might be necessary for the full protection of the rights of the slave-owner in the Territories, whenever the local Legislatures shall either attempt to destroy his right by unfriendly legislation or shall fail to pass such laws as are necessary for his protection."[27]

But Harlan equally opposed secession. He campaigned tirelessly to keep Kentucky loyal and, when war did break out, raised an infantry regiment. He was commissioned into the Union army as a colonel and distinguished himself in battle until, upon his father's death in 1863, he returned home to tend to his family's needs. Fighting arm in arm with German immigrants and Catholics, Harlan emerged from the war with his Know-Nothing sentiments abandoned. His defense of slavery, however, was unaltered. He opposed the Thirteenth Amendment on the grounds that it was "'a flagrant invasion of the right of self government' and a breach of promise to the loyal slaveholders of Kentucky, but it also gave to 'a bare majority in Congress' the power to wipe out property rights guaranteed by the American Constitution."[28] His opinion of the Fourteenth and Fifteenth amendments was no better. He joined the Conservative Party and tried to balance his nationalism with his fierce commitment to property rights. If forced to choose between the two major parties, the Democrats would certainly have received his support.

With the presidential nomination of Ulysses Grant, however, an acquaintance of Harlan's during the war, Harlan made peace with the postwar amendments and switched allegiance to the Republicans. He decided finally that the Conservatives had no future and that the Democrats were attempting to once again fracture the nation.

A grateful Republican Party nominated Harlan for governor in 1871, and, with newly enfranchised African-Americans key to any Republican victory, he found himself not only soliciting black votes but actually changing his perspective on issues of equal rights. "I rejoice," he announced late in the campaign, "that [slavery] is gone; I rejoice that the Sun of American Liberty does not this day shine upon a single human slave upon this continent; I rejoice that these human beings are now in possession of freedom, and that that freedom is secured to them in the fundamental law of the land, beyond the control of any state." Then he added, noting his attitudes of the past, "Let it be said that I am right rather than consistent."[29]

Although Harlan lost the election, he garnered more votes than any other Republican in Kentucky's history. He was nominated again four years later. In this election, the Civil Rights Act of 1875 was a major issue. Harlan tried to avoid taking a definitive position but, when pressed, asserted "under the law of Kentucky, any one of the colored men within the sound of my voice has the same right that any white man possesses to ride in one of your cars from here to the city of Louisville."[30] Harlan lost once more, albeit by a narrower margin, and, the following year, was instrumental in gaining the presidential nomination for Rutherford B. Hayes. A grateful President Hayes offered him the post of ambassador to Great Britain. Harlan declined, citing family responsibilities. On October 16, 1877, the president nominated him to be associate justice of the Supreme Court. On Thanksgiving Day 1877, Harlan learned by telegram that he had been confirmed.

In early 1878, John Marshall Harlan took his seat on the high court, set, although he did not know it, on a collision course with Joseph P. Bradley.

NINE

A Jury of One's Peers:
Strauder and *Rives*

I n 1879, four years after the Civil Rights Act of 1875 had been enacted, not a single challenge to the equal access provisions of the law as described in Section 1 of the law had reached the Supreme Court. In the fall term of that year, however, the justices heard two Fourteenth Amendment cases brought under Section 4, jury access, that would bear heavily not only on the fate of the 1875 law but on the American notion of civil rights itself.

The first case involved the murder conviction of an African-American named Taylor Strauder in West Virginia in April 1874. Strauder had killed his wife, Anna, in a fit of jealous rage, a fact he did not deny. Moreover, he claimed to be justified in the act, since Mrs. Strauder had been almost obsessively unfaithful, sleeping more or less openly with a multitude of other men, bringing shame and obloquy on her husband. Local authorities evidently found Strauder's defense persuasive. Although he remained in jail, three terms of state circuit court passed without his case being brought before a judge. Only when Strauder's lawyers petitioned to have him released was he finally tried. In November 1874, he was found guilty by an all-white jury and sentenced to hang.[1]

Strauder's lawyers appealed to the West Virginia Supreme Court. Their claim, incredibly, included the assertion that their client had been indeed entitled to kill his wife. The only reason he was convicted, the lawyers maintained, was that West Virginia whites were so bigoted that a fair trial was impossible. As part of this latter point, the lawyers noted that, by statute, only white men were eligible to be jurors. Eventually the appeal reached the United States Supreme Court, by which time it had been reduced to the question of statutory exclusion of African-Americans from a jury.[2]

The second case involved two teenage brothers in Virginia, African-Americans, Lee and Burwell Reynolds, indicted for the murder of a white man, Aaron C. Shelton, in November 1877. The jury chosen to try them in state court was, again, all white, although in this case, blacks had been excluded by coincidence or contrivance rather than by law. Whatever vague sympathy had been engendered in the white community toward Taylor Strauder would certainly not be present in this case.

The brothers' lawyers initiated a petition of habeas corpus to a federal district court, alleging that "a strong prejudice existed in the community of the county against them, independent of the merits of the case and based solely upon the facts that they are negroes and that the man they were accused of having murdered was a white man. From that fact alone, they were satisfied they could not obtain an impartial trial before a jury exclusively composed of the white race." They further posited that "their race had never been allowed the right to serve as jurors, either in civil or criminal cases, in the County of Patrick, in any case, civil or criminal, in which their race had been in any way interested."[3]

The judge who received the petition, Alexander Rives, had a history of integrating juries by order from the bench. In November 1878, Rives, using the authority granted him by Section 3 of the civil rights law, ruled that the brothers be removed from state jurisdiction on the grounds that, for African-Americans, all-white juries were in violation of Section 4 and therefore the equal protection clause of the Fourteenth Amendment. Reaction in the Old Dominion was immediate and intense. That Judge Rives had opposed secession and renounced the Democratic Party for Lincoln's Republicans in the 1850s only compounded white Virginia's fury. In January 1879, the state's legislature passed a series of resolutions denouncing Judge Rives's order as "unwarranted by the Constitution . . . destructive of the rights of the people of each state to protect life, liberty, and property in their own way, by their own courts and officers." The resolutions further stated, "All acts of Congress, and particularly those known as the Civil Rights Bill and the Enforcement act, which attempt . . . to provide for the performance by the United States of duties and obligations belonging to the States, are unconstitutional and void."[4] The legislature instructed the state's attorney to sue to have the prisoners returned.

Rather than back down, Rives provided further provocation to his many enemies in Virginia by ordering the arrest of five state court judges who "purposefully refused" to seat black men on juries. "The fact that colored men are seldom seen on Virginia juries," Rives observed, stating the obvious, "raises the presumption that they are, on account of race or color, left off the list of names furnished to the Sheriffs by Corporation and County judges from which to draw juries."[5] Virginia brought suit to have the case returned to state court. By the time the case, *Virginia v. Rives*, reached the Supreme Court, Judge Rives was under twenty-four-hour protection by federal troops.

The two decisions were eagerly anticipated, as much for the barometer they would provide to the Court's mood as for resolution of the issues themselves. How tightly the justices would draw the knot around the postwar amendments had not yet been fully established. Justice Miller, for example, one of the Lincoln appointees, who had supported the president in his extension of federal powers, including the suspension of habeas corpus, had by this time become an outspoken advocate of limited national power, as his 1873 opinion in the *Slaughterhouse Cases* attested. Rulings in *Strauder* and *Rives*, therefore, promised to have broad impact, stretching beyond the judiciary into the political system at large.

There would hardly have been an outcry from an outraged nation if the justices ruled against the African-Americans. While the venom directed at Judge Rives in the South was predictable, feelings in the North were little different. According to the *Brooklyn Daily Eagle*, the issue was "whether the Federal Government can force upon Southern States measures or proceedings which are not attempted to be forced upon Northern States . . . whether a colored man, on trial for a criminal offense which is clearly within the exclusive jurisdiction of a State court, has a right to demand a jury composed in whole or in part of men of his own color." As the article soon made clear, the real issue cut closer to home. "If such a right exists in Virginia, it also exists in New York." The law, then, "does not concern the negroes of the South alone, but the negroes of the North as well, together with the Chinese, the Irish, the Germans and men of all other nationalities." Decrying the possibility that members of minority groups might demand participation on a jury by members of that group, the article observed, "This reduces the point to absurdity." The newspaper proposed a remedy: "It is clear enough to plain people that justice and the Fourteenth Amendment are satisfied . . . if the two colored men [in the murder case] receive the same protection of the law that white men receive . . . The Constitution as it stands forbids discrimination against the negro, but does not compel discrimination in his favor."[6]

The *Chicago Daily Tribune* described Judge Rives's behavior as "a war on State Courts" and added, "That the judge is not dismayed by the adverse criticism of his conduct, not only in the State, but throughout the country, is certain."[7] Even the *New York Times*, staunchly Republican, after defending Judge Rives's actions, acknowledged the difficulty in proving blacks had been excluded from juries strictly as a result of race. The *Times* did note that this case would be "one of the most important questions of constitutional law that has arisen since the war."[8]

On March 1, 1880, the Court issued rulings on both appeals. Both opinions were written by Justice Strong, the abolitionist from Pennsylvania who, like Judge Rives, had switched from the Democrats to the Republicans in the 1850s.

Despite the change in political winds, equal rights' advocates took hope that Strong might remain an unshakable champion for black Americans. In *Strauder*, the first of the decisions rendered, he did not disappoint. The justice wrote:

> The very fact that colored people are singled out and expressly denied by a statute all right to participate in the administration of the law, as jurors, because of their color, though they are citizens, and may be in other respects fully qualified, is practically a brand upon them, affixed by the law, an assertion of their inferiority, and a stimulant to that race prejudice which is an impediment to securing to individuals of the race that equal justice which the law aims to secure to all others. The right to a trial by jury is guaranteed to every citizen of West Virginia by the constitution of that state, and the constitution of juries is a very essential part of the protection such a mode of trial is intended to secure.[9]

Strauder was ordered to have a new trial, with African-Americans sitting on the jury.[10] As much as the ruling itself, the breadth implied in Strong's opinion, acknowledgment that "brands of servitude" were a concrete and not an ethereal concept, signaled that there were definite limits to the Court's willingness to disembowel the Fourteenth Amendment.

Two justices dissented. One, Stephen Field, who had taken an expansive view of the Fourteenth Amendment to protect butchers in the *Slaughterhouse Cases*, stated bluntly, "The fourth section of the act of 1875, so far as it applies to the selection of jurors in the State courts, is unconstitutional and void. Previous to the late amendments, it would not have been contended by anyone familiar with the Constitution that Congress was vested with any power to exercise supervision over the conduct of State officers in the discharge of their duties under the laws of the State, and prescribe a punishment for disregarding its directions."[11] Field's dissent was the first time a Supreme Court justice had gone on record in attesting a portion of the Civil Rights Act of 1875 unconstitutional. His reasoning certainly suggested that, if asked, his view would extend to the entire statute. For the moment, Field remained in the minority, but he was an influential voice of the Court and eventually it was likely that other justices would come to agree with his assessment. If the 1875 law was eventually declared unconstitutional, the power and scope of the Fourteenth Amendment itself would be narrowed as well. Southern whites, even in a case they lost, could therefore find encouragement in *Strauder*. Whether they would, however, find further encouragement in *Rives* depended on whether the Court viewed the Civil Rights Act, and thus the Fourteenth Amendment guarantees, broadly, in the spirit in which they were enacted, or narrowly, hiding behind verbiage to limit their impact.

Strong began his *Rives* opinion by agreeing that "[the Civil Rights of 1875] rests upon the Fourteenth Amendment of the Constitution and the legislation to enforce its provisions." He then added, "The plain object of these statutes, as of the Constitution which authorized them, was to place the colored race, in respect of civil rights, upon a level with whites. They made the rights and responsibilities, civil and criminal, of the two races exactly the same."

But then the justice pointed out, "The provisions of the Fourteenth Amendment of the Constitution we have quoted all have reference to State action exclusively, and not to any action of private individuals." Applying the narrow definition that Justice Bradley had promulgated in his circuit court *Cruikshank* opinion, Strong insisted that the Fourteenth Amendment, and by extension the Civil Rights Act of 1875, provided "protection against State action, and against that alone."

But to Strong, *Rives* was unlike *Strauder* in that there was no specific state action on which Fourteenth Amendment protections might be invoked. "The petition of the two colored men . . . did not assert, nor is it claimed now, that the Constitution or laws of Virginia denied to them any civil right, or stood in the way of their enforcing the equal protection of the laws. The law made no discrimination against them because of their color, nor any discrimination at all." De facto discrimination, Strong had announced, whether or not it had been obvious to Judge Rives, was not in the Court's purview. No statute, no case. Thus, as in *Cruikshank*, those choosing to discriminate against the freedmen would have had to *announce* their intention to do so in advance in order to be subject to Fourteenth Amendment prohibitions.

Justice Strong did allow that, under Section 1 of the Civil Rights Act, if an "officer to whom was entrusted the selection of the persons from whom the juries for the indictment and trial of the petitioners were drawn" has misused his authority, that officer would be liable to penalties.

The Fourteenth Amendment was broader than the Civil Rights Act, the justice asserted, and therefore the latter did not apply to all cases in which discrimination might take place. Strong, the onetime abolitionist, concluded, incredibly, "The statute authorizes a removal of the case only before trial, not after a trial has commenced. It does not, therefore, embrace many cases in which a colored man's right may be denied. It does not embrace a case in which a right may be denied by judicial action during the trial, or by discrimination against him in the sentence, or in the mode of executing the sentence."

In other words, reading the Civil Rights Act properly, only *before* a jury was chosen could a defendant assert that the jury was chosen unfairly. Once jury selection had begun, the defendant's right to question its composition was lost.

But the impact of Justice Strong's decision went farther than even this Kafkaesque stipulation. If a question about jury selection, or any other question of fairness, did arise after proceedings had begun, since this went beyond the purview of the law in question, remedy could only be sought in *state* courts. So, while not going so far as the Virginia resolutions of January 1879, or Justice Field's assertion in *Strauder* that the Civil Rights Act was unconstitutional, Justice Strong, with a stroke of his pen, annulled one of its key provisions. Justice Field, who seemed to think there were two Fourteenth amendments, one for business and one for freedmen, wrote a separate concurring opinion. "The equality of protection assured by the Fourteenth Amendment to all persons in the State," he noted, "does not imply that they shall be allowed to participate in the administration of its laws, or to hold any of its offices, or to discharge any duties of a public trust."[12]

Judge Rives was overruled. The decision was unanimous.* Justice Harlan joined Strong in both opinions without comment, as did Justice Bradley. The Court therefore held that "the fact that no blacks had ever served on a local jury was not evidence that they had been systematically excluded," once again making it virtually impossible, lacking a statement of discriminatory intent, to press a successful challenge to state voting laws in federal court.[13] In a case the following year, Harlan wrote an opinion in which Bradley joined, once again overturning a statutory prohibition in the jury selection process.[14] But states had learned well. In the future, they would avoid explicit discriminatory provisions in favor of those without discriminatory language that achieved the same ends.

Strauder and *Rives* were Strong's farewell to the Court. On December 14, 1880, he resigned. His reasons were never fully spelled out, although he timed his resignation to allow a lame-duck President Hayes to appoint his successor. Strong later wrote two articles for the *North American Review* in which he decried the burgeoning case load of the Court and urged the establishment of additional lower federal courts to ameliorate the problem.[15]

Hayes first nominated Stanley Matthews, but the Senate balked as Matthews was seen as "tied too closely to corporate interests." Hayes withdrew the Matthews nomination and offered William Burnham Woods, a former Union general who had settled in Alabama after the war. Woods was confirmed in January 1881, part of a major reconstitution of the Court that would accelerate in the months to come.

---

* *Strauder v. West Virginia* and *Virginia v. Rives* are the first of nine decisions generally lumped together as voting rights cases decided between 1880 and 1903. Referred to as the *Strauder-Powers Cases*, they espouse the principle that only statutory discrimination in jury selection or for determining voter eligibility is actionable under the Fourteenth Amendment. As will be seen in chapter 14, however, which discusses one of the latter cases in this group, *Williams v. Mississippi*, the sociopolitic climate in the South had changed so radically during the intervening period that not evaluating the cases separately vastly diminishes the appraisal of their impact.

TEN

DECONSTRUCTION:
THE *CIVIL RIGHTS CASES*

IN 1880, DURING THE TERM the *Strauder* and *Rives* decisions were handed down, the appeals of five of the unsuccessful suits brought under Section 1 of the 1875 Civil Rights Act finally reached the Supreme Court. One of the cases dated to 1876, just months after the law had been passed. As the *Chicago Daily Tribune* had predicted, none of the five cases came from the Deep South. One originated in California, where "a colored person [was refused] a seat in the dress circle of Maguire's theatre in San Francisco," and a second in New York City, where "a person, whose color was not stated, [was denied] the full enjoyment of the accommodations of the theatre known as the Grand Opera House."[1] The remaining three cases originated in Missouri, Kansas, and Tennessee.

The Court dithered, refusing to hear any of the cases for an additional three years, citing procedural snags or simply declining to place the appeals on the docket. The delay worked against other potential African-American plaintiffs, who could not be heard in lower courts with a Supreme Court decision pending, while encouraging whites to continue to disregard the law's prohibitions.

When the Court finally heard arguments on March, 29, 1883, America's repudiation of Reconstruction was more or less complete and the mood of the country had turned decidedly anti-Washington. One commentator wrote, "I have no intention to impeach the patriotism of those who hold opinions which grew out of the excitements of civil war. But, in their eagerness to extend the jurisdiction of the General Government, they went too far, and exposed the country to unforeseen dangers."[2]

Democrats in the newly seated Forty-eighth Congress controlled the

House by almost eighty votes. Although Republicans nominally controlled the Senate, the party had by this time fully aligned itself with the commercial interests that had begun to coalesce into the giant plutocracies that would run with laissez-faire glee through American political economy for the next three decades.[3] Much of the party had turned against African-Americans, and Republican candidates were openly courting white votes in the South. "The wing of the Republican party that raised the loudest outcry against Hayes's policy of deserting the Negro promptly abandoned him [after Hayes left office] and threw support to . . . any white independent organization available."[4]

In 1880, Rutherford B. Hayes had declined to seek the second term he could not have won. On the thirty-sixth ballot at the Republican convention, Representative James A. Garfield of Ohio narrowly bested former President Ulysses Grant. His running mate was Chester Arthur of New York, forced on Garfield by party king-maker Roscoe Conkling, as the price for the Empire State's thirty-five crucial electoral votes. Garfield and Conkling, who had first backed the malleable Grant, loathed each other, and the nominee and his running mate were barely civil. In the general election, with Conkling's support, Garfield defeated the Democrats' Winfield Scott Hancock, a brilliant general during the Civil War. The difference was fifty-nine electoral votes (New York thereby providing the margin of victory), although Garfield won the popular vote by a mere 1,898 votes out of almost nine million cast.

Almost immediately after the new president took his oath of office, Associate Justice Noah Swayne resigned. Garfield, still in the throes of assembling a cabinet, nominated Stanley Matthews to fill Swayne's seat on the Court. Matthews, unsuccessful as a Hayes nominee, squeaked through after renomination by Garfield.

Then, 199 days after taking office, James Garfield was dead, assassinated by a disgruntled and likely deranged job seeker named Charles Guiteau. Chester Arthur, described generously as a "political spoilsman," succeeded to the office. Arthur attempted to rise to the needs of his office and, in fact, for three years, led the nation quietly and with a surprising degree of competence.[5] But Chester Arthur was of the Gilded Age, and while he did his best to restrict the blatant patronage and payoff politics of Roscoe Conkling, the enforcement of the civil rights of African-Americans lay so far down on his list of priorities as to be nigh unto invisible.

But where Arthur couldn't match Garfield's feat of appointing a Supreme Court justice during a six-month stint in office, the new president did have the opportunity to make two appointments during his three years in the White House. In July 1881, Justice Nathan Clifford died, the last holdover from the pre–Civil War Court. The following January, Ward Hunt followed suit after a term on the high court of only nine years. After President Arthur filled the seats, four of the nine justices had been on the bench less than five years.

To replace Clifford, Arthur, perhaps to signal that his administration would not be as brazenly political as Grant's, nominated Horace Gray, a justice of the Massachusetts supreme judicial court. Gray was a scholar, not involved in politics to any significant degree. As thorough as Joseph Bradley, but not as dour, he nonetheless had a technocrat's view of the law and his role in interpreting it. As a contemporary noted, "Law is more than justice. It is order as well, established that the citizen may know, surely and before-hand, what will be the consequence of his acts, so that he may direct them accordingly. In not a few matters, it is better that the law should be settled than that it should be right. Horace Gray had a strong sense of order."[6]

For Hunt's seat, Arthur reverted to type and nominated Roscoe Conkling, once again evoking outrage in the press and among the public at large. Conkling was quickly confirmed but, likely reluctant to take a position of diminished influence, once again declined to sit on the Court. Arthur finally settled on the circuit court judge Samuel Blatchford, another New Yorker. Blatchford had been a prominent patent and maritime attorney before being elevated to the federal bench. One of five justices appointed within the previous three years, he personified the "new" Republicans, a man more focused on the needs of commerce than on those of Negro Americans. In March 1883, when the *Civil Rights Cases* were heard, it was before a Court representing an America even farther removed from freedmen's rights.

Two months before hearing arguments in the *Civil Rights Cases*, however, the Court issued an opinion in another inflammatory case, *United States v. Harris*, often referred to as the *Ku Klux Klan Case*.

In August 14, 1876, in Crockett County, Tennessee, Deputy Sheriff William Tucker had in custody four black men charged with a variety of criminal offenses, although none had yet been tried. A group of twenty men, one of whom was a farmer named R. G. Harris, either broke into or were let into

Senator Charles Sumner
(Library of Congress Prints and Photographs Division)

Representative Thaddeus Stevens
(Library of Congress Prints and Photographs Division)

Chief Justice
Roger Brooke Taney
*(Library of Congress Prints
and Photographs Division)*

Chief Justice Salmon P. Chase *(Library of Congress Prints and Photographs Division)*

Louis Agassiz

Herbert Spencer

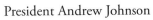

William Graham Sumner

President Andrew Johnson

Chief Justice Morrison R. Waite

President Ulysses Grant

Associate Justice Joseph P. Bradley
(Library of Congress Prints and Photographs Division)

Associate Justice John Marshall Harlan

President Rutherford B. Hayes
(Library of Congress Prints and Photographs Division)

Chief Justice Waite administering the oath of office to President-elect
Rutherford B. Hayes. *(Library of Congress Prints and Photographs Division)*

Engraving that appeared in *Harper's Weekly* depicting an agent of the Freedmen's Bureau as a peacemaker between blacks and whites after the Civil War.

MENDING THE FAMILY KETTLE.

COLUMBIA—"*Now, Andy, I wish you and your boys would hurry up that job, because I want to use that kettle right away. You are all talking too much about it.*"

Cartoon appearing in *Leslie's Illustrated Weekly* during Reconstruction.
(Library of Congress Prints and Photographs Division)

Albion Tourgée

Associate Justice Henry Billings Brown
(Library of Congress Prints and Photographs Division)

Chief Justice
Melville Fuller
*(Library of Congress Prints
and Photographs Division)*

Associate Justice Oliver Wendell Holmes
(Library of Congress Prints and Photographs Division)

W. E. B. DuBois

the jail where the four were held. The black men were dragged outside and beaten so severely that one of them died. Harris and his nineteen companions were charged under federal law for violating the Enforcement Act of 1871, commonly referred to as the Ku Klux Klan Act, which forbade "two or more persons from . . . going in disguise upon the public highway, &c. to deprive any person or class of equal rights, &c. under the laws; or to prevent the State authorities from protecting all in their equal rights."[7] Harris and his fellow defendants asked that the indictments be dismissed on the grounds that the federal government had no right to legislate the activities of private persons. That right was reserved to the states. In circuit court, the judges divided on the issue, so the case had been referred to the Supreme Court, which, as it had done with most other Fourteenth Amendment cases, deferred the case. Five years after the fact, newly seated Justice Woods was given the task of writing the opinion.

After referring to *Cruikshank* and *Reese* to establish the limitations on federal enforcement of the Fourteenth Amendment, Woods observed that "it is perfectly clear from the language of the first section [of the amendment] that its purpose also was to place a restraint upon the action of the states."[8] Then, taking Justice Bradley's circuit court opinion out of context, Woods quoted the passage "It is a guarantee of protection against the acts of the state government itself. It is a guarantee against the exertion of arbitrary and tyrannical power on the part of the government and legislature of the state, not a guarantee against the commission of individual offenses, and the power of Congress, whether express or implied, to legislate for the enforcement of such a guarantee does not extend to the passage of laws for the suppression of crime within the states." Of course, in his opinion Bradley had come to quite a different conclusion, that, under limited circumstances, the federal government was entitled to ensure the rights of citizens against encroachment through the commission of ordinary crimes.

After noting Chief Justice Waite's extension of the doctrine in his *Cruikshank* opinion, Woods cited the man he replaced, Justice Strong, writing in *Rives*. "These provisions of the Fourteenth Amendment have reference to state action exclusively, and not to any action of private individuals." From there, it was a simple matter to find that the Ku Klux Klan Act was not constitutional. If a state did not mind that its citizens dragged helpless, unarmed men out into the street and beat them to death, the federal government would not mind either, since the Fourteenth Amendment was not really enacted to curb such behavior.

The decision was unanimous.

The opinion in the *Civil Rights Cases* was not delivered until October. Scant optimism could be found in the African-American community or among those remaining whites who hoped to realize Charles Sumner's and Thaddeus Stevens's vision of an America dedicated to equal rights for all its citizens. A string of unanimous decisions disemboweling both civil rights legislation and the Fourteenth Amendment on the altar of federalism and strict construction did not leave room for much suspense on how the Court would rule on the Civil Rights Act of 1875.

When the decision was handed down, however, there was one surprise. The Court's ruling was as predicted; what had not been expected was that the decision was not supported by all nine members of the Court. One justice dissented. Chosen to write the opinion for the majority was the man who always seemed present when a vital issue was to be decided, Joseph Bradley. The dissent was penned by John Marshall Harlan.

Bradley opened with his conclusions, striking in their simplicity (in contrast to the remainder of his opinion).

1. The 1st and 2d sections of the Civil Rights Act passed March 1st, 1876, are unconstitutional enactments as applied to the several States, not being authorized either by the XIIIth or XIVth Amendments of the Constitution.

2. The XIVth Amendment is prohibitory upon the States only, and the legislation authorized to be adopted by Congress for enforcing it is not direct legislation on the matters respecting which the States are prohibited from making or enforcing certain laws, or doing certain acts, but is corrective legislation such as may be necessary or proper for counteracting and redressing the effect of such laws or acts. The XIIIth Amendment relates only to slavery and involuntary servitude (which it abolishes), and, although, by its reflex action, it establishes universal freedom in the United States, and Congress may probably pass laws directly enforcing its provisions, yet such legislative power extends only to the subject of slavery and its incidents, and the denial of equal accommodations in inns, public

conveyances, and places of public amusement (which is forbidden by the sections in question), imposes no badge of slavery or involuntary servitude upon the party but at most, infringes rights which are protected from State aggression by the XIVth Amendment.[9]

Bradley's absolutist view of the Fourteenth Amendment is a stark departure from his circuit court *Cruikshank* opinion. There, while his criteria for federal legislation that created limits or prohibitions on individual action were extensive, he had specifically, citing *Prigg*, recognized that in some cases, where a right had been granted by "the mother country," such legislation was permissible. If he had held to that position, however, he then would have been forced to evaluate the Civil Rights Act of 1875 on its merits. By taking Morrison Waite's *Cruikshank* opinion instead of his own, he could simply cast the law out without further explanation.

The crux of the legal argument had, of course, always been one of federalism. The Tenth Amendment read, "The powers not delegated to the United States by the Constitution, nor prohibited by it to the States, are reserved to the States respectively, or to the people." The Court had increasingly hardened into the position that since nowhere in the Constitution was there any provision allowing the national government to mandate behavior by private individuals, except in very specific cases, none of which were germane to this law, regulation of private behavior was constitutionally reserved to the states. During oral arguments, Solicitor General Samuel F. Phillips demurred, claiming that the Fourteenth Amendment's insistence on "equal protection of the laws" superseded the Tenth by defining new areas "delegated to the United States."[10] Equality, then, as defined in the Fourteenth Amendment, was appropriate to be ensured by Congress. Attorneys for the defendants stood their ground, accusing Phillips of overreaching, of artificially broadening the amendment to achieve an end not reflective of either Congress's intention or the Constitution's.

Bradley agreed with Phillips as to where the crux of the case lay. "No one will contend that the power to pass [the law] was contained in the Constitution before the adoption of the last three amendments," he wrote. "The power is sought . . . in the Fourteenth Amendment."[11]

But that was the only area of agreement between the justice and the solicitor general. The Fourteenth Amendment, to Bradley, certainly did not extend to Congress the power to regulate the private behavior that was

alleged in any of the five cases before the Court. "[The amendment]," he re-
iterated, "does not invest Congress with power to legislate upon subjects
which are within the domain of State legislation, but to provide modes of
relief against State legislation, or State action, of the kind referred to." Bradley was, in essence, choosing broad construction for the Tenth Amendment
and strict construction for the Fourteenth. "Individual invasion of individual rights," Bradley asserted with finality, "is not the subject matter of the
amendment."

After Bradley had continued, repetitively and at great length, to provide
constitutional justification for his opinion, all of which he derived from precedents established by the very justices with whom he had served, he could
not restrain himself from appending a sociological statement. He began in
the section of his opinion that categorically dismissed the notion of extending the Thirteenth Amendment, which prohibited slavery, to apply to the
type of discrimination alleged in these cases as "badges of servitude." "It would
be running the slavery argument into the ground," Bradley wrote, "to make
it apply to every act of discrimination which a person may see fit to make as
to the guests he will entertain, or as to the people he will take into his coach
or cab or car, or admit to his concert or theatre, or deal with in other matters
of intercourse or business."

Then, seemingly to scold those who would attempt to adjudicate equal
rights, Bradley wrote, "When a man has emerged from slavery, and, by the
aid of beneficent legislation, has shaken off the inseparable concomitants of
that state, there must be some stage in the progress of his elevation when he
takes the rank of a mere citizen and ceases to be the special favorite of the
laws, and when his rights as a citizen or a man are to be protected in the ordinary modes by which other men's rights are protected."[12]

It is difficult to view this astounding statement—made despite numerous
incidents of beatings, murder, and intimidation of African-Americans by
whites; despite the reign of terror wrought by the Ku Klux Klan and other
violent Redeemer groups; despite the most blatant ploys to deny the vote
instituted by whites against blacks; despite vagrancy laws, rigged juries, and
rampant violation of contract rights—and not conclude that this was the
Court's point all along. The justices who concurred with Bradley had all but
announced that they wanted to be out of the business of protecting a class
of Americans whom they held to be of no value. Stop complaining to us,

Bradley seemed to be saying. And if it took contortions of the Constitution or Byzantine, self-serving applications of the law to get the Court out of the equal rights business, so be it.

As Oliver Wendell Holmes would later write, "The very considerations which judges most rarely mention and always with an apology, are the secret root from which the law draws all the juices of life. I mean, of course, considerations of what is expedient to the community concerned. Every important principle which is developed by litigation is in fact and at bottom the result of more or less definitely understood views of public policy."[13] Given the string of tortuous interpretations of both the postwar amendments and Congress's efforts to enforce their provisions, the Court's view of public policy in the area of freedmen's rights is quite easy to appreciate.

Bradley was joined in his opinion by seven of the eight remaining justices, but, finally, another voice was heard. John Marshall Harlan, the former slave owner from Kentucky, had joined in the series of decisions leading up to the *Civil Rights Cases*, but his willingness to countenance the torturing of the Constitution was at an end. Harlan did not issue his dissent at the Court session, but rather filed it later, stating that the need to write an opinion had taken him by surprise. This is an odd admission, seeing that the case had been heard long before and the feelings of the other justices were hardly a secret. It has been suggested that Harlan had been struck by a severe case of writer's block. In any case, Harlan eventually penned his dissent on the same inkstand as Chief Justice Taney had written the infamous *Dred Scott* opinion.

What Harlan wrote was to become one of the most praised opinions in the Court's history.

Harlan began unambiguously. "I cannot resist the conclusion that the substance and spirit of the recent amendments of the Constitution have been sacrificed by a subtle and ingenious verbal criticism." Then, quoting Edmund Plowden, a famed English legal theorist, from 1574, Harlan added, " 'It is not the words of the law, but the internal sense of it that makes the law; the letter of the law is the body; the sense and reason of the law is the soul.' " Whether Harlan was taking an intentional swipe at Bradley's well-known devotion to bloodless logic, or merely stating his own philosophy, he never let on. But to Bradley, who was well aware of his reputation, the line almost certainly would have been interpreted as a personal rebuke.

Harlan continued, "Constitutional provisions, adopted in the interest of liberty and for the purpose of securing, through national legislation, if need be, rights inhering in a state of freedom and belonging to American citizenship have been so construed as to defeat the ends the people desired to accomplish, which they attempted to accomplish, and which they supposed they had accomplished by changes in their fundamental law . . . The court has departed from the familiar rule requiring, in the interpretation of constitutional provisions, that full effect be given to the intent with which they were adopted."

Harlan clearly was suggesting that his colleagues had resorted to sham legal interpretation to achieve a social goal that they had predetermined. In this Harlan had turned the contemporary argument on its head. "Activism" or "legislating from the bench" has been a clarion by which conservatives have decried liberals for attempting to make social policy by artificially extending constitutional provisions. Harlan here accused conservative judges of legislating from the bench, making social policy by artificially narrowing constitutional provisions.

> My brethren say that when a man has emerged from slavery, and by the aid of beneficent legislation has shaken off the inseparable concomitants of that state, there must be some stage in the progress of his elevation when he takes the rank of a mere citizen, and ceases to be the special favorite of the laws, and when his rights as a citizen, or a man, are to be protected in the ordinary modes by which other men's rights are protected. It is, I submit, scarcely just to say that the colored race has been the special favorite of the laws. What the nation, through congress, has sought to accomplish in reference to that race is, what had already been done in every state in the Union for the white race, to secure and protect rights belonging to them as freemen and citizens; nothing more. The one underlying purpose of congressional legislation has been to enable the black race to take the rank of mere citizens. The difficulty has been to compel a recognition of their legal right to take that rank, and to secure the enjoyment of privileges belonging, under the law, to them as a component part of the people for whose welfare and happiness government is ordained.

Harlan added, "I insist that the national legislature may, without transcending the limits of the Constitution, do for human liberty and the fundamental rights of American citizenship, what it did, with the sanction of this court, for the protection of slaves and the rights of the masters of fugitive slaves."

The justice closed with this famous passage:

Today it is the colored race which is denied by corporations and individuals . . . rights fundamental in their freedom and citizenship. At some future time, it may be that some other race will fall under the ban of race discrimination. If the constitutional amendments be enforced according to the intent with which . . . they were adopted, there cannot be, in this republic, any class of human beings in practical subjection to another class . . . The supreme law of the land has decreed that no authority shall be exercised in this country upon the basis of discrimination . . . against freemen and citizens because of their race, color, or previous condition of servitude. To that decree—for the due enforcement of which, by appropriate legislation, Congress has been invested with express power—everyone must bow, whatever may have been, or whatever now are, his individual views as to the wisdom or policy either of the recent changes in the fundamental law or of the legislation which has been enacted to give them effect.

History may have vindicated Justice Harlan, but his contemporaries surely did not. That the dissent would not be welcomed in the South was no surprise. But Harlan's words were unwelcome in the North as well. The *New York Times* was pleased to find its prediction that the Court would overturn the law vindicated. In an editorial that appeared on October, 16, 1883, the *Times* agreed with Bradley that "the prohibition of the amendment is specifically directed against the making and enforcing of laws by the States which shall abridge the privileges and immunities of citizens. Assuming that these include the right to equal accommodations in public conveyances and places of entertainment, it does not appear that in any of these cases any State has in its legislation or the enforcement of its laws made the discriminations complained of."

The *Times* also pointed out that "the decision is unlikely to have any considerable practical impact, for the reason that the act of 1875 has never been enforced. The general practice of railroads, hotels and theatres has remained unchanged and has depended mainly on the prevailing sentiment of the communities in which they are located."

Then the *Times* observed, "it is doubtful if social privileges can be successfully dealt with by legislation of any kind," a point of view that would be echoed thirteen years later by Henry Billings Brown in *Plessy v. Ferguson.* "At any rate," the *Times* concluded, "the whole matter is now remanded to State authority in which it rightfully belongs."[14]

The *Brooklyn Daily Eagle* was more succinct. "There was a time when this decision would have created some excitement, but that time passed years ago . . . The Negro gained nothing by the passage of the Civil Rights act, and he will lose nothing by having it declared a dead letter. The decision simply gives him notification . . . that his advancement from a position of mere dependency on his white neighbor was to be brought about, not by fulminations of politicians but by self-respect, patience, hard work and general good behavior on his own part."

The *Daily Eagle* then noted, "The decision is interesting as another proof that the Supreme Court continues to be . . . true to the spirit and structure of our Government. The partisan spirit has never been able to debase the Supreme Court. There, if nowhere else . . . loyalty to the fundamental law of the land has found a home.[15]

A telling commentary appeared in *Harper's Weekly.* Since "the long and terrible Civil War sprang from the dogma of State sovereignty, invoked to protect and perpetuate slavery, it was that, at its close, the tendency to magnify the National authority should have been very strong, and especially to defend the victims of slavery . . . In calmer times, the laws passed under that humane impulse are reviewed, and when found to be incompatible with strict constitutional authority, they are set aside. It is another illustration of the singular wisdom of our constitutional system."[16]

The *Atlanta Journal Constitution* crowed. A RADICAL RELIC RUBBED OUT, the headline proclaimed. SPECIAL RIGHTS FOR NONE BUT EQUAL RIGHTS FOR ALL. A TRIUMPH OF LAW AND SENSE WHICH STRENGTHENS THE DECREE THAT THE REPUBLICANS MUST GO.[17]

Not every white newspaper praised the decision. The *Hartford Courant* lamented, "We regret that the judicial authority of the land has felt a duty . . . to wipe out of existence a law that for nearly ten years has worked no harm to anybody, and has been a testimony on the part of the American people of their sincerity in demanding equal rights for all men."[18]

The *Chicago Daily Tribune*, which had been so prescient in predicting the eventual outcome, said simply, "The decision of the United States Supreme Court was not unexpected." The newspaper added, "The persons who have manifested the greatest interest in the decision are the Washington hotelkeepers. The hotels since the law was passed have not received colored persons. No prosecution has been attempted."[19]

The black press, of course, saw the matter differently. Black newspapers were unanimous in their outrage at the decision. The *Boston Hub* charged that the Court had deliberately cast the power of the judiciary against equal rights. The *Louisville Bulletin* exclaimed, "Our government is a farce, and a snare, and the sooner it is overthrown and an empire established upon its ruins the better." The *New York Globe* denounced Bradley as reaffirming the "infamous decision of infamous Chief Justice Taney [in *Dred Scott*] that 'a black man has no rights that a white is bound to respect.'"[20] There were occasional black voices that said the decision was wise in that it eliminated the artificial distinction between black and white, or the artificial association of prosperous, educated blacks with African-Americans lower on the socio-economic ladder, but these views were isolated.

Curious was the reaction of some of Justice Harlan's peers. William Strong, now retired and in private practice, told Harlan, "At first I was inclined to agree with the Court but since reading your opinion, I am in great doubt. It may be that you are right. The opinion of the Court, as you said, is too narrow—sticks to the letter, while you aim to bring out the Spirit of the Constitution."[21]

ELEVEN

FLOODGATES: THE REBIRTH OF WHITE RULE

THE COURT'S DECISION in the *Civil Rights Cases* legitimized a de facto process that had begun virtually the day the Civil War ended and had stalled but by no means ended during Radical Reconstruction. "Almost immediately, whites began to map out a new master-servant relationship, one they hoped would look as much as possible like the old—excepting little other than its element of actual human ownership."[1] When Justice Bradley announced both that private individuals were immune from the postwar constitutional amendments, and that African-Americans could not seek redress in federal courts, except in cases where state governments officially announced their intentions to discriminate, he helped usher in a period of de jure racial discrimination that would last almost a century and was virtually as odious as slavery itself.

Even during Radical Reconstruction, whites had experimented with a number of strategies to maintain the South's traditional social structure, ranging from restrictive voting requirements or rules for jury service to the creation of what were in effect private armies, such as the Ku Klux Klan, the Order of the White Camellia, and the White Rose. The United States Army, Redeemers quickly realized, could not be everywhere at once. Territory could be claimed by the federal government but, except in the cities or other densely populated areas, not held.

Redeemers had also been the serendipitous beneficiaries of the Radicals' insistence on universal male suffrage. In addition to African-Americans, many poorer whites who had been shut out of the voting process by property qualifications gained access to the ballot box for the first time. The question of whether they would vote their economic interests and side with blacks against the monied class, or their racial interests and side with the monied class against blacks was answered quickly and definitively. Poor whites preferred white aristocrats to African-Americans. As a result, the Democratic Party gained thousands of new voters, and so, even when elections were overseen by federal ballot watchers, much of the South tilted away from the Republican Party. Republicans eventually tried to counter by openly courting white voters over black, but Democratic gains in the old Confederacy proved deep and unshakable.

Still, granting the franchise to freedmen resulted in tangible gains for black Americans in local, state, and even national government unimaginable before the war. Virtually all black office holders were elected or appointed as Republicans. So, with poor whites voting overwhelmingly Democratic, whatever their intention, the Radicals had actually succeeded in creating the seeds of a vibrant two-party system in the South.

Those seeds could only sprout, of course, if voting rights were protected equally for both races. If black Americans could not vote, participation in other vital civil functions, such as serving on juries, testifying against whites, entering into contracts, or even mixing in white society could be suitably restricted by whites. A good deal of the physical intimidation by the Klan and other violent Redeemer groups was aimed at suppressing if not eliminating the African-American vote. Where Democrats controlled state or local governments, more peaceful but equally unsubtle means of turning blacks away from the polls were employed. Achieving electoral supremacy under the watchful eye of the federal courts was less convenient than simply writing discriminatory regulations into law, but the South was a defeated power so subtlety, as far as it went, was required. Even after federal troops had been withdrawn from the South, "it seemed more expedient to control and suppress the Negro vote than to try to reduce it legally."[2]

The Court's decision in the *Civil Rights Cases*, however, not only fully validated the blatant ploys to disenfranchise black Americans and relegate them to some shadow existence between freedom and slavery, but also threw open the door to a more codified approach to removing African-Americans first from the voting rolls and then from mainstream civil life. If the Court would merely wink at racism, Redeemers across the South could, with a minimum of effort, establish a white supremacist society guaranteed with the authority of the printed word. Still, Jim Crow society did not burst forth and overwhelm the legal systems in the southern states. The process was gradual. "Before the writing of actual laws, the customs that would harden into legal Jim Crow had begun to permeate nearly every corner of Southern life."[3]

While schools rarely contained members of both races, and public transportation had begun to separate blacks and whites, the main efforts to suppress African-Americans continued to focus on the ballot box. Some of the contrivances to deny blacks the vote would have been almost laughable if the impact was not so tragic. South Carolina, for example, introduced a device called the "eight-box ballot," a box with eight separate slots, each designated for a specific candidate or party. A voter was required to match the ballot to the slot or his vote would be invalidated. The manner in which the ballot and the ballot box were labeled rendered it virtually impossible for someone not literate to cast a valid vote. Whites unable to read were given assistance by poll workers, whereas blacks were left to try to decipher the system on their own. Despite the obvious intent of disenfranchising African-Americans, the eight-box ballot law, because it was enacted without language that specifically discriminated against blacks, would have been perfectly acceptable to the nine white men—or at least eight of the nine—sitting on the Supreme Court in Washington.

The tactics employed by white southerners grew so blatant, so ludicrous, that in 1890, Thomas Brackett Reed of Maine, the sitting Speaker of the United States House of Representatives, published an article in a national magazine outlining some of the more egregious practices.

Reed opened, "No form of government can be based on systematic injustice; least of all a republic. All governments partake of the imperfections of human nature and fall far short not only of the ideals dreamed of by good men, but even of the intentions of ordinary men. Nevertheless, if perfection be unattainable, it is still the duty of every nation to live up to the principles of simple justice, and at least follow the lights it can clearly see."[4]

The Speaker went on to outline some of these "systematic injustices," during which he quoted liberally from pronouncements from southern officials themselves. Of the practice of threatening black voters, Reed wrote, "When the interesting collection of gentlemen in a Southern district go forth to fire guns all night, in order, as the member from that district phrased it in open House, 'to let the niggers know there is going to be a fair election the next day,' they are guilty of intimidation."[5]

Of the eight-box law, the Speaker cited an 1888 speech by John P.

Richardson III, governor of South Carolina. "We have now the rule of a minority of four hundred thousand [whites] over a majority of six hundred thousand [blacks]," Richardson had said. "No army at Austerlitz or Waterloo or Gettysburg could ever be wielded like that mass of six hundred thousand people. The only thing which stands to-day between us and their rule is a flimsy statute—the Eight-Box Law—which depends for its effectiveness upon the unity of the white people."[6]

Southern officials were willing to openly defend—and brag about—such practices as tissue ballots, ballot boxes with false bottoms, and ballot box stuffing, and Reed took them on as well. "Where else on earth," Reed wrote, "would you get such a declaration as came from John P. Finley, of Greenville, Miss., for twelve years treasurer of his county—a declaration made in the presence of his fellow-citizens—that he did not consider ballot-box stuffing a crime, but a necessity; that in a case of race supremacy a man who stuffed a ballot box would not forfeit either his social or business standing; and that ballot-box stuffing, so far as he knew, was looked upon by the best element in the South as a choice between necessary evils?"

Speaker Reed had another example. "You would search far before you would find the parallel of what Watt K. Johnson said. 'I would stuff a ballot-box,' said he, 'if required to do it, to put a good Republican in office, as I would a Democrat, as my object is to have a good honest government.' 'Good honest government' by ballot-box stuffing!"[7]

Where contrivance was not sufficient, there was always raw fear to fall back on. After the army withdrew, going to the polls became an increasingly risky venture as "violence, especially Klan terror, kept untold numbers of blacks from the polls, particularly those living in rural areas where African-American numerical strength was at its highest."[8]

But after a century of being denied, even these machinations, widespread as they were, could not be counted on to suppress African-Americans' will to vote. Blacks continued to endure abuse and risk bodily harm in order to try to cast ballots. White southerners were also all too aware that just because the Supreme Court had drifted away from freedmen's rights, this was no guarantee that they might not one day drift back again.[9] For white society to permanently breathe easy, they would need to find a way to imbed in law what was practiced in the community. In order to comport with the law, that no discrimination be prescribed by statute, whites sought "a means of disenfranchisement which, on its face, would be noncoercive and nonviolent."[10]

Rather than a hit-and-miss approach, Mississippi took the tactic employed by the Radicals twenty years before and threw it back in their faces. If the Reconstruction South had been forced to adopt new Constitutions, the Redeemer South would do the same, revising those state constitutions, "principally with a view to changing suffrage qualifications."[11] A move began in Mississippi to convene a constitutional convention to find a means of denying the vote to African-Americans while not disenfranchising illiterate whites. Any revision of the state constitution, which had been forced on Mississippi during Radical Reconstruction, would have to pass judicial muster, of course, but given the Court's recent guidelines, the task was not thought to be particularly onerous. The state legislature eventually passed a resolution calling for a constitutional convention to meet in Jackson in February 1890.

Mississippi's African-Americans were under no illusions as to the purpose of the convention. Whites, in fact, had made no secret of their intentions. A movement began by the Republican Party, particularly among blacks, to elect as many delegates to the convention as possible. The difficulty, of course, was that in a state where voting fraud was as common as magnolias, Democrats had no difficulty ensuring a rigged election. Of the 135 delegates chosen to attend the convention, two were Republicans of whom only one was black, Isaiah Montgomery, a wealthy landowner on record as supporting disenfranchisement.[12]

At the meeting itself, the delegates were remarkably frank. A judge named J. J. Chrisman observed, "Sir, it is no secret that there has not been a full vote and a fair count in Mississippi since 1875. In plain words, we have been stuffing the ballot boxes, committing perjury, and here and there in the state carrying the elections by fraud and violence until the whole machinery for elections was about to rot down."[13]

But Chrisman wasn't lamenting the actions of Mississippi officials for denying equal rights to African-Americans; he was pointing out the need for a codified means of denying the vote to blacks so white Mississippians no longer would be required engage in such practices in order to ensure a proper election result.

The new state constitution that emerged had substantially stiffened voting qualifications. Provisions included a two-year residency requirement, an annual poll tax, and an elaborate test, which required an applicant to read and interpret a section of the state constitution chosen by a local official. This last qualification purported to be a test for literacy, but the actual purpose of the "understanding and interpretation" test was not only to prevent any new registration by Mississippi's extensive African-American population, but also to disqualify those already on the rolls. In practice, whites were given the most simple clauses to read (and were often helped along by agreeable poll workers), while African-Americans were given serpentine, incomprehensible clauses, which had been inserted into the document for that very purpose.* When African-Americans were off the voting lists, they would be stricken from jury rolls as well. Just to be certain nothing was left to chance, a new electoral system was created, as well as a reapportionment of the counties to ensure a majority of white constituencies, and the new constitution mandated a complete, statewide reregistration of voters.

Finally, to ensure the new constitution's adoption, the state legislature changed a law that required the document to be submitted to the voters and instead allowed a vote among the very delegates who had drawn it up to be sufficient.

The drafters made little secret as to their intent. James K. Vardaman, later to be elected both governor and United States senator, observed delicately, "There is no use to equivocate or lie about the matter. Mississippi's constitutional convention of 1890 was held for no other purpose than to eliminate the nigger from politics . . . let the world know it just as it is."[14]

When Mississippi's new constitution did not arouse ire in the federal courts, whites in other southern states understood that they had been handed a blueprint for success. In 1898, for example, Louisiana convened a constitutional convention "for the express purpose of disfranchising the Negro in order 'to establish the supremacy of the white race.'"[15] The resulting document provided three paths to registration as a voter. The first was the ability to read and write and to fill out an application form without assistance. The Louisiana courts ruled that a perfectly filled-out application was needed to satisfy this requirement. Most blacks were either illiterate or semiliterate and thus unable to qualify. Alternately, an applicant might demonstrate ownership of property assessed at least at $300, and produce a record of paying property taxes. The last means of qualification, meant to open the polls to

---

* Race-baiting Senator Theodore Bilbo, during his campaign for reelection in 1946, remarked, "The poll tax won't keep 'em [blacks] from voting. What keeps 'em from voting is section 244 of the constitution of 1890 that Senator George wrote. It says that a man to register must be able to read and explain the constitution when read to him . . . And then Senator George wrote a constitution that damn few white men and no niggers at all can explain." *Collier's,* July 6, 1946, p. 18.

the many whites who could not meet the first two criteria, was a grandfather clause. As in Mississippi, the 1898 Louisiana constitution was not submitted to the voters for ratification, but simply adopted by the delegates to the convention that drew it up.

The results were all that whites could have hoped for. Statistics in Louisiana, kept in a remarkably thorough fashion, revealed on "January 1, 1897, Number of Negro voters 130,344, Number of White voters 164,088. On March 17, 1900 Negro 5,320, White 125,437." The numbers were broken down further as to the qualifications under which these voters registered in 1900. "Under the 'educational' qualification: White 86,157; Negro 4,327. Under the 'property' qualification: White 10,793; Negro 916. Under the 'grandfather' clause: White, 29,189; Negro, 0."[16]

South Carolina adopted a constitution in 1895 that required a literacy test, a poll tax, and disqualified from voting anyone convicted of crimes that were disproportionately committed by African-Americans. That constitution also, for the first time, mandated segregated schools—"Separate schools shall be provided for children of white and colored races, and no child of either race shall ever be permitted to attend a school provided for children of the other race"—and prohibited "marriage of a white person with a Negro or mulatto or a person who shall have one-eighth or more of Negro blood."

In Alabama, a constitution was adopted in 1901 that stipulated that an applicant to vote must be able to read and write a section of the American Constitution (a requirement inserted, as far as one can tell, without irony) or own property assessed for taxation at $300 or more. Grandfather clauses allowed poor illiterate whites to avoid either alternative.

New constitutions were not the only method employed by whites to return the South to a de facto antebellum state. In 1890, the same year that Mississippi enacted its new constitution, the Louisiana legislature passed an act that became known as the "Separate Car Law," a provision of which would set the stage for the most significant test of racial equality since the end of the Civil War.[17] The law demanded, by statute, a separation of the races on public railways. But to avoid running afoul of the one prohibition the Supreme Court had maintained for equal rights legislation, the law stipulated that the respective railway cars to which the races might be assigned be "equal." Thus the concept of "equal but separate," as it was first described, entered American jurisprudence, aimed inevitably for a test in the United States Supreme Court.

TWELVE

BLURRING THE BOUNDARIES: THE EXPANSION OF DUE PROCESS

DURING THE 1870S AND 1880S, the Supreme Court had narrowed both the scope of the Fourteenth Amendment and the federal government's powers to enforce its provisions, all on the altar of federalism, the Tenth Amendment, and the states' right of "police power."[1] After the ruling in the *Civil Rights Cases*, the amendment would have virtually no real application in the lives of African-Americans. But by no means would the Fourteenth Amendment fade into oblivion as a constitutional anachronism. Rather, the amendment, particularly its notion of due process, would be given new life by the justices, not as was originally intended, in the protection of the rights of freedmen, but in the affairs of members of that new oppressed class, the American corporation. Beginning almost at the moment the Court decided that the Fourteenth Amendment must give way to the Tenth in cases involving the rights of African-Americans, they began, without a touch of disquiet, to take precisely the opposite view in cases where states attempted to use this newly expanded police power to regulate the activities of businesses, particularly railroads.[2]

The phrase "due process of law" appears twice in the United States Constitution, in the Fifth Amendment as well as the Fourteenth. In the former, the promise that "no person . . . shall be deprived of life, liberty, or property without due process of law" is taken as a prohibition against misconduct by the federal government; in the latter, virtually the same phrase applied the principle to the various states but, as the justices had made clear, not to individuals or private entities within those states.

"Due process of law" appears a straightforward enough term, and, indeed, general understanding exists that it represents merely a guarantee that laws will be applied fairly, that the full range of legal rights of every citizen must be respected. The government can neither annul these rights nor apply them selectively.

The origin of due process seems to have been Magna Carta, the English charter of laws of 1215. Although Magna Carta is widely considered a triumph of individual liberty over the arbitrary power of the state, the document had little to do with protection of individual rights, which could be pretty much trampled on as much after as before its adoption. Magna Carta was primarily an enumerated list of restrictions on the power of the stupendously incompetent King John over his barons. Chapter 39 states, "No free man shall be taken or imprisoned or disseised of his Freehold, or Liberties, or free Customs, or be outlawed, or exiled, or any other wise destroyed, nor will we go upon him nor send upon him, except by the lawful judgment of his peers or by the law of the land."

Only in the seventeenth century, when the great English legal theorist Sir Edward Coke insisted that the provisions of Magna Carta applied to all subjects of the crown, not merely the nobility, did due process gain wider application. His common law interpretations survived well into the next century and had no small impact on American legal thought. During the constitutional period, "Coke had taught, and Americans believed, that due process of law meant accordance with regularized common law procedures, especially grand jury accusation and trial by jury."[3] The inclusion of the phrase in the Bill of Rights was, of course, primarily the work of James Madison and was intended to establish the guarantees to which Coke referred.[4] The definition under which Madison worked has changed very little in the ensuing centuries. The 2004 edition of *Black's Law Dictionary* defines due process as "The conduct of legal proceedings according to established rules and principles for the protection and enforcement of private rights, including notice and the right to a fair hearing before a tribunal with the power to decide the case." A similar definition, slightly more fleshed out, is the assurance of "fair procedure when the government imposes a burden on an individual. The doctrine seeks to prevent arbitrary government, avoid mistaken deprivations, allow persons to know about and respond to charges against them, and promote a sense of the legitimacy of official behavior."

In the law, however, where parsing of language often trumps obvious intent or commonsense understanding, any vagueness, no matter how slight, will invariably create a good deal of mischief. So it has been with due process, which has been wielded by the justices for well over a century to gain advantage for one or another point of view.

Application of due process became complicated during the 1870s because, classically defined, the phrase only encompassed guarantees on how legal proceedings would be conducted, not on what they would be conducted about. But in many of the equal rights cases that came before the Court, the justices insisted on applying their own, sometimes quixotic, interpretations of the amendments' intent. They strangled the language, restricting application of procedural standards to only the most obvious enumerated rights; for example, that states could not, by statute, restrict the right to vote on racial grounds. Once the Court ruled that the actions of private individuals were not covered under the Fourteenth and Fifteenth amendments, or that state laws, unless explicitly discriminatory in language, were exempt from federal intervention, granting African-Americans specific rights was no longer a question of procedural guarantees, but rather whether or not a right or protection was *implicit* in the amendment even though it wasn't precisely spelled out. Once Fourteenth and Fifteenth Amendment guarantees became less than absolute, rights claimed by African-Americans inevitably came into conflict with rights claimed by opposing groups, state legislatures, for example. The Court's focus then shifted from deciding whether proper procedures had been followed with respect to a specific plaintiff to deciding which of competing rights would apply.

To resolve the conflict the justices had themselves created, a strict application of "procedural" due process suddenly would not do. To sort out this notion of implied rights, one must apply the hazier first derivative of procedural due process, something called "substantive due process."

Specifically, substantive due process is the extension of procedural guarantees to encompass those rights that might not be specifically enumerated in the Constitution but are fundamental to our notions of freedom; as Justice Benjamin Cardozo wrote in 1937 in *Palko v. Connecticut*, such rights that are "implicit in the concept of ordered liberty."[5] Obviously, the more broadly substantive due process is applied, the greater the number of people or institutions that will claim protection under its aegis, the greater the number of disputes will be thereby engendered, and the greater the influence of the judiciary in deciding which side will prevail. When expanded to sufficient breadth, the judiciary will be in the position to pick and choose whose rights to protect and whose to ignore on a rather grand scale. That an entire class of people, African-Americans, say, could therefore be deprived of fundamental rights on the altar of conflict resolution was and is perfectly acceptable under the law.

Given the ambiguities in wording inevitable in a document with such complex application as the American Constitution, that the concept of implied rights is an ongoing source of debate is hardly surprising. Still, the expansion of due process to encompass implied rights has been a source of outrage among conservative judges. That an "activist" judiciary can simply make up rights to suit its own social or economic agenda, "legislate from the bench" as it were, is anathema to judges who would define themselves as "strict constructionists" or "originalists." Most galling in recent jurisprudence is an implied right of privacy in the Fourth Amendment, on which Justice Harry Blackmun based his majority opinion in *Roe v. Wade.* Conservatives are fond of enunciating other travesties that have occurred when judges moved from the enumerated to the implied.

Robert Bork, for example, attempted to categorize *Dred Scott* as an example of the application of substantive due process. Bork wrote, "How, then, can there be a constitutional right to own slaves where a statute forbids it? Taney created such a right by changing the plain meaning of the due process clause of the fifth amendment . . . He knew [slave ownership was a constitutional right] because he was passionately convinced that it must be a constitutional right. Though his transformation of the due process clause from a procedural right to a substantive requirement was an obvious sham, it was a momentous sham, for this was the first appearance in American constitutional law of the concept of 'substantive due process,' and that concept has been used countless times since by judges who want to write their personal beliefs into a document that, most inconveniently, does not contain those beliefs."[6]

In decrying selectivity, however, Judge Bork descended to it. To annul the Missouri Compromise in *Dred Scott,* Chief Justice Taney relied on the principle of judicial review, a power that John Marshall wrote into the United States Constitution, which, most inconveniently for Judge Bork, does not contain that power. That judicial review is a right every bit as implied as that of privacy has escaped Judge Bork's notice, however.

But it is characteristic of critics of judicial expansionism that they will decry only the instances in which the result is one with which they philosophically disagree, and will defend or rationalize those with which they are in support. At issue, then, is not whether one justice or one Court has unfairly usurped legislative, executive, or state power, but rather whether one approves or disapproves of the power that the Court has claimed for itself. Jurisprudence is, after all, hardly a value-free science.

Yet Judge Bork's main point, in principle at least, is well taken. To extend or contort the Constitution willy-nilly to suit political fashion would surely threaten to undermine the very system of laws under which Americans sought to live by drafting a Constitution. Yet those extensions and contortions seem to be integral to American history. What's more, to attempt to apply objectivity to as inexplicit a document as the Constitution, as Judge Bork clearly favors, inevitably fails.[7] Leonard Levy observed that "legal rules, legal logic, legal erudition, legal research, and legal precedents do not decide questions involving the ambiguous or vague clauses of the Constitution, the very clauses usually at issue in those cases whose outcome helps to determine justice, shape public policy, and measure the degree of liberty or equality that exists in this country."[8]

In *Dred Scott*, legal historians have been virtually unanimous in their condemnation of Chief Justice Taney's extension of due process to justify and protect slavery. In *Roe v. Wade*, a case Judge Bork equates with *Dred Scott* for misuse of judicial authority, opinion splits. In theory, the rift is whether a "right of privacy" is implicit in the Fourth Amendment, but in fact, the disagreement has little to do with legal philosophy but is rather simply a question of whether or not one agrees that abortion is a political right.

In the same vein, during the period the Court was asphyxiating the Fourteenth and Fifteenth amendments, the justices felt no need to redefine due process of law. Instead, they simply redefined the amendments, thus moving the issues before the Court from the relative clarity of procedural due process to the more subjective substantive due process, then applied strict, and many would say arbitrary, standards on where and how substantive due process could be applied. One need only recall Justice Field's ringing condemnation of state police power when used against the New Orleans butchers in the *Slaughterhouse Cases*—and his defense of precisely the same power when concurring in *Cruikshank, Rives,* and the *Civil Rights Cases*—to recognize how subjective the meaning of the Fourteenth Amendment could be.

The notion of "implied rights" does not exist in constitutional law, Justices Field, Bradley, Waite, and others insisted again and again in Court rulings narrowing application of the postwar amendments in equal rights appeals. They constantly rejected arguments that the Thirteenth, Fourteenth, and Fifteenth amendments had application beyond the absolutely strictest reading. Thus, such amorphous and questionable notions as "badges of servitude" were given short shrift. In a rather substantial irony, some commentators have praised the justices' rulings during this period for applying "restraint," for voluntarily restricting their own power rather than resorting to "activism" to artificially rewrite the Constitution.

In fact, the justices were engaging in nothing of the sort. They were hardly restricting their own power, as their pivot in the railroad cases would later demonstrate, nor were they applying restraint. The judges were simply finding justification, no matter how flimsy, for declining to enforce constitutional amendments with whose principles they philosophically and politically disagreed. When freedmen's rights were disposed of and the subject of Supreme Court appeals began to shift to regulation of America's burgeoning corporate class, the justices' position on substantive due process shifted right along with it.

In early cases involving state police power and economic rights, the Court had no choice but to take the same position as it had in equal rights decisions. In the *Slaughterhouse Cases*, the Court ruled that Louisiana's granting of a monopoly to regulate butchers outweighed the butchers' rights to freedom of contract, thus once again elevating the Tenth Amendment at the expense of the Fourteenth.[9] But at the time the *Slaughterhouse Cases* were being decided, the bulk of Tenth versus Fourteenth Amendment cases were for freedmen's rights, and the justices would have been hard-pressed to allow states Tenth Amendment powers to create, say, an obviously discriminatory literacy test while denying its power to keep animal waste out of the New Orleans drinking supply.

By the time the next round of economic cases came before the Court, Grover Cleveland was president, the first Democrat to hold the post since Andrew Johnson, and the Court had become amenable to considering the Fourteenth Amendment in a different light. During arguments of a nondescript railroad case, *San Mateo County v. Southern Pacific Railroad*, the attorney for the defense, United States senator turned corporate lawyer Roscoe Conkling made a stunning claim to the panel of justices whose company he had twice declined.[10] Holding up an old book that he claimed was his handwritten journal, Conkling, a member of the joint congressional committee that had drafted the Fourteenth Amendment, insisted the word "person" had been used in the amendment's wording instead of "citizen" because the committee members had intended to apply the amendment's guarantees to corporations rather than freedmen. The committee, he told the justices, reading from the purported journal, was "reacting to individuals and joint stock companies . . . appealing for congressional and administrative protection against invidious and discriminating State and local taxes."[11] Although Conkling's pronouncement, later dubbed a "conspiracy theory" by historians, proved to be utter hogwash, none of the nine justices saw fit to question him.[12] And since the case itself was dismissed on technical grounds, the matter received no comment in Chief Justice Waite's opinion.

But what Conkling had done was introduce into the Court's thinking the legal concept of "economic substantive due process," a second derivative of the original concept. It applied protections of the Fourteenth Amendment to the amorphous notion of "freedom of contract." This extension of substantive due process does not refer to the freedom to enter into contracts, but rather interprets contract rights to prohibit government regulation, minimum wage laws, unionization, and any number of other provisions that might restrict or limit the manner in which a corporation does business. Under a strict application of economic substantive due process, a law prohibiting child labor, for example, would be in violation of the Constitution.[13]

The seed that Conkling planted did not take long to sprout. Just two months after hearing *San Mateo*, the Court decided *Stone and Others v. Farmers' Loan & Trust Co.*, which became known as the *Railroad Commission Cases*. At issue was whether or not the Mississippi railroad commission could enforce provisions of a bylaw it enacted in 1884 that attempted "from time to time to fix, regulate, and receive, the tolls and charges by them to be received for transportation."[14] Among the grounds under which the railroads appealed was that "the statute under which the commissioners are to act impairs the obligation of the charter contract of the Mobile & Ohio Railroad Company," which had been chartered in Alabama. Another was that the Mississippi law "denies the company the equal protection of the laws, and deprives it of its property without due process of law."

The Court, speaking through Chief Justice Waite, upheld the Mississippi law. But the chief justice also set in motion the process by which states would lose virtually all their power to control businesses. Waite asserted, "From what has thus been said, it is not to be inferred that this power of limitation or regulation is itself without limit. This power to regulate is not a power to destroy, and limitation is not the equivalent of confiscation. Under pretense of regulating fares and freights, the state cannot require a railroad corporation to carry persons or property without reward; neither can it do that which in law amounts to a taking of private property for public use without just compensation or without due process of law." The chief justice added, damning with faint support, "General statutes regulating the use of railroads in a state or fixing maximum rates of charges for transportation, when not forbidden by charter contracts, do not necessarily deprive the corporation owning or operating a railroad within the state of its property without due process of law within the meaning of the Fourteenth Amendment of the Constitution of the United States nor take away from the corporation the equal protection of the laws." Whether Conkling had pried open the door to economic substantive due process or Waite had come to it on his own is not clear, but by even allowing the possibility of economic application of the Fourteenth Amendment, Waite created a potential land rush of appeals against state regulation.

Justices Harlan and, predictably, Field dissented, both desirous of throwing open the door to economic interpretation much wider than had Waite. Harlan asserted, "I am of opinion that this statute impairs the obligation of the contract which the state made with these companies, in this, that it takes from each of them the power conferred by its charter of fixing and regulating rates for transportation . . . and confers upon a commission authority to establish from time to time such rates as will give a 'fair and just return.'" Field added, "The act of Mississippi is so plain an impairment of this essential right [of contract] that I should not have supposed there could be any question on the point did I not find that a majority of my associates are of opinion that it is an entirely constitutional proceeding on the part of the legislature, in no wise interfering with the contract of the company."

In another 1886 case, Chief Justice Waite dropped his conditions, making official (if not quite de jure) what the Court had implied de facto in the Mississippi railroad commission case. In *Santa Clara County v. Southern Pacific Railroad Company*, a unanimous Court, speaking through Justice Harlan, ruled that a railroad could not be taxed for fences that had been erected by the state and were therefore not part of the railroad's property. The decision was unremarkable except for a comment made during oral argument by the chief justice that was included in the case summary, but not in Harlan's opinion. Waite asserted, "The court does not wish to hear argument on the question whether the provision in the Fourteenth Amendment to the Constitution, which forbids a State to deny to any person within its jurisdiction the equal protection of the laws, applies to these corporations. We are all of the opinion that it does."[15]

In fact, corporations had begun to enjoy quite a bit more protection under the Fourteenth Amendment than African-Americans ever did. With a lukewarm endorsement of police power, two key dissents in the Mississippi case, and Morrison Waite's extension of the Fourteenth Amendment to guarantee the rights of inanimate objects, attorneys for the railroads pressed their advantage. They argued that "when the reasonableness of legislative rates is questioned, 'due process' requires that the Courts shall finally decide the matter; that is that the question of reasonableness of legislative rates is a judicial one, under the Fourteenth Amendment's guaranty of 'due process of law.' "[16]

A more blatant example of an "implied right" than a constitutional guarantee of a profitable return on investment would be hard to imagine. Yet the Supreme Court, which had rejected the right to an equitable literacy test as not specified in the Fourteenth or Fifteenth Amendment, had given every indication that it would look favorably on extending its enforcement of due process to include deciding what was and was not a "reasonable" freight rate that a railroad could charge its customers. "Dismissing . . . its earlier concern for the federal equilibrium, this tribunal began a reinterpretation of the Fourteenth Amendment in the light of the principles of Lockian individualism and of Spencerian *Laissez Faire*, which traverses the results it had previously reached at every point."[17]

In 1890, economic substantive due process once again came to the fore in the decisive case of the *Chicago, St. Paul & Milwaukee Railroad v. Minnesota*.[18]

Both the nation and the Court had changed since *Santa Clara*. Benjamin Harrison was president, having defeated incumbent Grover Cleveland in 1888, although without gaining a majority of the popular vote.[19] Republicans, ceding the South to the Democrats, had not even campaigned there. Three new justices had been impaneled on the Court. Morrison Waite had died late in Cleveland's term, and William B. Woods had died a year before. For chief justice, President Cleveland chose Melville Fuller, a corporate attorney from Illinois with no judicial experience. Fuller was described by a critic as the "fifth best lawyer in the city of Chicago," not meant as a compliment to either the man or the city. The *New York Times* praised Fuller's affability, his friends in both parties, the social prominence of his wife, his friendship with President Cleveland, and the number of his visits to plead cases before the Supreme Court as an attorney. Missing from the *Times* article and most other descriptions of Fuller was any praise for excellence or an incisive legal mind.[20] Fuller's record on equal rights was extremely conservative. He had "led legislative opposition to Lincoln's Emancipation Proclamation, had supported state constitutional provisions that rejected black suffrage and black migration, and had helped segregate Chicago schools."[21]

To replace Woods, Cleveland had chosen the wonderfully named Mississippian Lucius Quintus Cincinnatus Lamar, the first and only erstwhile officer in the Confederate army to serve on the Court. While Lamar had been a postwar supporter of African-American participation in the political process, his judicial credentials were as suspect as Fuller's had been. Even Lamar admitted he had misgivings about accepting the position since he had "always acted on the principle that a man should not undertake the duties of any position to which he is not consciously equal."[22] His active, enthusiastic service in the Confederacy, however, aroused little debate in the Senate. He had claimed a conversion to Unionism and was pronounced a man of sufficient integrity to be taken at his word. Many Republican newspapers, however, attacked Lamar for his refusal to apologize for his rebel past and, more significantly, that he was "naturally and spontaneously to the side of the strong against the weak." He was, in fact, "a friend of monopolies."[23] Eventually, however, Lamar was confirmed by a 32–28 vote in a Republican-controlled Senate, the first Democrat to sit on the Court in a quarter century.

Benjamin Harrison had also made an appointment, the first of four justices he would have the opportunity to select. Stanley Matthews died in March 1889, just two weeks after Harrison's inauguration, and, for his seat, the new president appointed David Josiah Brewer, the Court's first Kansan. Brewer possessed unquestioned intellectual credentials, but, a nephew of Justice Field, he shared his uncle's veneration of property rights and would become perhaps the Court's most conservative justice.

Another uncle, Henry Martyn Field, the justice's brother, was a prominent Presbyterian minister and travel writer with prewar abolitionist credentials. In 1886, he had a written book titled *Blood Is Thicker Than Water*, a record of his travels through the South. At one point, he quoted a North

Carolina farmer, who observed, "A negro works with his hands rather than his brain: he is a good field hand—good at the hoe or the plow. But set him to watch a loom, where he has nothing to do but keep his eyes wide open, and before he knows it, those eyes will be shut and he will be fast asleep." Field in no way contradicted this view, but, rather, supported it, referring later in the same paragraph to the black man's "natural indolence" and then describing blacks as "a simple and docile race."[24]

Reverend Field's sentiments were hardly unusual, even for an abolitionist. By the standards of the time, they would not have even been considered racist. One would have been hard-pressed to find more than a tiny minority of American whites in the 1890s who did *not* believe black people were as the reverend described. Whether Justice Brewer ascribed to a similar view of African-Americans is not known, but the family was close and Brewer certainly never gave any indication that he believed differently. As a justice in state supreme court, Brewer dissented in a case that invalidated school segregation, making it clear that he thought neither state law nor the Fourteenth Amendment prohibited racial separation in education.[25]

The son of missionaries of the Congregational Church, Brewer himself was born in Smyrna, Asia Minor, where his father had been assigned to attempt to convert Jews and Orthodox Greeks to Protestantism.[26] Brewer's own Protestant roots ran deep, and he had been steeped in the virtues of hard work, honesty, individual achievement, and private enterprise. Government regulation had little place in his ethos, except to prevent intrusion on freedom of action. Brewer attended Yale, where one of his classmates was another laissez-faire advocate named Henry Billings Brown. In his twenties, Brewer settled in Leavenworth, Kansas, making a name for himself as an attorney and then on the state bench. When appointed to the Court, Brewer's pro-business bent and expansive view of contract rights were a matter of public record, and he thus could be expected to embrace the newly popular economic substantive due process.

At issue in *Chicago, St. Paul, & Milwaukee Railroad v. Minnesota* was whether a state law, "an act to regulate common carriers, and creating the railroad and warehouse commission of the state of Minnesota, and defining the duties of such commission in relation to common carriers," was in violation of the due process clause of the Fourteenth Amendment. The specific complaint was that the railroad had charged excessive rates for the transportation of milk, which the state commission had reduced. The railroad had sued in state court and been rebuffed. The railroad's Supreme Court appeal was specifically on Fourteenth Amendment grounds, using the very arguments that railroad attorneys had been making since the *Santa Clara* case. How the justices ruled would determine whether or not economic substantive due process would be given force of law.

The majority opinion, delivered by Justice Blatchford, noted with typical judicial clarity, "it is the expressed intention of the legislature of Minnesota, by the statute, that the rates recommended and published by the commission . . . are not simply advisory, nor merely prima facie equal and reasonable, but final and conclusive as to what are equal and reasonable charges . . . under the statute, the rates published by the commission are the only ones that are lawful, and therefore, in contemplation of law, the only ones that are equal and reasonable . . . In other words, although the railroad company is forbidden to establish rates that are not equal and reasonable, there is no power in the courts to stay the hands of the commission, if it chooses to establish rates that are unequal and unreasonable."

Blatchford, with only slightly diminished verbosity, explained his explanation. "[The state law] deprives the company of its right to a judicial investigation, by due process of law, under the forms and with the machinery provided by the wisdom of successive ages for the investigation judicially of the truth of a matter in controversy, and substitutes therefore, as an absolute finality, the action of a railroad commission which, in view of the powers conceded to it by the state court, cannot be regarded as clothed with judicial functions, or possessing the machinery of a court of justice."[27]

But the Constitution contains no mention whatever of the Supreme Court's right to intervene in a state regulatory matter, even if "the wisdom of successive ages" supported it. What's more, the railroad had not in the least been denied a "judicial investigation." The Minnesota state courts had investigated the matter fully and found the commission had been acting within its legal rights. The only "finality" was in the railroad's losing its appeal. What Blatchford had conveniently omitted in the paragraph was the word "federal" before "judicial," thus denying, or at least eviscerating, Minnesota's Tenth Amendment right to set rules for the behavior of individuals and businesses residing or engaging in commerce within its borders, unless specifically forbidden to do so by federal statute. This was precisely the same state power, of course, that the Court had viewed so expansively in the past—and would in the future—in questions surrounding the rights of African-Americans.

Blatchford, seemingly unmindful that his colleagues had insisted in equal rights cases that the Court could not and should not usurp any state prerogative guaranteed under the Tenth Amendment, made his argument even more broad, agreeing with the railroad attorneys to add the vague and utterly meaningless standard of "reasonableness" to the judgment.

"The question of the reasonableness of a rate of charge for transportation by a railroad company, involving, as it does, the element of reasonableness both as regards the company and as regards the public, is eminently a question for judicial investigation, requiring due process of law for its determination. If the company is deprived of the power of charging reasonable rates for the use of its property, and such deprivation takes place in the absence of an investigation by judicial machinery, it is deprived of the lawful use of its property, and thus, in substance and effect, of the property itself, without due process of law, and in violation of the constitution of the United States; and, in so far as it is thus deprived, while other persons are permitted to receive reasonable profits upon their invested capital, the company is deprived of the equal protection of the laws."

Not only, then, could a state not decide what was fair and reasonable within its borders, but it must cede that power to a court sitting more than one thousand miles away, whose familiarity with local needs and standards fell somewhere between vague and nonexistent. The absurdity of the Supreme Court establishing itself as freight rate board has not been lost on scholars. "If thereby property values were stabilized and guaranteed against serious governmental impairment through the legerdemain of equating 'due process' with 'reasonable' laws and 'just compensation,' of transferring from the legislature to the judiciary the control over rates, of converting 'personal liberty' into 'freedom of contract' and 'contract' into 'property,' of extending the immunities designed for the property-less Negro to the vast assets of that corporate 'person' known as the Southern Pacific Railroad Company [in *Santa Clara*], it must be remembered that no great contemporaneous public protest was made."[28]

The Court's ruling was not unanimous, however. Justice Miller concurred in the decision but would have voted differently if the railroad operated only within state borders. Joseph Bradley, joined by Justices Gray and Lamar, disagreed entirely. "The legislature has the right, and it is its prerogative, if it chooses to exercise it, to declare what is reasonable. This is just where I differ from the majority of the court. They say in effect, if not in terms, that the final tribunal of arbitrament is the judiciary. I say it is the legislature. I hold that it is a legislative question, not a judicial one." But Bradley had gone from standard setter to dissenter. *Chicago, St. Paul & Milwaukee* was to be his last important opinion.

Economic substantive due process was now the law of the land, because the Supreme Court had declared it to be so. Laissez-faire and Social Darwinism reigned triumphant. *Chicago, St. Paul & Milwaukee* opened the gates. From there, wielding due process like a shotgun, "to 1936 . . . the Supreme Court arrogantly, artlessly, and inconsistently manipulated doctrines of constitutional law against an array of statutory reforms that sought to protect consumers, trade unions, farmers, unorganized workers, women, and children from the exploitation and abuses of economic enterprise."[29] One might have added that the Court also "arrogantly, artlessly, and inconsistently" upheld statutory deprivations of the most fundamental rights of black Americans. The American historian Brooks Adams, grandson of one president and great-grandson of another, noted that the Court seemed determined to "dislocate any comprehensive body of legislation whose effect would be to change the social status."[30]

In the end, the issue of whether or not "substantive due process" was used or misused by the justices in limiting the right of state governments to regulate corporations operating within its borders is moot. The real question is whether or not the justices simply had sought, and ultimately found, legal cover for advancing their own personal political and social agendas. When the Court chose to limit federal power in civil rights cases and expand it to protect railroads, the justices seemed quite plainly merely to be expressing antipathy for African-Americans and approval of railroad magnates. "Corporations succeeded to the rights which those who framed the Fourteenth Amendment thought they were bestowing upon the negro. This outcome is not entirely devoid of irony."[31]

And while the justices were busy granting the protections to commerce that they had denied to freedmen, African-Americans were being progressively denied the right to vote, convicted on trumped-up charges by all-white juries, consigned to substandard schools, forced to use filthy public toilets, shunted off to second-rate accommodations on railroads and streetcars, denied entry to hotels and theaters, dragged from their homes and beaten, hanged, or burned to death.

After the Civil War, blacks could no longer be considered property. The Supreme Court, it seemed, now considered them something less than property.

THIRTEEN

CONFLUENCE: *PLESSY V. FERGUSON*

O N SEPTEMBER 1, 1891, a political committee was formed in New
Orleans. The group consisted of doctors, lawyers, newspaper publishers,
and prominent businessmen. Its leader, Louis Martinet (both names pronounced in the French style), held degrees from both medical school and law
school, and edited a local weekly. The committee raised $30,000, quite a
large sum of money in those days, to pursue a single aim. The group Martinet formed was called, unambiguously, the "Citizens' Committee to Test the
Constitutionality of the Separate Car Law." Louis Martinet and all the other
members of the committee were black.

By 1891, like an outmanned army cut off from retreat, reduced to forming
small, ultimately hopeless pockets of resistance, New Orleans had become
virtually the last bastion of organized African-American resistance in the
South. Surrounded, their options shrinking with the territory they held,
these last desperate fighters sustained themselves either with the delusion of
strength or the illusion of a coming miracle.

That the African-American community in New Orleans was the most
vibrant and accomplished in the South, perhaps in the entire nation, made
the events to come all the more tragic.[1] Since the early eighteenth century,
the city, under rule by the French, whose racial attitudes were less severe,
had boasted a population of educated, able free blacks. They referred to
themselves as "Black Creoles," or "*gens du coleur libre*." Even after the Louisiana Purchase in 1803, free Negro society in New Orleans continued to flour-
ish. Although technically classified as "colored" by whites, many members of
the New Orleans African-American community, as a result of a substantial
amount of both official and unofficial intermarriage, looked a good deal

more white than black. Through generations of mixed-race births, many of their number had quite limited African blood: mulattoes, one half black; quadroons, one quarter; octoroons, one eighth. Octoroons in particular often appeared so Caucasian that they could come and go in white institutions without anyone questioning their lineage. Because of achievement and a rather snobbish view of themselves as compared to slaves and less accomplished free blacks, links with the African-American elite in the North were a good deal stronger in New Orleans than in any other southern city.

These men, who had prospered both before the Civil War and during Reconstruction, who had sent their children to college, who had visited Europe, who had sometimes owned slaves of their own, with the passage of the Separate Car Law, also known in Louisiana as Act 111, would now be subject to the same humiliating treatment as field hands.[2] And the Separate Car Law was but one facet of the general onslaught against the freedoms that Black Creoles had enjoyed since before the United States became a nation. Louis Martinet and his associates faced the potential denial of their right to property, free access to public facilities, and even their right to vote.

Martinet's committee, aware that their chances in state court were virtually nonexistent, intended to use the $30,000 they had raised to force a test case in the United States Supreme Court. Martinet, as an attorney himself, was doubtless aware that the high court also offered scant chance of success. Perhaps Justice Harlan had issued his ringing dissent in the *Civil Rights Cases*, but he had subsequently concurred in a number of other cases that left his support of equal rights problematic. The other eight justices had either concurred in the 1883 decision or, if they had been appointed since, gave little indication that they would take a favorable view of yet another test of what were already becoming known as Jim Crow laws.[3]

Moreover, the socioscientific climate made any equal rights challenge even more tenuous. The racial views of the justices, as well as the vast majority of Americans, continued to be steeped in quack scholarship. Social Darwinism was more popular than ever, counting among its devotees a rising star on the Supreme Judicial Court of Massachusetts named Oliver Wendell Holmes Jr. The theory was regularly employed to buttress economic or sociological arguments. Pseudoscience abounded in the 1890s; everything from phrenology, which asserted that one's personality could be deduced by the shape and size of his or her skull, to theosophy, which claimed insight into the mind of God and postulated spiritual evolution and reincarnation. Few

white Americans questioned the premise that one race predominated because it deserved to. Arguments were made that any attempt to "civilize"
African-Americans would cause more problems than it solved. "Going a step
further in the investigation," one academic wrote, "we will find, not only
that the negro is more criminal in the North than in the South, but that,
dividing the South into groups of States, he is most criminal in the States
where he is best educated."[4] In this climate, to expect the Court to mandate
that the black race be forced to mix on equal terms with the white was just
short of fantasy.[5]

But Martinet did not intend to pursue his challenge as an equal rights
case, at least not at first. Providing separate facilities for blacks and whites
also had economic overtones. One potential ally, unlikely though it would
seem at first blush, might be the railroads themselves. Providing dual accommodations was an expense, particularly for those lines in which white and
colored cars were each filled to less than capacity. Martinet could only hope
that, despite its predilection for white supremacy, the Court would be reluctant to rule against equal rights if the decision would also erode the laissez-
faire power of corporations.

The Court had put its toe in the water on the notion of "equal but separate"
in 1877, while the Civil Rights Act of 1875 was still in force. Josephine De-
Cuir, a well-to-do black woman and plantation owner, had purchased a valid
first-class ticket on a steamboat going up the Mississippi from New Orleans
to Vicksburg, Mississippi, although she herself was only traveling to her
home in Hermitage, Louisiana. During the trip, she had been denied access
to the "ladies cabin" on the top deck and directed to the cabin below decks
set aside for African-Americans. Ms. DeCuir sued under an enforcement act
guaranteeing a section of the 1869 Louisiana constitution that provided "all
persons shall enjoy equal rights and privileges upon any conveyance of a
public character." She was awarded damages in state court, a judgment upheld by the Louisiana Supreme Court, at that time still dominated by Reconstruction Republicans. The court ignored the intrastate nature of Ms.
DeCuir's passage and instead focused on the law itself, which, the judges
insisted, created no burden on interstate commerce, and thus did not run
afoul of the Constitution's commerce clause, but rather remained within
Louisiana's Tenth Amendment jurisdiction.

In a unanimous decision in *Hall v. DeCuir*, the United States Supreme Court overturned the decision. Morrison Waite wrote the majority opinion and, in typically Byzantine fashion, concluded that Ms. DeCuir's suit put a burden on *interstate* commerce because she herself was traveling *intrastate*. Since white passengers in the ladies' cabin had booked passage with the expectation of traveling in a whites-only facility, if Louisiana compelled the steamboat to seat Ms. DeCuir in the same cabin, Louisiana would have altered the terms of the contract with its interstate passengers. This, according to the chief justice, would impose a burden on interstate commerce beyond Louisiana's authority. Of course, if Ms. DeCuir had been an interstate passenger, the steamboat line would have had no authority to bar her from the ladies' cabin under the Civil Rights Act of 1875. That the Court, to that point, had been dodging challenges to the 1875 law was not addressed by the chief justice.[6]

The more powerful statement, and the more prescient, was made in a concurring opinion by Justice Clifford. Ignoring the 1875 law entirely, Clifford asserted, "Substantial equality of right is the law of the state and of the United States; but equality does not mean identity . . . there was and is not any law of Congress which forbids such a carrier from providing separate apartments for his passengers." Clifford did not stop with public conveyances. "Equality of rights," he wrote, "does not involve the necessity of educating white and colored persons in the same school any more than it does that of educating children of both sexes in the same school, or that different grades of scholars must be kept in the same school, and that any classification which preserves substantially equal school advantages is not prohibited by either the state or federal Constitution, nor would it contravene the provisions of either."

Although *DeCuir* seemed to provide an opening to invalidate forced segregation in interstate travel on economic grounds, the next serious test of "equal but separate" didn't arise for more than a decade. Then, in 1890, the same year that the Court decided *Chicago, St. Paul & Milwaukee*, it issued an opinion in another enforced segregation case, *Louisville, New Orleans & Texas Railway Co. v. Mississippi*.[7]

In 1888, two years before Louisiana enacted its own separate car law, Mississippi had included a similar provision in a law establishing a commission to oversee railroad travel within the state. The Louisville, New Orleans & Texas Railway refused to comply, unwilling to undergo the expense of providing extra cars, and, as in *DeCuir*, the railroad traveled interstate routes, although some passengers embarked and disembarked in Mississippi. If the Court had followed *DeCuir*, the Mississippi law would have been seen as a burden on interstate commerce and thus been struck down. But Justice Brewer, writing for a 7–2 majority, saw things differently.

Dancing on the head of a pin, Brewer wrote, "The [*DeCuir*] decision, was . . . carefully limited to those cases in which the law practically interfered with interstate commerce. Obviously whether interstate passengers of one race should, in any portion of their journey, be compelled to share their cabin accommodations with passengers of another race was a question of interstate commerce, and to be determined by Congress alone. In this case, the Supreme Court of Mississippi held that the statute applied solely to commerce within the state, and that construction, being the construction of the statute of the state by its highest court, must be accepted as conclusive here. If it be a matter respecting wholly commerce within a state, and not interfering with commerce between the states, then obviously there is no violation of the commerce clause of the federal Constitution."

Two justices dissented. Joseph Bradley merely had the record reflect "that in his opinion the statute of Mississippi is void as a regulation of interstate commerce." Justice Harlan, however, committed his reasoning to the record. While lacking the bite of his dissent in the *Civil Rights Cases*, Harlan was equally devastating in this case simply employing logic: "In its application to passengers on vessels engaged in interstate commerce, the Louisiana enactment forbade the separation of the white and black races while such vessels were within the limits of that state. The Mississippi statute, in its application to passengers on railroad trains employed in interstate commerce, requires such separation of races while those trains are within that state. I am unable to perceive how the former is a regulation of interstate commerce and the other is not. It is difficult to understand how a state enactment requiring the separation of the white and black races on interstate carriers of passengers is a regulation of commerce among the states, while a similar enactment forbidding such separation is not a regulation of that character."

Brewer's narrowly drawn majority opinion has been characterized as "nimble mental gymnastics," in which "the Court revealed a greater commitment to the flourishing of segregation than to the flourishing of commerce."[8] But whatever its logical virtues, or lack thereof, the practical impact of Justice Brewer's opinion was widespread. In addition to Louisiana,

Alabama, Tennessee, Kentucky, and Arkansas all passed similar separate car legislation soon after *Louisville Railway* was decided, modeling their laws on Mississippi's because it had been "tested in the courts."

With a civil rights basis seemingly impossible and *Louisiana Railway* the most recent precedent, Martinet and his fellow committee members needed to divine some alternative strategy that could persuade the justices to overturn the Louisiana law. They hired two attorneys, both white, they hoped would be up to the task. The first, James C. Walker, was a local criminal lawyer who had been involved in a number of equal rights cases, albeit with quite limited success. The second was a quixotic carpetbagger-turned-civil rights advocate named Albion Tourgée.

Tourgée, a one-eyed novelist, attorney, and thrice-wounded Union army veteran, had moved from New York to North Carolina in 1865 and eventually been appointed to the local bench. He became known for demanding fair treatment for African-Americans in his courtroom and had thus aroused the enmity of the local Ku Klux Klan. He ignored the risk to his own life, but after the Klan threatened his wife and daughter, Tourgée moved back North. He wrote a novel detailing his experiences titled *A Fools Errand by One of the Fools*, which sold over two hundred thousand copies, providing him both fortune and national reputation. Tourgée accepted Martinet's invitation to lead the expected appeal, taking the case without pay but, because of illness, was forced to remain in rural New York State. The one-eyed northerner was a passionate advocate and noted lawyer, certainly, but his strategic decisions were to prove questionable.

Tourgée and Martinet agreed that, for their test, whoever boarded the train had to be arrested in New Orleans so that the man (Tourgée's notion of sending a woman was discarded quickly) wasn't simply beaten and thrown off.[9] Martinet discovered soon after floating the idea around town that the railroads were, in fact, none too keen to provide extra cars to accommodate the South's race laws. The Louisville and Nashville Railroad agreed to host the test, promising that deputies would be on board, prepared to arrest Martinet's surrogate before the train left New Orleans.

Over Martinet's objections, Tourgée decided to employ a light-skinned black man to create the test case. Tourgée wanted to make certain that the conductor, who, according to the law, was actually required, on pain of committing a misdemeanor, to ask the passenger to move, could be seen to be acting arbitrarily. The committee chose Daniel Desdunes, the son of one of its members, whose skin and features were indistinguishably white. On February 24, 1892, young Desdunes purchased a first-class ticket for Mobile, Alabama, entered the first-class compartment, and announced to the conductor that he was, in fact, black. Desdunes added that he held a ticket to an out-of-state destination, since *DeCuir* was still the best hope of providing a precedent. With deputies waiting in the car, the conductor ordered Desdunes to move. Desdunes refused to leave the car and was duly arrested and removed from the train.

As the date for Desdunes's trial approached, however, James Walker began to wonder about the strategy. *Louisville Railway* had undercut the interstate passenger defense. Perhaps a Fourteenth Amendment appeal would be better after all. But *Louisville Railway* had been decided on extremely narrow grounds, so Walker was persuaded by Martinet to stick to the original plan. Tourgée, still in New York, had misgivings of his own. A victory on interstate passenger grounds would leave segregation in Louisiana intact. "What we want is not a verdict of not guilty, nor a defect in this law," Tourgée wrote to Walker, "but a decision whether such a law can be legally enacted and enforced in any state and we should get everything off the track and out of the way for such a decision."[10]

Matters were taken out of Desdunes's attorneys' hands when, in an unrelated separate car case, the Louisiana Supreme Court ruled that the law could not apply to interstate passengers. Only the United States Interstate Commerce Commission, the judges ruled, could regulate travel across state lines. The case against Desdunes was therefore moot, eliminating any possibility for the committee to test the law in the federal courts. But although their specific test had failed, Walker, Tourgée, and Martinet could be heartened that their plan had been vindicated by the Louisiana Supreme Court. What was more, *Louisville Railway* might not, in fact, preclude a challenge even on intrastate travel. Martinet's newspaper, the *Crusader*, naively proclaimed, "Jim Crow is as dead as a doornail."

Walker, Tourgée, and Martinet almost immediately set in motion another challenge, this one by a passenger whose entire journey would be within state lines on a railway that operated entirely within Louisiana. Chosen for the task was an octoroon, a thirty-four-year-old shoemaker named Homer Adolph Plessy. As with Daniel Desdunes, not even the most race-baiting white man would have guessed that Homer Plessy was anything but a well-spoken, well-dressed, hardworking white man.

On June 7, 1892, Homer Plessy purchased a first-class ticket on the East Louisiana Railroad for a thirty-mile journey from New Orleans to Covington. After he was shown to his seat, he informed the conductor of his racial background.[11] As in the previous occurrence, both the railroad and the local police had agreed to cooperate in the test. The conductor instructed Plessy to repair to the smoky, dingy, dilapidated car just behind the locomotive. (Whites who were drunk, unruly, or insulted women could be banished to this "Jim Crow car" as well.) As before, if the conductor failed in his duty, he was subject under the law to fine or imprisonment. Homer Plessy refused to move to the colored car and was arrested and taken to the parish jail. Everyone involved—the conductor, the police deputy, and Plessy himself—had been courteous and respectful. Bail was soon posted and Plessy released.

Homer Plessy was arraigned on October 13, 1896, in front of Judge John H. Ferguson, a relocated New Englander, who had also agreed to be a party to the proceedings. James C. Walker, appearing for the defendant, as he had for Daniel Desdunes, filed a fourteen-point brief asking for a dismissal, omitting, of course, any reference to interstate travel. At Tourgée's insistence, Walker did not address the obvious lack of equality in the accommodations.

Assistant District Attorney Lionel Adams objected to the dismissal, and, as everyone had agreed, Judge Ferguson ruled against Plessy and allowed the prosecution to proceed. Originally, Walker and Tourgée had planned to allow Plessy to go to trial and then ask for a writ of habeas corpus in federal court. Instead, Walker immediately filed a petition for dismissal in state supreme court, thereby bypassing the trial process altogether.

The Louisiana Supreme Court agreed to hear Walker's plea, and both he and Adams filed extensive briefs. Within a month, the court had ruled for the state against Plessy, thus reinstating the criminal complaint. In January 1893, Plessy's attorneys filed an appeal with the United States Supreme Court in *ex parte Plessy*, as it had been called in Louisiana, on a writ of error, which would necessitate a review of the record from state court.

The Supreme Court that Albion Tourgée, James Walker, and Samuel Phillips, who had been hired to handle the federal appeal, encountered had changed by one third since the last significant transportation cases, *Chicago, St. Paul & Milwaukee* and *Louisville Railway*. Benjamin Harrison was in his last days as president, having lost his 1892 rematch with Grover Cleveland. But since appointing Justice Brewer, Harrison, in his one term, had appointed three more justices to the Court.

Joseph Bradley had died in January 1892. Harrison replaced the author of the *Civil Rights Cases* opinion with George Shiras Jr., an attorney with a long record of representing corporate interests, who had never before sat as a judge at any level. Lucius Q. C. Lamar died just days after Plessy's case was heard. (He would be succeeded by another southerner, Howell Edmunds Jackson, who was sworn in on the same day as Cleveland was inaugurated. Jackson would serve only three years before his death in 1895.)

Predating both of these appointments, however, was the death in October 1890, after twenty-eight years on the Court, of Justice Samuel Freeman Miller. As his replacement, President Harrison appointed David Brewer's old Yale classmate, Henry Billings Brown.

Henry Brown was born in South Lee, Berkshire County, Massachusetts, in 1836, to a family that had settled in America in the early 1700s. One of his forebears was brought to trial for witchcraft. Brown wrote, "I was of a New England Puritan family in which there had been no admixture of alien blood for two hundred and fifty years. Though Puritans, my ancestors were neither bigoted nor intolerant—upon the contrary some were unusually liberal."[12]

His father owned lumber mills, and young Henry "had a natural fondness for machinery and was never so happy as when allowed to 'assist' at the sawing of logs and shingles and the grinding of grain in [his] father's mills."[13] The elder Brown sold his businesses and, when Henry was eleven, informed his son that he was to become a lawyer. At age sixteen, Henry enrolled at Yale. The college, dingy and grim at that time, with only seven hundred students, was perfect for a Calvinist temperament.

> The rooms, though not particularly uncomfortable, were shabby and received but slight attention from the "Professor of Dust and Ashes." All the accessible parts of the woodwork had been profusely illustrated by the pocket knives of former generations. The sanitary arrangements, if such they can be called, were primitive to the last degree. The hours of work were equally so. In winter we rose before dawn, attended morning prayers and a recitation by gaslight, then just introduced into the public rooms, but not into the dormitories, and sat down to breakfast about sunrise. A daily walk to the post office was all the exercise we could afford except on

Wednesday and Saturday afternoons. Attendance at chapel twice a day on Sunday was compulsory.[14]

After he graduated in 1856, his father paid for a year's tour of Europe. Henry visited France, Italy, and Germany, discovering a facility for language and a reverence for European history and tradition. Upon his return, he studied law at Yale and Harvard, leaving, as most law students did, before gaining a degree. He migrated west to seek his fortune in Michigan. Brown gained employment in a local law firm, where he impressed the partners with his diligence and quick mind. He began to make a study of maritime law, a subject on which he would remain expert for the remainder of his career. Although in 1860 he believed "the situation of the country is dreadful and civil war appears almost inevitable," he nonetheless voted for Lincoln.

Often dour, Brown was given to fits of depression; his eyes were sufficiently bad, perhaps from glaucoma, that for long periods he could not read and could barely see to get about on the streets. He would lose the sight in one eye in his thirties and feared losing sight in the other for the remainder of his life. Although he neglected to mention it in his memoirs, Brown avoided military service in the Civil War by hiring a substitute, a common enough practice, but one of which, despite the difficulties with his vision, Brown was apparently ashamed.

But Henry Brown was no coward. In 1884, "Mr. and Mrs. Brown were awakened by a masked man standing by Mrs. Brown with a pistol pointed at Mr. Brown and telling them to keep quiet while he proceeded to look for valuables. There chanced to be a pistol in the commode loaded and left there by a young naval officer who had been a visitor. Irritated by the burglar's seizure of a watch, Brown jumped from the bed and took the pistol and fired at the burglar. The fire was returned, but neither one hit, and the burglar speedily fled."[15]

During the war, he had remained in Detroit, where business boomed. In 1864, Brown married the daughter of a wealthy lumberman, another New England transplant. They would have no children. But a good marriage and a successful practice were springboards to the judiciary. Brown was appointed to the district attorney's office, then the district court bench, then to appeals court, and, finally, in 1890, after fifteen years as a federal judge, was nominated by Benjamin Harrison to the United States Supreme Court.

By then, Henry Brown had become known as a fierce defender of property rights, although politically he was considered a centrist.

In his social attitudes, Henry Billings Brown was a man of his times. His views of women, Jews, Native Americans, and Asians could be described as every bit as "unenlightened" as his opinion of African-Americans. A Yankee Calvinist with an unshakable reverence for the letter of the law, Brown believed, along with most of his colleagues on the Court, that race considerations per se had no place in the administration of justice.

Eschewing an argument as to the equality of accommodations, and with the interstate passenger argument not at issue, Plessy's counsel was forced to attack the Separate Car Law on the very grounds that offered the least chance of success: that the law was in violation of both the Thirteenth and Fourteenth amendments of the United States Constitution. Since being banished to a "colored car" was a bond of servitude, Plessy's attorneys asserted, the law was repugnant to the Thirteenth Amendment, which banned slavery, and that Plessy's being forced to relocate strictly because of race violated the Fourteenth Amendment provision that demanded "equal protection of the laws."

Tourgée told the Court, "The [Separate Car Law] itself is a skillful attempt to confuse and conceal its real purpose. It assumes impartiality. It fulminates apparently against white and black alike. Its real object is to keep Negroes out of one car for the gratification of whites—not to keep whites out of another car for the comfort and satisfaction of the colored passenger."[16]

Even here, however, the arguments were muddled. Tourgée, who had insisted on using a light-skinned African-American for this very reason, spent a good bit of time asserting that the Separate Car Law did not define how racial makeup would be determined, thus giving light-complexioned blacks an advantage over those with darker skin. He also observed that the law placed an undue burden on the conductor to make the determination. The inequality, therefore, was between different castes of Negro. But even in this context, refusal to extend their discussion to the most obvious inequality, that of the accommodations themselves, left the arguments dangling. Tourgée was aware of the difficulties the omission would engender, but chose voluntarily to bypass them. He noted that the law mandated "substantial equality of accommodation," which was obviously lacking on the railroad cars. But he added that equality of accommodation was not relevant to his constitutional challenge. "The gist of our case," Tourgée told the justices, "is the unconstitutionality of the assortment: not the question of equal accommodation."[17]

The decision may have been sound on philosophical grounds and pleasing to Tourgée's sense of justice, but even in the poisoned atmosphere in which he was making his case, it was a terrible blunder. Tourgée unilaterally denied himself what was potentially the only strategy that might have had some small chance of success. The Supreme Court, as hesitant to disturb the railroad's right of contract as it was to affirm civil rights, might conceivably have seized the opportunity to avoid ruling on the constitutionality of the Separate Car Law by simply agreeing with the plaintiff that "equal meant equal." Tourgée might have suggested that if the accommodations were truly equal, they could be swapped. Had the Court so mandated, as whites would never be willing to spend their journey breathing in smoke and soot in the Jim Crow car, the law would have become moot. The railroads would have been pleased with such a result and lobbied for its application in other jurisdictions. But a tactical victory was not sufficient for Tourgée. He wanted a moral statement or nothing. As a result, he would get nothing.

Counsel for Louisiana had it a good deal easier. Adams simply insisted that under the concept of "police power" implicit in the Tenth Amendment (substantive due process), the state was within its rights to pass any law necessary to maintain public order and provide for the safety and well-being of its citizens. And since the law also forbade whites from riding in the colored car—as if anyone would want to—Act 111 was, in fact, evenhanded and fair. (That unruly whites could be banished to the colored car was not raised by either party.) The state, never under pressure to defend the character of the accommodations, was able to merely stipulate their equality.

After the filings, which were completed in February 1893, the case languished. Tourgée, who initially thought to move for an expedited hearing, decided to allow the case to come up "when it will." He seemed to have realized for the first time that the Court, as constituted, presented highly unfavorable odds. "Of the whole number of justices, there is but one known to favor our view," he noted, an obvious reference to Justice Harlan. Of the remaining eight (Justice Jackson had been seated by then), four were likely to vote against

Plessy and four were certain to. Those latter four would "probably stay where they are until Gabriel blows his horn," was how Tourgée put it.[18]

Tourgée suddenly put his hope on attrition among the justices and a shift in popular sentiment.[19] "The Court has always been the foe of liberty until forced to move on by public opinion," Tourgée observed. But public opinion among the white population was moving farther away from Tourgée with every passing day.

As a result of a heavy docket, a three-year delay between filing and oral argument was standard, and the Court did not hear arguments in what was now *Plessy v. Ferguson* until April 13, 1896. Tourgée and Phillips appeared for the plaintiff, and Louisiana attorney general Milton J. Cunningham and Washington attorney Alexander P. Morse for the defense.

Once again, the panel of justices had changed. In place of Samuel Blatchford, who had died in July 1893, Grover Cleveland had appointed Edward Douglass White, a Louisiana Democrat who had served in the Confederate army as a teenager, although in what capacity was unclear, and he may or may not have been a prisoner of war.[20] White, who would later serve as chief justice, was known for conservative views on both race and business. Howell Edmunds Jackson had died in 1895, replaced by Rufus Peckham, a strong advocate of economic substantive due process.

The arguments to the Court largely followed the briefs, Tourgée stressing the Thirteenth and Fourteenth Amendment questions, which he categorized as an inappropriate extension of state police power, as well as the inconsistency of classifying an octoroon as colored. Cunningham and Morse focused on the wording of the law, which, to them, passed constitutional muster in every way. Justice Brewer was not present during oral arguments and so would not participate in the decision, a small advantage for Plessy as Brewer was one of the justices whom Tourgée had been certain would vote against him.

Drafting of the opinion was assigned to Associate Justice Brown. Why Chief Justice Fuller chose Brown is unknown, and Brown never revealed whether he was assigned the case or requested it, but the *Plessy* opinion ensured that Henry Billings Brown, who might otherwise have passed quietly into history, became, for all time, a notorious champion of segregation, a manifestation of racial intolerance.

On May 18, 1896, five weeks after the arguments had been presented, the

Court delivered its verdict. By a 7–1 majority, to the surprise of no one except perhaps the plaintiffs, the justices found against Homer Plessy.

For a man of Brown's beliefs, the issues were clear. He saw little of merit in any of the plaintiff's arguments. The Thirteenth Amendment claim, that the Separate Car Law imposed "bonds of servitude" on nonwhites, he found particularly silly.

> The Thirteenth Amendment . . . abolished . . . slavery. Slavery implies involuntary servitude—a state of bondage; the ownership of mankind as a chattel, or at least the control of the labor and services of one man for the benefit of another, and the absence of a legal right to the disposal of his own person, property and services . . . A statute which implies merely a legal distinction between the white and colored races—a distinction which is founded in the color of the two races and which must always exist so long as white men are distinguished from the other race by color—has no tendency to destroy the legal equality of the two races, or reestablish a state of involuntary servitude. Indeed, we do not understand that the Thirteenth Amendment is strenuously relied upon by the plaintiff in error in this connection.[21]

Through Justice Brown, then, the Court announced that, at least for this decision, it was returning to the strict-construction philosophy of *Cruikshank* and *Harris*, which had been abandoned in the *Railroad Commission Cases* and *Chicago, St. Paul & Milwaukee*. There would be no application of substantive due process in *Plessy*.

On the Fourteenth Amendment question, Brown agreed with Clifford's *DeCuir* opinion that equality does not require identity. He wrote, "The object was undoubtedly to enforce the absolute equality of the two races before the law, but, in the nature of things, it could not have been intended to abolish distinctions based upon color, or to enforce social, as distinguished from political, equality, or a commingling of the two races upon terms unsatisfactory to either. Laws permitting, and even requiring, their separation in places where they are liable to be brought into contact do not necessarily imply the inferiority of either race to the other, and have been generally, if not universally, recognized as within the competency of the state legislatures in the exercise of their police power." But for precedent, instead of *DeCuir*, Brown cited a case in which a state supreme court mandated the legality of enforced segregation in one of its cities' school systems. The city was Boston.*

Legal separation, the Massachusetts court had ruled, did not imply inequality.[22] Could not the needy be served by different institutions than the wealthy? The young different than the old? Boys different than girls? All that was necessary was that equality before the law be paramount; that access to and treatment by the courts be equal. Thus mere separation of the races did not, on its face, represent inequality. Brown wrote:

> So far, then, as a conflict with the Fourteenth Amendment is concerned, the case reduces itself to the question whether the statute of Louisiana is a reasonable regulation. In determining the question of reasonableness, [the state legislature] is at liberty to act with reference to the established usages, customs, and traditions of the people, and with a view to the promotion of their comfort and the preservation of the public peace and good order. Gauged by this standard, we cannot say that a law which authorizes or even requires the separation of the two races in public conveyances is unreasonable, or more obnoxious to the Fourteenth Amendment than the acts of Congress requiring separate schools for colored children in the District of Columbia, the constitutionality of which does not seem to have been questioned, or the corresponding acts of state legislatures.

Unlikely as it may have been that the justices would have ruled for Plessy under any circumstances, Tourgée's refusal to test the obvious inequality of the accommodations allowed Brown to ignore the practical applications

---

* *Roberts v. City of Boston.* 5 Cush. (59 Mass.) 198 (1849). "In 1847, Sarah Roberts, a five-year-old black girl, applied for admission to a white public school in Boston primarily because she had been excluded from a neighborhood school near her home and would have had to travel a greater distance in order to attend an assigned Afro-American school. Charles Sumner and his black associate lawyer, Robert Morris, represented the plaintiff and argued for equality before the law. They contended that separate schools for blacks were based on deep-rooted prejudice, and that blacks were inconvenienced by a system that created a feeling of degradation. Massachusetts Supreme Court Chief Justice Lemuel Shaw rejected the plaintiff's classical equality argument as pure theory and impractical when applied to the American environment. In regard to the plaintiff's psychological and sociological arguments, Shaw remarked that racial prejudice was 'not created by law, and probably cannot be changed by law.' The Roberts case did not consider equal facilities, the second half of the 'separate but equal' doctrine; rather, Roberts provided a legal tradition for public supported separate schools for blacks based upon the judicial principle of reasonable classification." David W. Bishop, "Plessy v. Ferguson: A Reinterpretation," *Journal of Negro History* 62, no. 2 (Apr. 1977), p. 128.

of the law. The task of supporting Louisiana's mandated segregation was therefore made that much easier. Since Louisiana, under Tenth Amendment police power, had both the right and the obligation to provide public tranquillity, to, in fact, protect property, there seemed little choice but to deny Plessy's claim.

Brown could not resist, as a coda, advancing his own social views. "The argument also assumes that social prejudices may be overcome by legislation, and that equal rights cannot be secured to the negro except by an enforced commingling of the two races. We cannot accept this proposition. If the two races are to meet upon terms of social equality, it must be the result of natural affinities, a mutual appreciation of each other's merits, and a voluntary consent of individuals. If one race be inferior to the other socially, the Constitution of the United States cannot put them upon the same plane."[23]

The dissent was once again filed by Justice Harlan. As he had in the *Civil Rights Cases*, Harlan used his opinion not only to produce one of this nation's great enunciations of individual liberty and racial equality, but also to destroy the flimsy camouflage laid on by Louisiana and accepted by the majority, that a law mandating separation of the races was not discriminatory since it applied equally to both races.

> It is said in argument that the statute of Louisiana does not discriminate against either race, but prescribes a rule applicable alike to white and colored citizens. But this argument does not meet the difficulty. Everyone knows that the statute in question had its origin in the purpose not so much to exclude white persons from railroad cars occupied by blacks as to exclude colored people from coaches occupied by or assigned to white persons. The thing to accomplish was, under the guise of giving equal accommodation for whites and blacks, to compel the latter to keep to themselves while traveling in railroad passenger coaches. No one would be so wanting in candor to assert the contrary.

Then Harlan declared famously, "In view of the Constitution, in the eye of the law, there is in this country no superior, dominant, ruling class of citizens. There is no caste here. Our Constitution is color-blind, and neither knows nor tolerates classes among citizens. In respect of civil rights, all citizens are equal before the law. The humblest is the peer of the most powerful. The law regards man as man, and takes no account of his surroundings or of his color when his civil rights as guaranteed by the supreme law of the land are involved."

But even Justice Harlan was not as color-blind as he claimed the Constitution to be. In the passage that preceded the one above, he observed, "The white race deems itself to be the dominant race in this country. And so it is in prestige, in achievements, in education, in wealth and in power. So, I doubt not, it will continue to be for all time if it remains true to its great heritage and holds fast to the principles of constitutional liberty." So, it seems, even to Harlan, the black man was not *inherently* equal, but simply equal under a benevolent set of laws created by whites.

Social views aside, Harlan's dissent still represented a subjective view of the law, incorporating intent, effect, and even common sense into legal interpretation. Including in an argument the phrase "everyone knows" was anathema to the strict constructionism of the Fuller Court, as it would be to many justices today. Intent, in their view, had no place. Justice Brown's argument, "prolix, turgid, and obtuse" as it has been characterized, is nonetheless more in line with those who purport to believe in the strict application of law.

For a decision that was to have such profound impact on the nation, *Plessy* attracted almost no notice. In the *New York Times*, for example, the case rated only two short paragraphs in a section devoted to railroad news, being omitted completely from the column in which Supreme Court decisions were generally announced.[24] The *Boston Daily Globe* did not report the result of the case at all, nor did the *Chicago Daily Tribune*. The *Hartford Courant* gave it but two short paragraphs.[25] All four newspapers had previously been quite thorough in their reporting of equal rights cases. A few days after the decision, the *Daily Globe* did report on a meeting of Boston's Colored League, in which the decision was widely denounced.[26] But on the decision itself, none of the newspapers put forth an editorial comment. The *Atlanta Constitution* ran a short summary under the headline FOR BLACKS AND WHITES.[27]

In fact, *Plessy* was largely overlooked until it was partially overruled in 1954 by *Brown v. Board of Education*, in which Chief Justice Earl Warren categorically rejected both the wording of the Plessy decision and the reasoning behind it. "Separate but equal is inherently unequal," Warren wrote, at long last capitulating to the obvious.[28]

The year after *Brown*, a sociopolitical analysis of *Plessy* was put forth that has set the stage for debate ever since, when the luminescent southern historian C. Vann Woodward published his first edition of *The Strange Career of Jim Crow*. Woodward's thesis, which could not have been more provocative, was that both during and after Reconstruction, segregation was not nearly so prevalent in the South as had been previously assumed. He provided numerous examples of northerners or Europeans traveling in the old Confederacy who were shocked at the degree of cooperation and intermixing of races that they encountered. Racism, to Woodward, was largely a class issue in the antebellum South, and only with the compromise of 1877 and especially the *Plessy* ruling did Jim Crow roar in. *Plessy*, then, was a fulcrum, a point of departure for southern states, immensely significant in the struggle for equal rights.

Some body of evidence supported him. In Virginia, for example, the first state segregation law was not enacted until 1900 when the legislature passed a separate car law. Until that law was passed, "for more than thirty years following the end of the Civil War whites and Negroes, with increasing frequency, rode together in the same railroad and streetcars in Virginia."[29]

If Woodward was correct, then, the Supreme Court would bear a good deal of the responsibility for the triumph of Jim Crow in the early twentieth century.

This thesis, however, came in for immediate criticism, other scholars pointing out that de facto segregation was a good deal more pervasive than Woodward had acknowledged, and that separation of the races was increasing in the years leading up to the *Plessy* decision.[30] The objections to Woodward's assertions became so intense that in subsequent editions of *The Strange Career of Jim Crow*, Woodward modified his argument, acknowledging that the South was hardly a bastion of tolerance and racial understanding before 1896. Still, he continued to insist that actual segregation, the apartheid system that dominated the southern states in the first two thirds of the twentieth century, was by and large a by-product of Congress, the president, and especially the Supreme Court.

In 1989, in a scrupulously researched and detailed account of *Plessy*, the historian Charles A. Lofgren sought to demonstrate that, historical perspective and contemporary judgments notwithstanding, neither the *Plessy* opinion nor the Court's decision was in the least bit remarkable given the tenor of the times. Henry Billings Brown, Lofgren insisted, merely reflected the "conventional wisdom." *Plessy* was not, in fact, remarkable at all. In this, of course, Lofgren was quite correct. The *Plessy* decision was merely a continuation—and a reaffirmation—of a judicial and social philosophy that the Court had advocated for two decades.

Lofgren would have been fine had he stopped there. But he added, "Specifically, Brown's conclusions did not rest on bad logic, bad social science, bad history, or bad constitutional law, as later alleged."[31] In this, Lofgren fell victim to historical myopia. Brown's opinion, in fact, was all of those things. Perhaps it was not worse logic or worse social science or worse history or worse constitutional law than the Court had been practicing for three decades, but that is hardly the point. If Justice Harlan could see through the artifice, why not the other justices? The lynchings, the beatings, the trumped-up convictions were all widely reported in northern newspapers. The justices could not have failed to know that through both precedent and interpretation, *Cruikshank, Rives, DeCuir,* the *Civil Rights Cases,* and ultimately *Plessy* could have been decided differently. Yes, *Plessy* was unremarkable, just as Lofgren asserts. That it was so unremarkable is perhaps the most damning thing about it.

Whether Justice Brown ever regretted his decision in *Plessy* is not known. In 1903, he wrote, "In some criminal cases against negroes, coming up from the Southern States, we have adhered to the technicalities of the law so strictly that I fear injustice has been done to the defendant."[32]

But ten years later, after he had left the bench, he also wrote, "There is a large class of people in our country who love change for the sake of change, or who think they may profit by it individually. These ideas are a perpetual source of trouble, but, of course, all wrong. There are always a few in the District who are clamoring for a change to a popular government, but the phantom of negro suffrage stands inexorably in their path. No suffrage without the nigger—no suffrage, no nigger."[33]

FOURTEEN

ONE MAN, NO VOTE:
WILLIAMS V. MISSISSIPPI

TWO YEARS AFTER *PLESSY*, the Court agreed to hear a case that once again raised the specter of rigged voting rules in the South. Although *Rives* was on the books, as well as a series of later decisions, by 1898 the systematic exclusion of African-Americans from ballot boxes was impossible to overlook. Mississippi, for example, whose black population according to the coming census in 1900 was almost 60 percent of the state's total, boasted not a single black man in any significant position in state or national government. So in *Williams v. Mississippi*, the Court had the opportunity to revisit an issue where the Fifteenth Amendment had been, if not ignored, at least perverted.[1]

In June 1896, Henry Williams was indicted for murder in Washington County, Mississippi, by an all-white grand jury. His lawyer, Cornelius J. Jones, moved in state circuit court to quash the indictment based on the systematic exclusion of blacks from the voting rolls on which grand jury participation was based. His petition specifically cited the 1890 Mississippi constitutional convention, which, according to Jones:

> was composed of 134 members, only one of whom was a negro. That under prior laws, there were 190,000 colored voters and 69,000 white voters. The makers of the new constitution arbitrarily refused to submit it to the voters of the state for approval, but ordered it adopted, and an election to be held immediately under it, which election was held under the election ordinances of the said constitution in November, 1891, and the legislature

assembled in 1892, and enacted the statutes complained of for the purpose to discriminate . . . and but for that the defendant's race would have been represented impartially on the grand jury which presented this indictment.[2]

Jones's petition to the grand jury was rejected. Henry Williams was subsequently convicted and sentenced to be hanged, also by an all-white jury.

Cornelius Jones then appealed Williams's case on a writ of error to federal circuit court, claiming that "the laws by which the grand jury was selected, organized, summoned, and charged, which presented the said indictment, are unconstitutional and repugnant to the spirit and letter of the Constitution of the United States of America, Fourteenth Amendment." When this appeal was also denied, Jones brought the case to Washington. *Williams v. Mississippi* would be the first test of voting rights to be argued before the Court since the *Plessy* decision.

Jones claimed in his Supreme Court petition that the exclusionary effect of the property tax and literacy clauses of the Mississippi constitution had made it impossible for his client to be judged by a jury of his peers, thus attacking the very provisions of the 1890 Mississippi constitution of which James K. Vardaman had been so proud. As a citizen of the United States, Jones went on, Henry Williams was entitled to federal constitutional guarantees.

On April 25, 1898, almost one year to the day before the people of Atlanta would gather to watch the burning of Sam Hose, the Supreme Court issued its decision. The newest justice, Joseph McKenna, fresh on the Court after serving only three months as United States attorney general, wrote the opinion. McKenna, the son of Irish immigrants, had been born in Philadelphia but, like Henry Brown and David Brewer, had migrated west, although in his case, like Stephen Field, the man he replaced, all the way to California.[3] McKenna was only the third Catholic to serve on the Court. (Roger B. Taney had been the first.) Although he had sat on the federal appeals bench in addition to his stint as attorney general, McKenna's legal credentials were stunningly undistinguished. He had become so sensitive to charges during his confirmation hearings that he was, in fact, ignorant of many aspects of the law, that he had sat in on classes at Columbia University Law School before taking the bench.

McKenna's supporters attempted to paint the opposition to his nomination as religious bigotry. One claimed to "have no patience with men who held the opinion that Catholics necessarily must consult the Pope or some other high functionary of the Catholic Church in every important transaction of their lives."[4] Although some anti-Catholic bigotry certainly existed, opposition to McKenna was more political than theological, particularly the charge by the bar association in McKenna's native California "that large corporations had been instrumental in securing his nomination."[5]

Although McKenna had not expressed any particular sentiments about African-Americans, his prejudice against the Chinese was deep and severe. "As a politician and legislator on both state and national levels, McKenna consistently and enthusiastically advocated various types of anti-Chinese legislation, and as a federal judge in California he construed the law rigorously to enforce the exclusion of Chinese, including even those who presented evidence of American citizenship."[6]

Even McKenna's most outspoken advocates were lukewarm. That same supporter with little patience acknowledged that "he did not contend that Mr. McKenna was a giant in his legal attainments." The *Harvard Law Review* wrote, "Although some of his judicial decisions have been very unfavorably criticized, Justice McKenna has always conducted himself impartially and for the best interests of his office." (Some considered this an odd endorsement since McKenna, even during his confirmation, had been unabashed in his defense of business interests, particularly railroads.)

Williams v. Mississippi was the new associate's first opinion, and he doubtless wanted to impress a dubious legal community with his acumen. McKenna began with the same high tone that characterized all equal rights decisions. "[The Fourteenth Amendment] and its effect upon the rights of the colored race have been considered by this Court in a number of cases, and it has been uniformly held that the Constitution of the United States, as amended, forbids, so far as civil and political rights are concerned, discriminations by the general government or by the states against any citizen because of his race."

Then, predictably, McKenna retreated to the narrow, strict reading of the amendment. "But it has also been held [that] to justify a removal from a state court to a federal court of a cause in which such rights are alleged to be denied, that such denial must be the result of the constitution or laws of the state, not of the administration of them."[7]

That to be unconstitutional a law must actually pronounce its intention to deny a class of citizens their rights, no matter how transparent the intent, was not new. But McKenna, although in the negative, had added a new qualification, or rather acknowledged one. The question of administration had not been of issue in *Strauder* or *Rives*. But in a famous Chinese laundry case, *Yick Wo v. Hopkins*, a dozen years earlier, the Court had ruled that if a law was impartial on its face yet was applied and administered so as to operate as a denial of equal justice, it might indeed be declared in violation of the Fourteenth Amendment.[8] Thus, Justice McKenna seemed to be saying, if Williams could *prove* that the law had been administered in a discriminatory fashion, he would then have grounds for his action. But simply the potential for mischief was not sufficient.

For most laymen looking at the Mississippi voting rolls, that some chicanery had been afoot would have been all too obvious. Although specific records were not published by the Magnolia State, virtually none of its 907,000 black residents were eligible to go to the polls.[9] How the justices viewed this overwhelming statistic, to say nothing of the very public pronouncements state officials had made as to their intention to disenfranchise black voters, would determine whether or not the Court acknowledged that its previous voting rights' decisions had led to constitutional abuses. For example, with *Yick Wo* as precedent, the Court could easily have ruled that the "interpretation clause" of the Mississippi constitution was not, in fact, used to test literacy, but simply as a ruse to deny the vote to African-Americans.

But once again, the Court could not see past its own prejudices. Rather than accept what a child could not have missed, Justice McKenna granted wide discretion to Mississippi's administering officers (all of whom also were white) on their choices of what an applicant to vote should read and "interpret." If they chose a short simple phrase for whites—or even no phrase at all—and long, complex phrases for blacks; even if Mississippi officials had publicly proclaimed that those phrases had been inserted in the state constitution simply to trip up potential black voters, the burden remained on Williams to prove that these choices of phrase had been made intentionally, on a case-by-case basis, to deny blacks the right to register. And then, to raise the bar yet higher, even if a certain officer was discriminatory in the manner in which he administered the test, it was the fault of the man, not the constitution under which he was operating.

McKenna's opinion was dreadfully written and blatantly racist, even by the standards of the day. In a spasm of obscure logic, he cited a South Carolina ruling that declared "the negro race had acquired or accentuated certain peculiarities of habit, of temperament, and of character which clearly distinguished it as a race from the whites; a patient, docile people, but careless, landless, migratory within narrow limits, without forethought, and its criminal members given to furtive offenses, rather than the robust crimes of the whites," to conclude that the Mississippi constitution did not in itself discriminate. "Nor is there any sufficient allegation of an evil and discriminating administration of [it]."

As to discriminatory application, McKenna pointed out that the plaintiff had not accused any specific administrators of misapplying the law; his targets had instead been the delegates to the Mississippi constitutional convention. "There is no charge against the officers to whom is submitted the selection of grand or petit jurors, or those who procure the lists of the jurors." That Williams had absolutely no way of knowing which commissioners had done what at any given time to deny someone the right to vote bothered the justice not one whit.

McKenna then ruled, incredibly, that, despite the decrease in black registrants in Mississippi to almost zero, Williams had not shown convincingly that potential black voters had been dealt with in a discriminatory fashion. "The Constitution of Mississippi and its statutes do not on their face discriminate between the races, and it has not been shown that their actual administration was evil; only that evil was possible under them."[10]

Williams was denied. This vote was unanimous. Even Justice Harlan joined the majority.

Cornelius Jones, inexperienced and black, was later criticized for basing his suit on the equal protection clause of the Fourteenth Amendment rather than the first section of the Fifteenth.[11] But as in *Plessy*, the Court had chosen a paper-thin, even tortured, interpretation of the Fourteenth Amendment and turned a blind eye to the obvious. Given the credulity with which Justice McKenna asserted the lack of blatant discrimination in the application of literacy tests for voters, that a different strategy would have yielded a fairer result is extremely unlikely.

Like *Plessy*, *Williams* was accepted without criticism by the press, the public, and in legal journals. The case was not subject to critical analysis until many decades later and was, in fact, cited in a number of articles in the

Harvard Law Review as perfectly sound precedent. When *Plessy* was overturned in 1954, it was on social grounds—"separate but equal is inherently unequal"—not because of judicial error. *Williams* was never overturned by the Court at all, but rather was rendered moot by the Voting Rights Act of 1964.

FIFTEEN

MR. JUSTICE HOLMES CONCURS

Louis martinet had failed in *Plessy* to employ a test case to loosen the grip of Jim Crow, and his defeat had ushered in a new round of restrictive laws across the South. But facing state and local judicial systems in which judge and jury were implacable enemies, African-Americans seemed to have only one remaining strategy; the federal test case. Five years after the *Plessy* decision, it was tried again. On this occasion, the man behind the attempt was so unlikely for such an undertaking that he employed multiple levels of security to keep his name secret.

The public face of the test case was Jackson W. Giles, a Montgomery postal employee and president of the Colored Men's Suffrage Association of Alabama, a group formed specifically to protest the grandfather clause of the 1901 Alabama constitution. That provision, Clause 187 of Article 8, stipulated that anyone registered to vote before January 1, 1903, would remain on the voting rolls for life unless they became disqualified because of the commission of a felony. Anyone not registered before that date, which meant basically every black person in the state, would face a far more stringent set of requirements. He would need to demonstrate that he "shall have paid on or before the first day of February next preceding the date of the election at which he offers to vote, all poll taxes due from him," or owned forty acres of land with property taxes paid, and could "read and write any article of the Constitution of the United States in the English language."[1]

To make certain that state officials had sufficient grounds to disenfranchise any Alabama black man who might otherwise have slipped through, the constitution disqualified from voting "those who shall be convicted of treason, murder, arson, embezzlement, malfeasance in office, larceny, receiving stolen property, obtaining property or money under false pretenses, perjury, subornation of perjury, robbery, assault with intent to rob, burglary, forgery, bribery, assault and battery on the wife, bigamy, living in adultery, sodomy, incest, rape, miscegenation, crime against nature, or any crime punishable by imprisonment in the penitentiary, or of any infamous crime or crime involving moral turpitude; also, any person who shall be convicted as a vagrant or tramp."

Alabama registrars were clever enough not to disenfranchise every black person. Lifetime voting rights were granted to African-American veterans of the army or navy who presented valid discharge papers, a tiny percentage of the total black population, and other prominent African-Americans, such as Booker T. Washington, knowing that such drops in the bucket would have next to no impact on state and local elections.

Washington in particular was handled with care. In 1895, he had suddenly "moved out of the ranks of obscure young black men" by giving a speech before a mostly white audience at the Cotton States and International Exposition in Atlanta, in which he accepted segregation as a basis for interracial cooperation. In the "Atlanta Compromise," as it came to be known, Washington urged whites to encourage "ignorant and inexperienced" blacks by offering rudimentary opportunities in agriculture and industry. "As we have proved our loyalty to you in the past, in nursing your children, watching by the sick-bed of your mothers and fathers, and often following them with tear-dimmed eyes to their graves, so in the future, in our humble way, we shall stand by you with a devotion that no foreigner can approach, ready to lay down our lives, if need be, in defense of yours, interlacing our industrial, commercial, civil, and religious life with yours in a way that shall make the interests of both races one. In all things that are purely social we can be as separate as the fingers, yet one as the hand in all things essential to mutual progress."

Excoriated by W. E. B. DuBois, among others, for selling out to oppression and his willingness to overlook the heinous abuses heaped on his people by whites, Washington nonetheless became a national luminary, praised across the sociopolitical spectrum by white men from Theodore Roosevelt to Andrew Carnegie and John D. Rockefeller for his up-by-the-bootstraps approach. Booker T. Washington became widely viewed among whites as the one Negro who could help keep others in line. He was on record as accepting voting restrictions based on literacy, education, or personal net worth. Allowing Washington to vote, therefore, provided Alabama whites with justification to claim that their constitution applied the same standards to all. Still, Governor William Dorsey Jelks could not resist observing that "the appointees would carry out the spirit of the Constitution, which looks to the registration of all white men not convicted of crimes, and only a few Negroes." Jelks was also widely known for his advocacy of lynching as an appropriate means of disposing of African-Americans accused of rape.

To mount the challenge to the Alabama constitution, Jackson Giles himself decided to act as plaintiff. As a United States government employee, Giles, in theory, would not be fired from his job for initiating the lawsuit. As Giles was preparing his case, to his surprise, a prominent New York attorney, Wilford H. Smith, suddenly volunteered to handle the case pro bono. Giles accepted gratefully, unsure how his intentions had become known to a New York attorney.

But Wilford Smith was not just any New York attorney. He was Booker T. Washington's personal lawyer. Unbeknownst to Giles, Smith had been hired, with great secrecy, by the very same man whom Alabama whites had tried so hard to mollify. Washington, understanding that his ability to have any influence at all depended on his being accepted in his perceived role as accommodationist, directed that all correspondence between him and Smith be handled by his private secretary, Emmett J. Scott. Code was used to transmit important information, with Washington himself at first referred to with a series of aliases, like "Filipino," "His Nibs," or "the Wizard." When Washington observed that anyone reading the letters would know immediately to whom the aliases referred, Scott switched to pseudonyms like R. C. Black (for himself) and J. C. May (for Smith) and left references to Washington out altogether. Smith referred to himself as "McAdoo," his stenographer, in return telegrams. Washington constantly monitored the security arrangements to ensure that southern whites would not know of his involvement with a direct challenge to their authority.[2]

When Giles brought his suit against E. Jeff Harris and the other members of the Board of Registrars of Montgomery County, he named not only himself but also five thousand other African-Americans whom he claimed had been unfairly denied the right to register to vote. Washington was hoping for a favorable ruling locally, and so the action was initiated in federal district court before Judge Thomas G. Jones, a conservative, but appointed to the federal bench by Theodore Roosevelt at the express recommendation of Washington himself. To Washington's disappointment, although he could not say so publicly, Jones danced between loyalties and dismissed the suit, claiming a lack of jurisdiction.[3] Giles was then forced to initiate a series of appeals, each of which was also denied on technical grounds. During the appeal process, Giles was, in fact, fired from the postal service. On February 24, 1903, *Giles v. Harris* reached the Supreme Court.

The Court's composition had again changed in the five years since *Williams*. William McKinley's assassination in 1901 had cut short his term, restricting his legacy on the Court to Joseph McKenna. New president Theodore Roosevelt, on the other hand, quickly had two seats to fill. Justices Shiras and Gray had left the bench.[4] In place of Shiras, President Roosevelt had appointed McKinley confidant and former secretary of state William R. Day. In place of Justice Gray, Roosevelt appointed a scholar and legal philosopher, a war hero, a man destined to become almost as renowned as the Court on which he served. Oliver Wendell Holmes Jr. Holmes (whose physician father had been appropriated, at least in name, by Arthur Conan Doyle as a model for a fictional detective) would be lionized in a bestselling biography, *Yankee From Olympus*, and become the subject of an Oscar nominated film, *The Magnificent Yankee* (Louis Calhern lost for Best Actor to José Ferrer playing Cyrano de Bergerac). He would be portrayed as the quintessence of American fairness in another highly decorated film, *Judgment at Nuremberg*. His successor on the Court, Benjamin Cardozo, praised him as "probably the greatest legal intellect in the history of the English-speaking world."[5] After his death, Holmes was widely eulogized as a great liberal, progressive, and a staunch defender of democratic ideals.

Holmes, however, was a far more complex figure. A Social Darwinist and proponent of ethical relativism, he favored a "rejection of higher law principles in favor of a jurisprudence that explicitly accepted the right of the dominant power in the community to make law."[6] His social views, despite popular mythology, were hardly progressive. When Louis Brandeis was finally confirmed as an associate justice after a bitter floor fight, in which the notion of a Jew on the Court turned out to be not all that appealing to many in the Senate, Holmes observed ecumenically that he would rather "see power in the hands of the Jews than in the Catholics," although he really did not "want to be run by either."[7] Holmes's racial views would prove not a good deal more enlightened.*

Holmes, whose reputation as a legal scholar was already immense, was nominated in August 1902. Despite his reputation, the nomination was not greeted with universal approval. The *New York Times*, while acknowledging that Holmes's appointment would prove "extremely popular," also observed that "he is not to be numbered among the country's jurists of the first rank." The *Times* added generously, "He has the gift of expression."[8] There was, however, no serious opposition to the nomination, and as soon as Congress reconvened in December, Holmes was confirmed unanimously with no debate. He was sworn in on December 8, 1902, and immediately took his seat on the bench. The following February, Wilford Smith appeared for Jackson Giles. Although Smith did not know it, he was on a collision course with one of the greatest legal minds America has ever produced.

Aware that, in *Williams*, the Court had refused to provide relief on the grounds that the plaintiff could not demonstrate actual harm, Smith came prepared. He carefully compiled reams of statistics, newspaper reports, and affidavits, all to demonstrate that, as in *Yick Wo v. Hopkins*, a seemingly evenhanded law was being employed solely to discriminate against a specific class of individual, in this case black voters. Thus, those sections of Article 8 of the Alabama constitution that artificially restricted African-American registration (in contrast with Article 187, which enabled virtually all the whites) were in violation of the Fourteenth and Fifteenth amendments.[9] "[The] part taken by the state—that is, by the white population which framed the Constitution, consisted in shaping that instrument so as to give opportunity and effect to the wholesale fraud which has been practiced."[10]

Ten weeks later, the Court delivered its verdict. Associate Justice Holmes, the newest member of the Court, had been assigned to write the opinion.[11] Speaking for a 6–3 Court, Holmes, in an opinion that "ingeniously evaded reaching the merits of the allegations that the African American electorate had been disenfranchised," denied Giles's claim.[12]

The crux of Holmes's opinion is grounded in his belief of the supremacy

---

* What specifically were Holmes's views on social issues is hard to determine with finality. "Wanting more than a modest place in American history, Holmes took steps to ensure that its judgment of him would be favorable: He destroyed all personal papers that reflected poorly on his reputation." H. L. Pohlman, "Reviewed Work: Oliver Wendell Holmes, Jr.: Soldier, Scholar, Judge. Gary J. Aichele," *American Historical Review* 95, no. 4 (Oct. 1990), p. 1305.

of the legislature, a view that his detractors contrast with Madison's famous warning against the "tyranny of the majority." Still, even if one subscribes to the philosophical underpinning, Holmes's reasoning is head-shaking.

Holmes made two major objections to Giles' suit. The first was that:

> The plaintiff alleges that the whole registration scheme of the Alabama Constitution is a fraud upon the Constitution of the United States, and asks us to declare it void. But, of course, he could not maintain a bill for a mere declaration in the air. He does not try to do so, but asks to be registered as a party qualified under the void instrument. If, then, we accept the conclusion which it is the chief purpose of the bill to maintain, how can we make the court a party to the unlawful scheme by accepting it and adding another voter to its fraudulent lists?[13]

In other words, if the Court upheld Giles's complaint, the United States would have become party to a fraud by protecting the plaintiff's right as a citizen; in turning Giles down, the United States retained its purity by denying a citizen redress of a legitimate grievance. If this sort of twisted reasoning had come from, say, Henry Billings Brown, constitutional law scholars would have roared in derision. But from Oliver Wendell Holmes, tortured logic went unremarked on for decades.

Holmes seemed not unaware of his own rhetorical gymnastics. "We cannot forget that we are dealing with a new and extraordinary situation," he wrote, then added:

> If we accept the plaintiff's allegations for the purposes of his case, he cannot complain. We must accept or reject them. It is impossible simply to shut our eyes, put the plaintiff on the lists, be they honest or fraudulent, and leave the determination of the fundamental question for the future. If we have an opinion that the bill is right on its face, or if we are undecided, we are not at liberty to assume it to be wrong for the purposes of decision . . . unless we are prepared to say that . . . the registration plan of the Alabama Constitution is valid, we cannot order the plaintiff's name to be registered.

Holmes concluded, "It is not an answer to say that, if all the blacks who are qualified according to the letter of the instrument were registered, the fraud would be cured."

The justice was quite correct, of course, but Holmes had an alternative that he did not bother to enunciate. He could simply have declared the specific provisions in question void, and moreover asserted that any state provision that, in word or application, violated the fundamental tenets of equal access to the ballot box as asserted in the Fifteenth Amendment would also be void. Alabama would then have had the choice of either eliminating the offending provisions from its constitution, desisting in using them as a means to disenfranchise black voters, or no longer being able to conduct elections for national office. (For statewide offices, Holmes was correct in his later assertion that the Court had no standing to enforce its ruling.) But Holmes never thought to mention that alternative, even as a hypothetical.[14]

The second objection was more in line with Holmes's long-standing aversion to questioning legislative supremacy. He wrote, "The other difficulty is of a different sort, and strikingly reinforces the argument that equity cannot undertake now, any more than it has in the past, to enforce political rights." In some ways, this second point is more disingenuous than the first. Holmes asserted:

> The court has as little practical power to deal with the people of the state in a body. The bill imports that the great mass of the white population intends to keep the blacks from voting. To meet such an intent, something more than ordering the plaintiff's name to be inscribed upon the lists of 1902 will be needed. If the conspiracy and the intent exist, a name on a piece of paper will not defeat them. Unless we are prepared to supervise the voting in that state by officers of the court, it seems to us that all that the plaintiff could get from equity would be an empty form. Apart from damages to the individual, relief from a great political wrong, if done, as alleged, by the people of a state and the state itself, must be given by them or by the legislative and political department of the government of the United States.

Holmes thereby dismissed Giles's claim with an odd twist on the jurisdiction issue. Giles, according to the justice, had no standing to bring his case not because the monetary damages were insufficient but because the Supreme Court could not dabble in politics. Holmes "framed the case . . . as being about political rights as opposed to race. [He] suggested that political rights cases are not justiciable and that the political process itself must supply the remedy to political wrongs. If race cases are truly political rights cases, and political rights cases are not justiciable, then *Giles* clearly imports that claims alleging racial discrimination in the political process are also nonjusticiable."[15]

All of this is a remarkably convenient construction that allows the constitutionally guaranteed rights and liberties of a large group of citizens to be trampled on.[16] And to refuse to rule against a statute because the Court lacked the power of enforcement was just silly. The Court has no power of enforcement for *any* ruling. It has no dedicated constabulary, no power over Congress. The Court derives its only authority from the willingness of the parties to adhere to its rulings and to the Constitution. If one of the parties refuses, force of arms, a tool of the other branches of government, may be used to ensure compliance.

Holmes's opinion was not unanimous. Once again a dissent was filed by Justice Harlan, but only to take issue on the jurisdictional issue. Harlan would "not formulate and discuss [his] views upon the merits of this case. But," he added, "to avoid misapprehension, I may add that my conviction is that, upon the facts alleged in the bill . . . the plaintiff is entitled to relief in respect of his right to be registered as a voter."

The more substantive dissent was, surprisingly, filed by Justice Brewer.[17] Although Brewer also concerned himself mostly with the jurisdictional issue, he stated plainly, "The plaintiff was entitled to a place on the permanent registry, and was denied it by the defendants, the board of registrars in the county in which he lived."

As to Holmes's contention that Giles's disenfranchisement could only be reversed in the legislature, Brewer replied, "Neither can I assent to the proposition that the case presented by the plaintiff's bill is not strictly a legal one, and entitling a party to a judicial hearing and decision. He alleges that he is a citizen of Alabama, entitled to vote; that he desired to vote at an election for representative in Congress; that, without registration, he could not vote, and that registration was wrongfully denied him by the defendants. That many others were similarly treated does not destroy his rights or deprive him of relief in the courts. That such relief will be given has been again and again affirmed in both national and state courts."

Holmes's opinion, as with many of the equal rights decisions, passed into law largely without comment. For decades, neither politicians, legal scholars, nor journalists expressed indignation or rebuke. Recent characterizations, however, have been substantially more critical. *Giles* has been called "an especially noteworthy feat of judicial legerdemain . . . silently condoning states that had adopted new voting rules to deny blacks the vote at the end of the nineteenth century,"[18] and "cynical and disingenuous."[19]

Most apparent is that Justice Holmes, as had Justices Bradley, Field, Brown, and others before him, simply shoehorned the law into his own views of white racial superiority. The case has been made in two recent biographies that "as for race . . . Holmes' opinions were not only driven into intolerance by his social Darwinism, but were driven beyond the general intolerance of the age."[20] While little evidence exists that Holmes was more racist than the standard of the day, there is equally little evidence that he was less so. But the greater issue, as it had been for the previous three decades, was not the predilection of any particular justice, but the Supreme Court's abdication of its responsibility to protect an abused class of citizens simply because its members seemed to have quite clearly decided that those citizens did not deserve protection. Further, if the Constitution, either in the post–Civil War amendments or in the Tenth, seemed to disagree, then the Constitution must somehow be wrong.

SIXTEEN

MOVEMENT

BETWEEN 1890 AND 1903, 1,889 lynchings were conducted in the United States. In 1,405 of those cases, the victims were black. Although no specific statistics exist, estimates of the number of those lynchings that occurred in southern states range from 70 to 80 percent.[1]

In her pamphlet *Lynch Law in Georgia*, Ida B. Wells-Barnett wrote, "During six weeks of the months of March and April just past [1899] twelve colored men were lynched in Georgia . . . The real purpose of these savage demonstrations is to teach the Negro that he has no rights that the law will enforce."[2]

Southern blacks had certainly gotten the message. With the help of the Supreme Court, the white population of the old Confederacy achieved all it had sought in the decades after the collapse of Reconstruction. African-Americans were returned to quasi slavery, and the social structure of the antebellum South could be replicated by whites without fear of intervention. The era of federal mandate for equal rights was at an end. The Court had defended state laws that stripped racial equality away, and overturned federal laws that sought to defend it. Those citizens of Georgia who mutilated Sam Hose, who doused him with oil and allowed him to slowly roast to his death without making the least effort to determine whether he was even guilty of a crime, needed no longer to look over their shoulders; no legislative branch of state, local, or national government nor any court of law would be in pursuit. *Plessy, Williams*, and a host of other decisions had announced that the Constitution would not be used either to punish those responsible or to prevent others from sharing Sam Hose's fate.

The Democratic Party was ascendant in Congress and would remain so for most of the twentieth century. Democratic rule would ensure disproportionate influence as southern representatives and senators gained seniority by being returned again and again to office. If Reconstruction was viewed in the South as an era of occupation, the post-*Plessy* period represented victory over the occupiers.

In the years just prior to *Plessy* and especially in the years just after, the white South threw itself into Jim Crow with gusto. At the time Henry Billings Brown handed down his opinion, only Georgia mandated racial separation on street cars. By 1907, every southern state had followed suit. Laws designed to cement the disenfranchisement of black voters were passed or toughened. Each of the eleven states that had formed the Confederacy had instituted a poll tax by 1904, most in combination with a grandfather clause, and seven had demanded literacy tests. Poll taxes were generally assessed on a running total, so virtually no black applicant could pay. As the South devolved into one-party rule, laws mandating white primaries became widespread, so votes in general elections by the few African-Americans who had slipped through the net were certain to be meaningless. By 1904, only 1,342 of the 130,000 African-Americans who had registered to vote in 1896 in Louisiana were still on the rolls. By 1906, 83 percent of white males were registered to vote, compared to 2 percent of blacks.[3]

With voting rights denied and public conveyances secure, southern state governments proceeded to enact legislation designed to segregate virtually every aspect of public life. Georgia passed a public park law in 1905, and within a few years, blacks were excluded from virtually all park facilities throughout the South. Forced segregation was soon mandated at factory entrances, pay windows, movie theaters, restaurants, grocery stores, taverns, and, especially, schools, cemeteries, and public toilets. Blacks were effectively herded out of the white South into decrepit, slum-ridden ghettos called "Darktowns." To postulate that the Jim Crow restrictions were as severe as those for slaves—and much more so than for antebellum free blacks—would in no way be an exaggeration.

After the grand came the trivial. As C. Vann Woodward observed, "Up and down the avenues and byways of Southern life appeared with increasing profusion the little signs: 'Whites Only' or 'Colored.' Sometimes the law prescribed their dimensions in inches, and in one case the kind and color of paint."[4]

By 1910, southern white society had more or less secured racial separation. African-Americans had been denied proper education and, as a result, were suited only to perform low-skilled, low-paying jobs. Police departments and courts, dominated by whites, kept order through an apartheid legal system. For a few whites the guarantee of low-cost workers and a quiescent black population provided opportunities to attain wealth and position in an environment that was largely noncompetitive. But the victory was Pyrrhic. For most whites, African-American losses were theirs as well. As employers tapped into the pool of subsistence labor, poor whites came to realize that their own earning power had been depressed along with that of blacks. As in the slave era, southern industry became dependent on a workforce that came cheap and lacked skills. Upward mobility for whites low on the economic scale soon proved as elusive as it had been for the blacks they had been so eager to repress.

The subjugation of African-Americans again locked the South into agriculture. In 1910, Mississippi's male population was 651,391, of whom 574,279 were employed. Of that number, an incredible 437,643, or 76 percent, were engaged in "agriculture, forestry, or animal husbandry."[5] Of Mississippi's 641,789 females, 305,366 were employed, and 241,416, or 79 percent, worked the land. By contrast, in Massachusetts, of a population of 1,340,517 males, 1,086,787 were employed, with only 71,783, or 7 percent, in farming or forestry. Of the 444,301 Massachusetts females employed out of a population of 1,402,167, only 2,793 toiled in similar occupations. Other southern states fared little better than Mississippi. In Alabama, 65 percent of the men and 71 percent of the women worked on the land. In North Carolina, the numbers were 67 percent of men and 60 percent of women; in South Carolina, 70 percent of men and 71 percent of women; in Georgia 65 percent of men and 60 percent of women; and in Louisiana, slightly more than 50 percent of both men and women

Nor can the argument be made that the Northeast was an exception and the percentages were similar in northern farm states to what they were in the South. In Iowa, for example, while 49 percent of the men were engaged in farming, only 7 percent of the women were similarly employed. Jim Crow laws made it increasingly difficult for southern blacks to own property, so most who worked on the land were either tenant farmers or migrants. The low percentage of Iowa women working the land is an indication that Iowa men worked family farms while in the South, men and women were working fields they did not own.

Manufacturing in Mississippi employed only 59,250 men and 6,520 women, less than 1 percent of the workforce, while in Massachusetts more than half of those employed were in manufacturing and mechanical industries. Even in agrarian Iowa the total was above 20 percent.

According to C. Vann Woodward, "The abundance of natural resources and industrial opportunities [in the South] was widely advertised and the desperate need of an industrialized and diversified economy was acknowledged, but in spite of thirty years of intensive propaganda and effort, the South remained largely a raw-material economy, with the attendant penalties of low wages, lack of opportunity and poverty.[6]

What nonfarm industry did exist in the South was disproportionately owned by northern financial interests. "The large extent to which ownership of the South's transportation, communication, financial, and manufacturing corporations was centralized in the cities of the Northeast, as well as the considerable degree to which ownership of the region's natural resources and its certificates of public indebtedness was concentrated there, no doubt contributed much to the stability of the [neomercantilist] system."[7]

Jim Crow might have freed the South to maintain its social order, but the by-product was economic atrophy and burgeoning poverty. Whites suffered along with blacks. In 1912, per capita wealth in the northern states was $1,950, in the Middle Atlantic States, $2,374, and in the South only $993, and these figures include the vast amount of southern wealth owned by northern commercial and financial interests.[8] By 1919, the eleven states with the lowest per capita income were all in the South. Few had access to the high end of the labor pool. The competition for those skilled, high-paying jobs that did exist was fierce, and, even then, such jobs paid substantially less in the South than in the North. While some small number of whites emigrated to seek enhanced opportunity, most remained, "further intensifying the old problems of worn-out soil, cut-over timber lands, and worked-out mines."[9]

Plessy and *Williams* had thus become fulcra on which not only the establishment of institutionalized racism but both southern and northern political economies ultimately pivoted. Eventually, in response to the hopelessness that federal abdication had engendered, African-Americans, whose roots and traditions had until that point caused them to try to make a go of it in the South, finally began to leave. There can be little doubt that the equal rights decisions of the Supreme Court were in large part responsible for the creation of a refugee class in America.

Conventional wisdom asserts that what has been termed the "First Great Migration" of African-Americans occurred roughly from 1915 to 1925, in response to exploding demand in northern factories. That decade "witnessed a steady expansion of northern industry, at the same time as the outbreak of war in Europe drastically curtailed the immigration which had supplied much of the northern labor force."[10] Any movement of African-Americans from the South in the years preceding World War I has generally been characterized as the "Migration of the Talented Tenth," referring to politicians, businessmen, lawyers, doctors, the educated, and skilled workers. The movement of ordinary African-Americans, it was argued, was in response to an increase of opportunity in the North, rather than the choking off of opportunity in the South.

Acceptance of this thesis implies that, regardless of economic deprivation, lynchings, miscarriages of justice, constant humiliation, and disenfranchisement, African-Americans were either too docile, too hopeful, or too afraid to leave until the carrot of northern industry became just too plump to ignore.

The numbers, however, do not bear this argument out. Although migration did become pronounced after the outbreak of the First World War, African-Americans had begun to leave the South in great numbers in the years just before *Plessy*, and the flight increased drastically in the ensuing decade. "By 1890, substantial numbers of blacks were moving to northern cities then experiencing booming economies, though it would take a generation and a world war before the black stream northward was to become a flood."[11]

Between 1890 and 1910, the white population of the South increased from 20 million to 29.4 million, while the black population increased from 6.7 million to 8.7 million, a far smaller percentage gain. Add to this that the Census Bureau asserted a significant undercounting of blacks in the South in the 1890 census, perhaps by as much as 10 percent.[12] Given that birth rates were traditionally higher among the black population, even a 5 percent increase would indicate that a significant migration of African-Americans from the South was under way. The Census Bureau postulated "a very considerable dispersion of the Negro population born in the South through other sections of the country."[13] In every southern state, African-American population as a percentage of the total declined between 1900 and 1910, while in every northern state it increased.[14] Between 1890 and 1900, the African-American population increased in northern states by 182,926, or about 25 percent. Between 1900 and 1910, the increase was 167,311, or about 18 percent.[15] In 1910, of the 999,451 blacks living in the North, 451,533 had been born in the South.[16]

South Carolina had sustained a net loss of 72,000 black residents between 1900 and 1910. For the first time in their history, the black populations of Mississippi and Louisiana declined, and in every other southern state growth among the black population drastically decreased. So, while the South lost an additional 450,000 African-American residents in the second decade of the twentieth century, this flight was merely the continuation of a trend rather than the onset of one.[17]

The majority of the émigrés moved to northern cities. In 1900, the African-American population of Manhattan was 36,246; by 1910, 60,534. Of those, more than 46,000 had migrated from other states, almost all from the South. New York City as a whole contained 60,666 African-Americans in 1900, and 91,709 in 1910, only 26,977 of whom had been born in New York State.[18] During the period from 1900 to 1910, the black population of Chicago increased by one third, of Philadelphia by more than 40 percent, and of other northern cities like Cleveland, Pittsburgh, St. Louis, Kansas City, and Indianapolis by between 25 and 45 percent.[19] The "largest number of Negroes" who migrated north during the decade were of "the intelligent laboring class," workers with skills that could be leveraged into employment opportunities in their new homes.[20]

The eminent African-American scholar Carter G. Woodson, writing in 1918, described one phenomenon of the process.

> Some of these Negroes have migrated after careful consideration; others have just happened to go north as wanderers; and a still larger number on many excursions to the cities conducted by railroads during the summer months. Sometimes one excursion brings to Chicago two or three thousand Negroes, two-thirds of whom never go back. They do not often follow the higher pursuits of labor in the North but they earn more money than they have been accustomed to earn in the South.[21]

By 1910, 440,534 African-Americans born in the South had migrated north and west. Conversely, only 41,489 African-Americans born in the North and West had moved to the South. The net loss of blacks by the South to the North and West was, therefore, 399,045. Using the same method gives southern whites a net loss of only 46,839. The increase of the African-American population between 1900 and 1910 showed a wide distribution over the northern and western states. The largest gains in the North were in New York with 35,000, or 35 percent, Pennsylvania with 37,000, or 23 percent, and Illinois, with 24,000, or 28 percent.[22]

As to the "Talented Tenth," while virtually all of the prominent African-Americans who lived in New York City in 1915 had been born in the South, many others who had the means to leave did. Much of the black migration during those years was young, unskilled, and unmarried, members of the first generations born after the abolition of slavery.[23]

When the black laboring class began to flee the South for the North in ever-increasing numbers and the labor pool degenerated, southern whites became more and more desperate to discourage black emigration. They began to spread tales of northern poverty and hardship; to tell blacks that they would freeze to death in the winter.

In response, the *Chicago Defender*, the nation's most prominent African-American newspaper, widely read in southern states, struck a steady drumbeat to encourage blacks to abandon agriculture and Jim Crow and come north to high wages, improved social status, and opportunity. Editorials in the *Defender* assured its southern readers that their treatment by northern whites would be vastly improved over what they had experienced below the Mason-Dixon Line.[24] At one point, the *Defender* compiled a list of the African-Americans who had frozen to death in the *South* and asked, "If you can freeze to death in the north and be free, why freeze to death in the south and be a slave?"[25] Other black leaders praised the "liberal attitude of some whites, which, although not that of social equality, gives the Negroes a liberty in northern centers which leads them to think that they are citizens of the country."[26]

The *Defender* and other black newspapers had definite impact, even among a population where few could read. In parts of the South where illiteracy was high, groups gathered in barbershops or other meeting places to hear the *Indianapolis Freeman* or the *New York Age* read aloud. Copies of the papers would pass from hand to hand until they literally disintegrated.[27]

Further pressuring the southern labor pool, northern industrial firms dispatched agents to offer inducements to southern blacks, usually consisting of free transportation, the promise of high wages, and sometimes subsidized rent. Many southern communities eventually passed ordinances to ban such recruitment. Labor agents were sometimes beaten and jailed. Southern whites might not have wanted African-Americans living on equal footing, but neither did they want them gone entirely.

The efforts to halt the exodus failed, and the migration wrought by Jim Crow permanently altered American demographics. "In 1910, 75 percent of the nation's blacks lived in rural areas and nine-tenths lived in the South. [By 1970] three-quarters are in cities and half reside outside southern states."[28]

The most effective way to stem the degradation of the labor pool, of course, was to provide economic opportunity. The South, with its abundance of natural resources, favorable climate, and navigable rivers, should have been a magnet for manufacturing. Southern capital might easily have flowed out of "extractive industries" to take advantage of the immense opportunities engendered by rising worldwide demand for industrial products, demand enhanced by the sharp decrease in supply caused by the war in Europe.

But southerners were more interested in trying to maintain the past, to replicating, as near as possible, the social economy of the slave system. The more they struggled to maintain a dead status quo, the more they were throttled by it. Scant was the opportunity for blacks or whites in a society in which universal education was discouraged and the perpetuation of an antiquated, dysfunctional social order overwhelmed economic considerations.

While northern industry was the beneficiary of the migration of cheap labor, social institutions in the North were placed under stress by the sudden wave of refugees pouring into its cities. As population began to overwhelm housing stock, government services, and, eventually, the job market, competition for territory between the burgeoning black population and the whites they threatened to displace became intense. A series of race riots broke out, the worst being a four-day conflagration in Chicago in 1919. "The ghetto was already well-formed by the eve of World War I; the migration and riot merely strengthened both the external and internal forces that had created it."[29]

By 1920, 152,000 African-Americans lived in New York City, and by 1930, 327,000. Harlem had by then more or less completed its metamorphosis. "The migration of blacks to northern cities led to changes in almost every aspect of black northern life. By far the most important effect of the black migration was the rise of the northern urban ghetto. The most famous ghetto, New York's Harlem, was transformed from a genteel upper-class white community at the turn of the century to a black ghetto and slum by 1930."[30]

By contorting the Constitution to suit its social views, the Court therefore had a profound and lasting impact not simply on the political and social
status of African-Americans but on the fabric of America itself. Justices
Bradley and Brown were probably correct in their conclusion that equality
cannot be achieved solely by legislation. Still, had the Civil Rights Law of
1875 been upheld and forced segregation and disenfranchisement been
struck down, instead of the reverse, the United States might have looked far
different in 1920, 1930, and beyond. The South, forced to contend with both
an aggressive, politically active workforce and a vibrant two-party system,
might have broken the bonds of tenant farming that shackled it through
most of the twentieth century. The North, inundated only by a wave of
refugees from across the Atlantic, and not an additional invasion from the
South, might have seen its cities grow in a more manageable fashion. The
nine justices on the Court might have thought they were providing favor to
the white race in appointing themselves the last bastion of racial supremacy,
but they certainly provided no favor to the nation they had been appointed
to serve.

A Charade of Justice

T HAT SLAVERY IS AN indelible stain on America's past is beyond question, but, all the same, any number of historians have attempted— and still attempt—to at least partly rationalize away the Founders' failure to put a stop to it. In response to the hypocrisy of, say, Thomas Jefferson, a slave owner, declaring "all men are created equal," Jefferson's many defenders insist that to compare the late 1700s with modern times is shoddy scholarship and just plain unfair. Jefferson opposed slavery, they say (although a few acknowledge that he did consider blacks inherently inferior), but pragmatic considerations made it impossible for him to even consider demanding an end to the practice. Much the same argument is made for George Washington and other Founders.[1] And, with slavery common practice in the western hemisphere and much of Asia, as well as in Africa itself, the moral issues tended to be hazier in the Founding period than in more contemporary times. With very few exceptions, it is pointed out, most whites accepted the enslavement of Africans as, if not quite justified in Scripture as many slave owners contended, at least not as the monstrous evil we deem it today. What's more, if slavery had been faced head-on by the Founders, the United States likely would not have had a Declaration of Independence and most certainly not a Constitution. Washington, Jefferson, and even antislavery northerners like Benjamin Franklin and John Adams accepted continuation of an institution they opposed, even abhorred, as the price paid to have a country.

But Jim Crow cannot be similarly pushed aside as anachronism or political necessity. By the 1870s, slavery and the slave trade had been abolished by legislation in Europe and force of arms in America. The United States was, for the first time, actually united, albeit under a set of principles anathema to the majority of southern whites. Any practical impediments to the nation moving toward political and social equality for all men had been swept away. (Women's rights were still but a faint glimmer.) Radical Republicans, dominant in a federal government larger, more powerful, and more of a factor in the lives of its citizens than ever before, had moved single-mindedly, even ruthlessly, to achieve those very goals. A series of presidents, none of whom was especially enthusiastic about equal rights, were either persuaded to support the initiative or neutered.

Painful as it was to many Americans in the North as well as the South, the United States was lurching toward an era of equality inconceivable only two decades before. Only the courts could deter an America that would finally be as free for black as for white; the very courts that Alexander Hamilton had assured the people of New York would turn away tyranny and be the relentless defender of the weak against the powerful. Brutus's warnings that the judiciary itself would be an incubator of despotism, sniffed at in Federalist 78 and Federalist 80, had been ultimately discarded.

But Hamilton, alas, had been wrong and Brutus right.

Led by the nine justices of the Supreme Court, the judiciary allowed, or more accurately mandated, America to become the land of quasi slavery, to repress African-Americans every bit as much as free people as they had been as property. The Court's decision to enable a social order at odds with legislation Congress had passed, the president had signed, and the states had ratified was one of choice, not necessity. There were no mitigating factors, not even any real jurisprudence that demanded it, only the distaste by white America to share its freedoms with blacks, a distaste the Court chose to reinforce rather than dissuade.[2]

In a series of decisions spanning almost three decades, the Supreme Court announced that it considered popular will and its own notions of racial hierarchy more compelling than the promise of equality under the Constitution. On the altar of strict adherence to the law, they ruled time and again to deny fundamental rights to black Americans. In reading and interpreting statutes with self-enforced myopia, a shifting series of justices rewrote constitutional amendments to suit racial attitudes to which Americans of today express repugnance. In doing so, the Court ultimately helped create an America in which Sam Hose could be tortured and murdered with the full approbation of not only the state of Georgia but the government of the United States.

This is not to say that the justices of the Court bear direct responsibility for the atrocities of the Jim Crow era. No justice ever beat, tortured, or falsely imprisoned a black man, nor personally turned one away from the voting booth. Still, incidents such as the burning of Sam Hose, perpetrated with impunity under laws that the Court had declared comporting to the Constitution, were widely and luridly reported. The justices could not have helped but be aware of the horrific acts of violence and abuse suffered by African-Americans because their rights had been denied them by the very Supreme Court on which they sat. While the justices debated the minutia of subordinate clauses, refusing to consider the larger picture of the manner in which the United States was being governed under their aegis, men, women, and children were slaughtered.

Consequently, whether *Plessy*, *Williams*, or *Giles* spurred the acceleration of Jim Crow laws or were merely coincident to an existing trend is, to a great degree, beside the point. The decisions by the justices gave force of federal law to segregation; proclaimed that the government of the United States, the same government that had gone to war to preserve the Union, was now firmly of the belief that the southern part of that Union could again confine the black man to chattel status. That some substantial segment of the white population greeted the Court's segregation decisions with relief does not go to justify them. As Hamilton took pains to exposit, the very object of placing federal judges on the bench for life, or at least during "good behavior," was to insulate them from popular passions, allow them to issue rulings without fear of being deprived of their position by an arbitrary political breeze.

Some have pointed out that the Court ruled in favor of African-Americans on a number of occasions, when white action was particularly blatant and egregious. But these decisions are merely exceptions that prove the rule. The Court created a set of guidelines to facilitate both the deprivation of black Americans' rights and enforced segregation to which anyone but an imbecile could adhere.

A century afterward, when the magnitude of the injustice could no longer be ignored and America had finally repudiated the values that led to *Plessy* or *Williams*, it became convenient to anoint a villain or two, a Henry Billings Brown, for example, to bear the full weight of the dereliction of his fellows. But to simply focus on Justice Brown, or dismiss him as a bigot, avoids the greater issue, renders the man and the decision merely anachronisms, anomalies, yielding no deeper meaning, no message for the America of to-day. In *Plessy*, Justice Brown was merely reflecting not only an accepted view of race but also a judicial philosophy that claims dispassion while protecting the entrenched. Justice Harlan's rebukes notwithstanding, nothing the justice said or wrote was unrepresentative of a strict, albeit bloodless, interpretation of law. *Plessy* and *Williams* were not then aberrations, vestiges of an unenlightened time, but rather examples of a manner in which both to view and to apply the law that is very much with us today.

In the process of researching a book such as this, immediately apparent is the immense volume of available scholarly material. Literally hundreds of books, articles, and monographs have been produced on *Plessy*, the *Civil Rights Cases*, the *Slaughterhouse Cases*, and even decisions of lesser notoriety like *Williams* and *Rives*. Each opinion has been exhaustively analyzed and scrutinized for adherence to precedent, consistency of logic, and the quality of arguments presented to the Court. Justice Bradley's opinions, or Justice Brown's, or Justice Harlan's dissents have been praised, excoriated, or parsed by constitutional law professors, other judges, or historians. Some have seen reputations enhanced in the process, some have been diminished. Cornelius J. Jones in *Williams*, for example, has been criticized for his failure to cite Fifteenth Amendment grounds in his Supreme Court appeal; Justice Harlan taken to task for introducing "sentimentality" into his dissents. There are some similar observations in these pages, particularly with respect to Albion Tourgée's decision not to question the equality of accommodations in *Plessy*.

Tourgée notwithstanding, however, this sort of analysis merely helps perpetuate the charade that the equal rights appeals to the Supreme Court were lost because of failures either in the law or of counsel. But do any constitutional law scholars actually believe that if only Cornelius Jones had made a better argument, the Court would have ruled for Henry Williams and voided the voting rules in Mississippi? That if only the Civil Rights Act of 1875 had been worded differently, it would have passed constitutional muster with Justices Bradley and Waite? Or if only the Fourteenth Amendment had been presented with less ambiguity, the Court would have ruled against the white murderers in *Cruikshank*? Or upheld African-American voting rights in *Rives* or *Giles*? What should be apparent is that the Court did not render its decisions to conform to the law but rather contorted the law to conform to its decisions.

If the hoax of a fair hearing was so blatant, how could the Court have successfully perpetrated such a transparent fraud? It could do so by seeming to ground every decision strictly in precedent; by overwhelming analysis with sheer tonnage of verbiage and citations; by employing technically sound but eelish logic to justify a preordained decision; and, mostly, by cherry-picking from a vast array of potential paths to fashion and refashion the law to suit. *Prigg* would be cited, then ignored; the *Slaughterhouse Cases* would be precedent, then they would not be; the Fourteenth Amendment would apply to private individuals, then it would not; there would be implied rights in the Constitution, then there would not be. The body of jurisprudence is such that a justice can find support for virtually *any* opinion and anchor it strictly in rules of procedure. Constitution law is, after all, simply politics made incomprehensible to the common man.

The problem with judges who would claim to be "strict constructionists," even "originalists," is that both philosophies are artificial, constructs to allow their adherents to pass off personal prejudice as law. Originalism, for example, implies that if an extraterrestrial with a fluency in English was suddenly dropped into Washington, he, she, or it would interpret the Constitution in an obvious and comprehensible way. But what does "necessary and proper" actually mean? Or "equal protection of the law"? Or, for that matter, "good behavior"? In fact, all constitutional analysis is "broad construction," interpretive. Pure objectivity is impossible.

Article III of the Constitution is vague as to both the extent of the judiciary's power and its composition. As the United States evolved, the Supreme Court carved out impressive territory for itself, including the power to determine whether or not a law passed by Congress and signed by the president comports to the Constitution. It has wielded that power sometimes in the interest of justice, more often, as in *Dred Scott* or the *Civil Rights Cases*, in the interest of philosophical self-interest.

As black Americans came to realize, without a Supreme Court willing to come out from under the umbrella of legal gymnastics and demand enforcement of the laws protecting citizens' rights, even constitutional amendments are simply hollow verbiage. Perhaps it is true that American democracy has survived the skewing of checks-and-balances toward an unelected branch of its government, but for many of its citizens, often the very ones for whom Alexander Hamilton promised protection, that democracy has hardly flourished.

NOTES

PROLOGUE: A DEATH IN GEORGIA

1   See Gregory Mixon. "Henry McNeal Turner versus the Tuskegee Machine: Black Leadership in the Nineteenth Century," *Journal of Negro History* 79, no. 4 (Autumn 1994), pp. 363–80.

2   *Atlanta Journal*, Mar. 16, 1899.

3   *Atlanta Constitution*, Apr. 18, 1899.

4   Ibid.

5   *New York Times*, Apr. 24, 1899.

6   Ida. B. Wells-Barnett, *Lynch Law in Georgia: A Six-Weeks' Record in the Center of Southern Civilization, as Faithfully Chronicled by the "Atlanta Journal" and the "Atlanta Constitution"* (Chicago: Chicago Colored Citizens, 1899).

7   *New York Times*, Apr. 24, 1899.

8   Wells-Barnett.

9   James W. Clarke, "Without Fear or Shame: Lynching, Capital Punishment and the Subculture of Violence in the American South," *British Journal of Political Science* 28, no. 2 (Apr. 1998), p. 269.

10 This did not prevent newspapers in the North, including the *New York Times*, the *Chicago Daily Tribune*, and *Boston Evening Transcript*, from accepting the rumor as proof of Sam Hose's guilt.

11 *Atlanta Constitution*, Apr. 24, 1899.

12 Quoted in Emma Coleman Jordan, "A Dream Deferred: Comparative and Practical Considerations for the Black Reparations Movement," *New York University Annual Survey of American Law 2003 Symposium: A History Lesson: Reparations for What?*, p. 592.

13 The Lige Strickland affair was reported in remarkable detail by the *Brooklyn Daily Eagle*, Apr. 24, 1899, and *New York Times*, Apr. 25, 1899, and also by Louis Le Vin,

in his report to Ida Wells-Barnett, filed weeks after the event. The stories differ in certain particulars but agree on all major points.

14 This statement, thoughtful and reasoned, was likely apocryphal, since in the subsequent investigation, none of those present reported Strickland doing anything but protesting his innocence.

15 *New York Times*, Apr. 25, 1899. The *New York Journal* was one of the few northern newspapers to express outrage over mob rule in the South.

16 *Chicago Daily Tribune*, Apr. 24, 1899.

17 An editorial criticizing the sheriff of Newnan ran on Apr. 25, and a short column of mild rebuke against Georgia two weeks later.

18 *Brooklyn Daily Eagle*, Apr. 25, 1899.

19 Ibid., Apr. 24, 1899.

20 Reported in the *New York Times*, Apr. 25, 1899.

21 W. E. B. DuBois, *Autobiography of W. E. B. Du Bois: A Soliloquy on Viewing My Life from the Last Decade of Its First Century* (New York: International Publishers, 1968), pp. 221–22.

22 Brutus, whose identity remains unknown, is thought to have been Robert Yates, an anti-Federalist delegate to the Constitutional Convention who walked out of the convention in disgust when he realized that James Madison and his supporters intended to impose an entirely new system of government on the United States.

23 The Brutus essays actually came first. Hamilton, Madison, and John Jay, writing together as "Publius," were forced to respond to Brutus when his cogent anti-Federalist arguments threatened to derail ratification in New York.

24 The debate on the nature of the judiciary was equally fierce in the Virginia ratifying convention with proponents of the new Constitution, led by James Madison and, of the judicial role, John Marshall, with opposition spearheaded by the redoubtable Patrick Henry.

25 Free blacks in the North were hardly considered citizens on a par even with white paupers.

26 *American Law Review* 1 (Apr. 1867), p. 572.

27 The sole constitutional alternative for Supreme Court oversight is impeachment, a remarkably—and intentionally—cumbersome process. It has never been used successfully to remove a justice.

ONE: CONSTRUCTION AND RECONSTRUCTION: TWO GREAT EXPERIMENTS

1 Eric Foner, *Reconstruction: America's Unfinished Revolution, 1863–1877* (New York: Harper and Row, 1988), p. 23.

2 Mildred Bryant-Jones, "The Political Program of Thaddeus Stevens, 1865," *Phylon* 2, no. 2 (2nd Qtr. 1941), p. 149.

3 Equality for all American males would be more accurate. As events played out, the movement for women's suffrage would be a casualty of the postwar period.

4 Quoted in Bryant-Jones, p. 150.

5 Quoted in C. Vann Woodward, *The Burden of Southern History* (Baton Rouge, LA: Louisiana State University Press, 1968), p. 92.

6 Ibid., p. 97.

7 Quoted in Joseph H. Lackner, "The Foundation of St. Ann's Parish, 1866–1870: The African-American Experience in Cincinnati," *U.S. Catholic Historian* 14, no. 2, "Parishes and Peoples: Religious and Social Meanings, Part One" (Spring 1996), p. 14.

8 Quoted in C. Vann Woodward, "The Political Legacy of Reconstruction," *Journal of Negro Education* 26, no. 3, "The Negro Voter in the South" (Summer 1957), p. 231.

9 Lincoln favored a far more measured approach to readmission, one that would guarantee fundamental rights to freed slaves without arousing the undying enmity of southern whites.

10 *Congressional Globe*, 40th Cong., 2nd sess. (Dec. 3, 1867), p. 2. The message was delivered in an attempt to ward off impeachment. Johnson was successful that time. Two days after his message was read in Congress, the House of Representatives voted 108–57 against reporting a bill of impeachment. He would not be so fortunate two months later.

11 Ibid., p. 3.

12 An indication that Congress, at least in 1862, did not disagree with Andrew Johnson's nullity of secession hypothesis.

13 George P. Smith, "Republican Reconstruction and Section Two of the Fourteenth Amendment," *Western Political Quarterly* 23, no. 4 (Dec. 1970), pp. 829–53.

14 *Statutes at Large*, 39th Cong., 2nd sess., p. 27.

15 Johnson also made little secret that he believed that the law favored blacks at the expense of whites.

16 *New York Times*, May 19, 1866.

17 As it was for Robert E. Lee.

18 Technically, two thirds of each house are required merely to "propose" an amendment. Actual passage occurs in the states.

19 *New York Times*, June 15, 1866.

20 *Hartford Courant*, June 14, 1866. The article referred to Stevens's proposal of a section bluntly barring disenfranchisement of blacks.

21 Population trends were such that southern influence in Congress would only decrease over time regardless of which choice the states made.

22 This phenomenon is hardly unique. During the George W. Bush presidency, many in Washington were driven to change their positions on torture, gay rights, and wiretapping simply because the Bush administration appeared so extreme on the other side.

23 William W. van Alstyne, "The Fourteenth Amendment, the 'Right' to Vote, and the Understanding of the Thirty-Ninth Congress," *Supreme Court Review* 1965, (1965).

24 *Statutes at Large*, 39th Cong., 2nd sess., p. 428.

25 Ibid., p. 429.

26 Foner, *Reconstruction*, p. 276.

27 Rumblings of impeachment had already begun, although even Stevens and Sumner had not made the suggestion publicly.

28 *New York Times*, Mar. 25, 1867.

29 Ibid., July 10, 1868.

Two: Beyond Party or Politics: The Capitalists Ascend

1 Chester McArthur Destler, "Entrepreneurial Leadership Among the 'Robber Barons': A Trial Balance," *Journal of Economic History* 6, Supplement: The Tasks of Economic History (May 1946), p. 32.

2 Ibid., p. 33.

3 *Statistical Abstract of the United States*, 1878, United States Department of the Census, p. 152. Southern states were Virginia, North Carolina, Tennessee, South Carolina, Georgia, Florida, Alabama, Mississippi, and Louisiana.

4 Ibid.

5 Ibid., pp. 148–49.

6 Foner, *Reconstruction*, pp. 32–33.

7 *Statistical Abstract*, p. 4.

8 *Brooklyn Daily Eagle*, Feb. 12, 1867.

9 *New York Times*, Aug. 12, 1868.

10 *Hartford Courant*, Aug. 15, 1868.

11 Foner, *Reconstruction*, p. 21.

12 Garrison, of course, had also warned that such "coercion would gain nothing," words that proved prophetic in the decades to come.

13 Quoted in the *New York Times*, Mar. 31, 1870, p. 5. Grant did "call the attention . . . of our newly enfranchised race to the importance of their striving in every honorable manner to make themselves worthy of their new privilege."

14 Quoted in Foner, *Reconstruction*, p. 449.

15 Ibid., p. 446.

16 Quoted in the *Hartford Courant*, Feb. 2, 1870.

Three: Another Reconstruction: The Lincoln Court

1 *Dred Scott v. Sandford* (60 U.S. 393 [1857]), was the first case since *Marbury v. Madison* in 1803 in which the Supreme Court overturned an act of Congress as unconstitutional, in this case the Missouri Compromise of 1820. The ruling caused

Scott to be returned to slavery, but the impact of the decision was far greater. Taney asserted in his opinion that blacks were inherently inferior and could never be citizens of the United States. The decision also created major upheaval in federal territories since the Court denied Congress the power to prohibit slavery in any of them.

2   Quoted in Sherrill Halbert, "The Suspension of the Writ of Habeas Corpus by President Lincoln," *American Journal of Legal History* 2, no. 2 (Apr. 1958), p. 99.

3   Congress was not in session at the time, and Lincoln would not call them back until July 4.

4   17 F. Cas. 144 (1861).

5   Subsequent rulings have upheld Taney's position, first in *ex parte Milligan* (see below) and most recently in *Hamdi v. Rumsfeld*.

6   The legal arguments ended up having no practical impact on John Merryman. He was released from Fort McHenry to a future unrecorded by historians.

7   Marshall had taken precisely the opposite tack in *Marbury v. Madison*, opting for a strategic retreat, not issuing an opinion President Jefferson would simply ignore. Marshall had thereby not only ensured his own survival as chief justice but also strengthened the Court.

8   Abraham Lincoln, message to Congress, July 4, 1861, second printed draft, with changes in Lincoln's hand, pp. 12–13, Abraham Lincoln Papers at the Library of Congress, series 1, general correspondence, 1833–1916.

9   4 U.S. 37 (1800).

10   67 U.S. 665 (1862).

11   See, for example, *Bank of Commerce v. New York*, 67 U.S. 620 (1863).

12   See *ex parte Vallandigham*, 68 U.S. 243 (1864); *Roosevelt v. Meyer*, 68 U.S. 512 (1863).

13   Nine years later, the Court admitted it had incorrectly dodged the paper money question and was forced to rule on it.

14   Franklin Roosevelt's attempt to expand the Court was, of course, stillborn.

15   One of Field's brothers, Cyrus, would begin the Herculean task of laying the transatlantic cable. Another, Henry, would become a minister and famed travel writer whose views of African-Americans will be discussed in chapter 12.

16   *Philadelphia North American*, Oct. 14, 1864, quoted in Charles Warren, *The Supreme Court and United States History* (Boston: Little Brown, 1923), p. 112.

17   *New York Times*, Oct. 14, 1864.

18   *Chicago Tribune*, Oct. 14, 1864.

19   Chase's image graces the $10,000 bill, a piece of currency that few, including the author, have ever personally seen.

20   Rock had to be escorted by federal marshals to the train in order to return home, since travel by blacks within the nation's capital was restricted.

21 *Statutes at Large*, 39th Cong., 1st sess. (July 23, 1866). The following year, Justice Wayne would die, reducing the Court to eight.

22 71 U.S. 2 (1866). The full opinions were not published until December.

23 Ironically, although for the wrong reasons, Democrats, as Taney had been in *Merryman*, were on the right side of history.

24 Warren, p. 164.

25 Republicans asked, only part rhetorically, whether *Milligan* meant that the military tribunal that had convicted the assassins of Abraham Lincoln had, in fact, precipitated a lynching.

26 A threat that was made good in Johnson's case.

Four: Siege: Congress Counterattacks

1 71 U.S. 475 (1866).

2 Quoted in Warren, p. 178.

3 See ibid., p. 178–79.

4 Quoted in ibid., p. 181.

5 Georgia had, by then, joined the action.

6 *Georgia v. Stanton*, 73 U.S. 50 (1867).

7 Warren, p. 186.

8 Stanley I. Kutler, "Ex parte McCardle: Judicial Impotency? The Supreme Court and Reconstruction Reconsidered," *American Historical Review* 72, no. 3 (Apr. 1967), p. 839.

9 Justice Wayne had died on July 5, 1867, leaving the Court with only eight justices. Wayne, from Georgia, had served since 1835. He was a staunch Unionist, but no abolitionist. He had voted with the majority in *Dred Scott*.

10 *Congressional Globe*, 40th Cong., 2nd sess. (Jan. 14, 1868), p. 504.

11 The issuing of formal opinions months after the cases had actually been decided was commonplace.

12 Kutler, "Ex parte McCardle," pp. 840–41. The manner in which the repeal was introduced caused great umbrage in Congress. Representative James F. Wilson of Iowa slipped an amendment into an otherwise innocuous bill just before the chamber was to vote on it. The following day, Democrats accused Republicans of "devious methods." Another "contended that Congress had no 'right' to withdraw previously granted jurisdiction once a cause was pending." Wilson "retorted that Congress rightfully could take away what it had granted."

13 74 U.S. 514–15 (1868).

14 Quoted in Warren, p. 206.

15 74 U.S. 700, 720 (1867).

16 Ibid. Gabriel J. Chin has argued that *Texas v. White* upheld Presidential Reconstruction by reaffirming that the duties of states and citizens remained unimpaired.

See "The 'Vothing Rights Act of 1867': The Constitutionality of Federal Regulation of Suffrage During Reconstruction," *North Carolina Law Review* (June 2004), pp. 1581–1611. The author disagrees, but even if Chin's interpretation is correct, the decision came too late to have any meaningful impact on the political course.

17 Ibid.

18 Yerger was never tried. He died of natural causes in 1875.

19 See, for example, Stanley I. Kutler, *Judicial Power and Reconstruction Politics* (Chicago: University of Chicago Press, 1968). Kutler uses *ex parte Yerger* to demonstrate what he sees as the Court's far more aggressive and confrontational stance. But the real test of *Yerger* never came. Whether or not the justices would have demanded his release is only the stuff of conjecture. But even if one grants the premise, the Court's retreat in *Mississippi v. Johnson, Georgia v. Stanton,* and *ex part McCardle* was sufficient to stay the hand of congressional Radicals, who must, therefore, have been sufficiently satisfied with the Court's behavior to drop the matter.

20 Quoted in Kutler, "Ex parte McCardle," p. 845.

FIVE: BAD SCIENCE AND BIG MONEY

1 Louis Menand, "Morton, Agassiz, and the Origins of Scientific Racism in the United States," *Journal of Blacks in Higher Education* 34 (Winter 2001–2), p. 110.

2 Quoted in ibid.

3 Agassiz, born and educated in Europe, was the first man to postulate that the Earth had undergone an Ice Age, and was equally expert in geology, paleontology, climatology, and ichthyology. He was brilliant at classifying subspecies by physical, environmental, and functional attributes, a skill he unfortunately applied to the origins of the races.

4 Richard Hofstadter, *Social Darwinism in American Thought* (New York: George Braziller, 1959), p. 17.

5 *New York Times,* March 28, 1860.

6 Ibid.

7 "Design theory," its opposite, posited that species were initiated fully formed. Most, although not all, design theorists assumed that the initiation was done by God.

8 Francis Bowen, "Remarks on the Latest Form of the Development Theory," *Memoirs of the American Academy of Arts and Sciences,* new series 8, no. 1 (1861), pp. 106–7.

9 Darwin's second great work, *The Descent of Man, and Selection in Relation to Sex,* would put the final nail in the polygenist coffin. *Descent,* of course, in ascribing man's origins to other primates, was to arouse even more controversy than *Origin of Species* and supply no shortage of fodder to those who preached racial stratification.

10 Richard Hofstadter, "William Graham Sumner, Social Darwinist," *New England Quarterly* 14, no. 3 (Sept. 1941), p. 457.

11 Hofstadter, *Social Darwinism,* p. 5.

12 Ibid., p. 36.

13 Herbert Spencer, "Progress: Its Law and Causes," *Westminster Review* 67 (Apr. 1857), p. 446.

14 Ibid., p. 447.

15 Hofstadter, *Social Darwinism*, p. 39.

16 In *Principles of Biology* (1864).

17 Hofstadter, *Social Darwinism*, p. 41.

18 Spencer, pp. 455–56.

19 Hofstadter, *Social Darwinism*, p. 44.

20 Ibid., p. 45.

21 Which perhaps it was, seeing that Carnegie was speaking of his response to his growing disillusionment with accepted Christian theology.

22 *Autobiography of Andrew Carnegie* (Boston: Houghton Mifflin, 1920), p. 339.

23 Destler, p. 33.

24 Quoted by Richard Hofstadter, *Social Darwinism in American Thought, 1860–1915* (New York: George Braziller, 1959), p. 31.

25 The theories of both Spencer and Darwin had root in Thomas Malthus, who demonstrated that, if left unchecked, population growth would overwhelm the resources needed to sustain it and keep Man in a perpetual state of near subsistence.

26 Harry Elmer Barnes, "Two Representative Contributions of Sociology to Political Theory: The Doctrines of William Graham Sumner and Lester Frank Ward," *American Journal of Sociology* 25, no. 1 (July 1919), pp. 3–4.

27 Ibid., p. 5.

28 Quoted in *New England Quarterly* 6, no. 4 (Dec. 1933), p. 846.

29 Quoted in Hostadter, *Social Darwinism*, p. 58.

30 Quoted in Barnes, p. 8.

31 See Bruce Curtis, "William Graham Sumner 'On the Concentration of Wealth,'" *Journal of American History* 55, no. 4 (Mar. 1969), pp. 823–32, and, for an earlier perspective, Harris E. Starr, "William Graham Sumner: Sociologist," *Journal of Social Forces* 3, no. 4 (May 1925), pp. 622–26.

32 William Graham Sumner, *Folkways: A Study of the Sociological Importance of Usages, Manners, Customs, Mores, and Morals* (Boston: Ginn and Company), p. 174.

33 Lester Frank Ward, for example, saw sociology mainly as a discipline in which dynamic strategies should be developed to reduce poverty and improve the lot of humankind. Ward is largely dismissed as a sentimentalist today, but his notion of using social science for social benefit is no more "unscientific" than Sumner's or Karl Marx's laboratory rationalism.

34 It made them feel good about themselves, in the same way that some modern financial theories allow derivative traders to think that they are making their billions for the betterment of society.

Six: Corporate Presidency: Ulysses Grant and the Court

1 D. W. Griffith's 1915 epic, *Birth of a Nation*, was based on a racist potboiler, *The Clansman*, by Thomas Dixon, published ten years earlier.

2 Woodrow Wilson, "The Reconstruction of the Southern States," *Atlantic Monthly* 87, no. 519 (Jan. 1901), pp. 6–7.

3 See Foner, *Reconstruction*, chap. 9; Leon F. Litwack, *Been in the Storm So Long* (New York: Vintage Books, 1980), chap 6.

4 When W. E. B. DuBois published *Black Reconstruction in America*, in 1935, most reviews were scathing.

5 Although in the Grant presidency a number of methods were utilized, many unsavory, to provide financial well-being to public officials.

6 *Statutes at Large*, 41st Cong., 1st sess., pp. 44–45.

7 *New York Times*, Dec. 15, 1869.

8 Quoted in Warren, p. 224.

9 The other was George Edmunds from Vermont.

10 *New York Times*, Dec. 23, 1869.

11 Rumors abounded that Stanton had committed suicide, although his family insisted that he had perished from natural causes. Since he was never sworn in, he does not appear officially on the roster of justices.

12 *Statutes at Large*, 37th Cong., 2nd sess., p. 345.

13 $150 million was issued in 1862, and an additional $300 million by 1864.

14 *Roosevelt v. Meyer*, 68 U.S. 512 (1863).

15 Whether the Legal Tender Acts were actually needed at all has been the subject of a good deal of debate.

16 See especially *Bronson v. Rodes* (74 U.S. 229), also *Butler v. Horwitz* (74 U.S. 258) and *Lane County v. Oregon* (74 U.S. 71).

17 75 U.S. 604 (1869).

18 Ibid.

19 J. I. Clark Hare, "The Legal Tender Decisions," *American Law Register* 19, no. 2, new series 10 (Feb. 1871), p. 89.

20 Sidney Ratner, "Was the Supreme Court Packed by President Grant?" *Political Science Quarterly* 50, no. 3 (Sept. 1935), p. 351. Whether or not Grant "packed" the Court with justices guaranteed to uphold the Legal Tender Acts spawned a duel in constitutional law journals that went on for decades. While "packed" is a silly term when referring to only filling two vacancies, that Grant did his best to ensure that his views on the matter—or, at least those of his advisers—would be reflected in the Court's future decisions should be a shock to no one.

21 Quoted in, Ratner, p. 346.

22 John S. Goff, "The Rejection of United States Supreme Court Appointments," *American Journal of Legal History* 5, no. 4 (Oct. 1961), p. 365.

23 Hunt suffered a massive stroke in January 1879, which left him speechless and partially paralyzed. He never participated in Court proceedings again but refused to resign because his pension hadn't vested. Only after he was granted his full pension, in 1882, did Hunt agree to cede his seat.

24 83 U.S. 81 (1872).

25 The Tenth Amendment, which states, "The powers not delegated to the United States by the Constitution, nor prohibited by it to the States, are reserved to the States respectively, or to the people," is the basis of federalism. A strict reading would indicate that any power not *explicitly* granted the federal government is reserved to the states. A broad reading would indicate that a power can be denied a state that is *implicitly* included in a delegated power. This distinction will be discussed at length in chapter 12 as it applies to the "due process" clause of the Fourteenth Amendment.

26 Italics added.

27 See Warren, p. 346.

28 Goff, "The Rejection," p. 365.

29 *Brooklyn Daily Eagle*, Apr. 21, 1875.

30 Williams later wrote that he was "surprised, as was the President, at the opposition of some of the Republican Senators," although he claimed the reasons "were not those given in the newspapers." George H. Williams, "Reminiscences of the United States Supreme Court," *Yale Law Journal* 8, no. 7 (Apr. 1899), p. 299.

31 Ibid.

SEVEN: EQUALITY FRAYS: *CRUIKSHANK* AND *REESE*

1 *New York Times*, Apr. 18, 1873.

2 *Boston Daily Globe*, Apr. 17, 1873.

3 *Brooklyn Daily Eagle*, Apr. 16, 1873. The editorial was written in response to the *New York Times*' "outrageously partisan dispatch." The Brooklyn editorial writer neglected to mention that two separate dispatches from federal marshals and numerous eyewitness accounts refuted the version the *Eagle* offered to its readers. And, unlike the *Times*, the *Eagle* had no reporter of its own on the scene.

4 *Chicago Daily Tribune*, Apr. 19, 1873.

5 Circuit Court of the United States, District of Louisiana, Apr. term, 1874 (1 Woods, 308; 13 *American Law Register* [new series] 630). Nelson and Tillman were two of the victims. In another count, "banding" was changed to "conspiring."

6 Anthony Champagne and Dennis Pope, "Joseph P. Bradley: An Aspect of a Judicial Personality," *Political Psychology* 6, no. 3 (Sept. 1985), pp. 481, 485–86.

7 Quoted in ibid., p. 485.

8 Ibid., p. 482.

9 Bradley never even attended law school. Like many attorneys at the time, he received the bulk of his legal training on the job.

10   There were also distinct Second Amendment overtones, since one section of the defendants' motion concerned the right to bear arms.

11   "Circuit Court of the United States. District of Louisiana. The United States v. Cruikshank et al.," *American Law Register* (1852–91) 22, no. 10, new series 13 (Oct. 1874), p. 630.

12   Ibid., p. 709.

13   Ibid.

14   Ibid., p. 715. Italics added.

15   In fact, the case was sent to the Supreme Court because the circuit court judges were divided on the decision, but Bradley issued the opinion of record.

16   92 U.S. 552 (1875). Waite wrote, with respect to the Second Amendment, "The right to bear arms is not granted by the Constitution; neither is it in any manner dependent upon that instrument for its existence. The Second Amendment means no more than that it shall not be infringed by Congress, and has no other effect than to restrict the powers of the National Government."

17   Ironically, Bradley dissented in the decision. Along with Justices Clifford, Davis, and Hunt, Bradley agreed the indictments should be rescinded, but only because of vagueness. The Fourteenth Amendment, these justices insisted, could apply to private action under the same criteria as the Fifteenth.

18   *Independent*, April 13, 1876, quoted in Warren, p. 327.

19   Ibid.

Eight: 1876: Justice Bradley Disposes

1   *Congressional Globe*, 41st Cong., 2nd sess. (May 13, 1870), p. 3434.

2   Bertram Wyatt-Brown, "The Civil Rights Act of 1875," *Western Political Quarterly* 18, no. 4 (Dec. 1965), p. 765.

3   Ibid., p. 767.

4   Ibid., p. 770.

5   One seat from Louisiana would remain vacant until January 1876, but that too would be eventually claimed by a Democrat.

6   Wyatt-Brown, p. 772.

7   *Statutes at Large*, vol. 18 (1875), p. 335.

8   See C. Vann Woodward, *The Strange Career of Jim Crow*, 2nd ed. (New York: Oxford University Press, 1966), chap. 1.

9   Whether Jefferson meant those words to be applied to *all* Americans is, of course, open to doubt.

10   *New York Times*, Mar. 2, 1875.

11   *Chicago Daily Tribune*, Mar. 1, 1875.

12   Valeria W. Weaver, "The Failure of Civil Rights 1875–1883 and its Repercussions," *Journal of Negro History* 54, no. 4 (Oct. 1969), p. 369.

13 Ibid.

14 William H. Rehnquist, *Centennial Crisis: The Disputed Election of 1876* (New York: Alfred A. Knopf, 2004), p. 85 (note).

15 John Copeland Nagle, "How Not to Count Votes," *Columbia Law Review* 104, no. 6 (Oct. 2004), p. 1734.

16 The Ku Klux Klan, the most notorious of these groups, had become sufficiently pervasive to have inspired an act of Congress specifically designed to curb its reign of terror. The law, the Enforcement Act of 1871, would figure prominently in another key case, *United States v. Harris*, discussed below.

17 *New York Times*, Nov. 6, 1876.

18 Nagle, p. 1736.

19 *New York Times*, Nov. 8, 1876; Nov. 9, 1876.

20 Nagle, p. 1736

21 Roy Morris Jr., *Fraud of the Century. Rutherford B. Hayes, Samuel Tilden and the Stolen Election of 1876* (New York: Simon and Schuster, 2003), p. 218.

22 Democrats have compared the election of 2000 with that of 1876. Chief Justice Rehnquist even wrote a book on the 1876 election in the wake of *Bush v. Gore*, in which he, not surprisingly, defended the role of the justices of both Courts. *Bush*, however, at least involved an appeal in which the entire Court could cast a view. (That the resulting decision broke along party lines was not lost on its critics.) Bradley acted pretty much on his own.

23 Allan Peskin, "Was There a Compromise of 1877?" *Journal of American History* 60, no. 1 (June 1973), p. 63.

24 In 1951, the great historian C. Vann Woodward put forward a more complicated theory of the compromise, but for African-Americans the salient features were the same.

25 Quoted in Alan F. Westin, "John Marshall Harlan and the Political Rights of Negroes: The Transformation of a Southerner," *Yale Law Journal* 66, no. 5 (Apr. 1957), p. 640.

26 Ibid.

27 Ibid., p. 643.

28 Ibid., p. 653.

29 Quoted in ibid., p. 660.

30 Ibid., p. 666.

NINE: A JURY OF ONE'S PEERS: *STRAUDER* AND *RIVES*

1 Stephen D. Engle, "Mountaineer Reconstruction: Blacks in the Political Reconstruction of West Virginia," *Journal of Negro History* 78, no. 3 (Summer 1993), p. 155.

2 *New York Times*, Mar. 2, 1880. One can only wonder how the justices would have treated the initial argument of justifiable homicide.

3 100 U.S. 315 (1880).

4 Quoted in *New York Times*, Jan. 18, 1879. *Cruikshank* and *Reese* had narrowed the scope of the enforcement acts but had not ruled on their overall constitutionality.

5 Quoted in the *New York Times*, Apr. 12, 1879.

6 *Brooklyn Daily Eagle*, Oct. 20, 1879.

7 *Chicago Daily Tribune*, Mar. 20, 1879.

8 *New York Times*, Apr. 12, 1879.

9 100 U.S. 303 (1880).

10 The following year, West Virginia passed a law that guaranteed all male citizens the right to sit on a jury. The decision eventually worked even better for Taylor Strauder. He was eventually released and allowed to fade into history.

11 This statement was from *Ex parte Virginia*, 100 U.S. 354 (1880), although Field cited it in his *Strauder* dissent.

12 100 U.S. 313 (1879).

13 William M. Wiecek, "The Emergence of Equality as a Constitutional Value: The First Century," *Chicago-Kent Law Review*, 2007, p. 259.

14 *Neal v. Delaware*, 103 U.S. 370 (1881).

15 *North American Review* 151, no. 408 (Nov. 1890), pp. 567–75, and *North American Review* 132, no. 294 (May 1881), pp. 437–50.

TEN: DECONSTRUCTION: THE *CIVIL RIGHTS CASES*

1 109 U.S. 3 (1883). The New York plaintiff, William R. Davis, was a twenty-six-year-old employee of a black weekly newspaper, the *Progressive American*, who had been born a slave in South Carolina.

2 Horatio Seymour, "The Political Situation," *North American Review* 136, no. 315 (Feb. 1883), p. 155.

3 Democrats had controlled the Senate in the Forty-seventh Congress. In the Forty-eighth, Republicans held a 38–36 edge, but the "Readjuster Party," a group of anti-wealth, Virginia-based populists, much closer to Democrats than Republicans, held both Virginia seats, which threw the upper house into an effective stalemate.

4 C. Vann Woodward, *Origins of the New South, 1877–1913* (Baton Rouge, LA: Louisiana State University Press, 1951), p. 216.

5 Arthur was often described as having undergone a "Prince Hal" conversion, although just how profound that conversion was will never be known. Arthur destroyed virtually all his personal papers after leaving office and never gave the reason for such an extreme and unprecedented act.

6 Francis C. Lowell, "Horace Gray," *Proceedings of the American Academy of Arts and Sciences* 39, no. 24 (June 1904), p. 629.

7 *Statutes at Large*, 42nd Cong., sess. 1, chap. 22, p. 13.

8 106 U.S. 629 (1883).

9 109 U.S. 3 (1883).

10   A view of the amendment that would later, of course, be vindicated.

11   109 U.S. 10 (1883).

12   109 U.S. 24-5 (1883).

13   Holmes, *The Common Law* (Boston: Little Brown, 1881), p. 35.

14   *New York Times*, Oct. 16, 1883.

15   *Brooklyn Daily Eagle*, Oct. 16, 1883.

16   Quoted in Warren, p. 336.

17   *Atlanta Journal Constitution*, Oct. 16, 1883.

18   *Hartford Courant*, Oct. 16, 1883.

19   *Chicago Daily Tribune*, Oct. 16, 1883.

20   All quoted in Weaver, pp. 371–72.

21   Quoted in Westin, p. 668.

ELEVEN: FLOODGATES: THE REBIRTH OF WHITE RULE

1   Jerrold M. Packard, *American Nightmare: The History of Jim Crow* (New York: St. Martin's Press, 2002), p. 41.

2   William Alexander Mabry, "Disenfranchisement of the Negro in Mississippi," *Journal of Southern History* 4, no. 3 (Aug. 1938), p. 318.

3   Packard, p. 56.

4   Thomas B. Reed, "The Federal Control of Elections," *North American Review* 150, no. 403 (June 1890), p. 671.

5   Ibid., p. 672.

6   Ibid., p. 677.

7   Ibid., p. 675.

8   Packard, p. 67.

9   In 1890, Henry Cabot Lodge of Massachusetts had introduced a bill calling for federal oversight of congressional elections. The bill passed in the House but was defeated in the Senate. Whites in the South nonetheless viewed the continuing congressional interest in elections in the South with alarm.

10   Earl M. Lewis, "The Negro Voter in Mississippi," *Journal of Negro Education* 26, no. 3, "The Negro Voter in the South" (Summer 1957), p. 330.

11   Mabry, p. 319.

12   Marsh Cook, a white Republican campaigning to be a delegate, was ambushed and murdered on a country road for advocating black voting.

13   Quoted in Mabry, p. 319.

14   Quoted in Jerrold M. Packard, *American Nightmare: The History of Jim Crow* (New York: St. Martin's Press, 2002), p. 69.

15   These were the precise words used by the chairman of the judiciary committee at the convention to describe its purpose. "B. E. H. and J. J. K., Jr.," "Federal Protection of Negro Voting Rights," *Virginia Law Review* 51, no. 6 (Oct. 1965), p. 1066.

16   Ibid.

17   Tennessee had passed a similar law two years earlier.

Twelve: Blurring the Boundaries:
The Expansion of Due Process

1   The Thirteenth and Fifteenth amendments were narrowed as well, but the Fourteenth was beneficiary of most of the justices' attention.

2   See especially, Edward S. Corwin, "The Supreme Court and the Fourteenth Amendment," *Michigan Law Review* 7, no. 8 (1909), and Richard Cortner, "Plessy in Perspective: Lofgren's View," *Law and Social Inquiry* 13, no. 4 (Autumn 1988).

3   Leonard Levy, *Original Intent and the Framers' Constitution* (New York: Macmillan, 1988), p. 273.

4   Madison's commitment to a Bill of Rights was, of course, late in coming. Until his opposition to an enumerated list of guarantees threatened to derail his bid for a seat in the new Congress, Madison had taken the position that such an inclusion in the Constitution would leave any right *not* enumerated at the mercy of a despotic legislature.

5   302 U.S. 319 (1937), p. 325.

6   Robert Bork, *The Tempting of America: The Political Seduction of the Law* (New York: Simon and Schuster, 1997), p. 31.

7   As Herbert Spencer's attempt to reduce sociology to a quantitative science failed.

8   Levy, p. 357.

9   *Munn v. Illinois*, a granger case, was another famous case of the period in which the Court sided with the state.

10   116 U.S. 138 (1885).

11   Quoted in Kenneth Stampp, *The Era of Reconstruction* (New York: Alfred A. Knopf, 1965), p. 108.

12   In 1938, scholarship by Howard Jay Graham demonstrated unequivocally that Conkling's argument was a combination of distortions, half-truths, and outright lies. Howard Jay Graham, "The 'Conspiracy Theory' of the Fourteenth Amendment," *Yale Law Journal* 47, no. 3 (Jan. 1938) and 48, no. 2 (Dec. 1938).

13   The seminal economic substantive due process case was *Lochner v. New York*, 198 U.S. 45 (1905), in which the Court struck down a state law mandating an eight-hour day for bakers.

14   116 U.S. 307 (1886).

15   118 U.S. 396 (1886). Waite's pronouncement was not questioned or disagreed with by any of the other justices. Thus, while it did not actually have force of law, every attorney pleading before the Court understood the impact.

16   Corwin, p. 659.

17   Ibid., p. 646.

18   134 U.S. 418 (1890).

19   Allegations of fraud, particularly in the pivotal state of Indiana, would dog Harrison throughout his term.

20   *New York Times*, May 1, 1888. *Brooklyn Daily Eagle*, Apr. 30, 1888. The *Daily Eagle* was somewhat more praising of Fuller's qualifications than was the *Times*.

21   Michael J. Klarman, *From Jim Crow to Civil Rights: The Supreme Court and the Struggle for Racial Equality* (New York: Oxford University Press, 2004), p. 16.

22   Quoted in Willie D. Halsell, "The Appointment of L. Q. C. Lamar to the Supreme Court," *Mississippi Valley Historical Review* 28, no. 3 (Dec. 1941), p. 401.

23   *San Francisco Chronicle*, Dec. 18, 1887, quoted in ibid., p. 404.

24   Henry M. Field, *Blood Is Thicker Than Water: A Few Days Among Our Southern Brethren* (New York: George Munro, 1886), pp. 18–19.

25   Klarman, pp. 16–17.

26   Now Izmir, Turkey.

27   134 U.S. 456 (1890).

28   Edwin Borchard, "The Supreme Court and Private Rights," *Yale Law Journal* 47, no. 7 (May 1938), pp. 1057–58.

29   Levy, p. 369.

30   Quoted in ibid., p. 369.

31   Corwin, p. 672.

Thirteen: Confluence: *Plessy v. Ferguson*

1   For a vivid and detailed description of the Plessy-era African-American community in New Orleans, see Harvey Fireside, *Separate and Unequal: Homer Plessy and the Supreme Court Decision That Legalized Racism* (New York: Carroll and Graf, 2004), chap. 4.

2   The number of free blacks, particularly mulattoes, in Louisiana dwarfed that of any of the other antebellum southern states. In 1850, 17,462 free blacks lived in Louisiana, compared to fewer than 2,000 in neighboring Mississippi. *Negro Population, 1790–1915* (Washington, D.C.: Bureau of the Census, 1915), p. 65.

3   The origin of the phrase "Jim Crow" has never been definitively established. Many historians believe it a derivation of a 1830s minstrel song, "Dancin' Jim Crow," or "Jump Jim Crow," performed in blackface by the white comedian T. D. Rice, in which black men were depicted in demeaning caricature.

4   John Roach Straton, "Will Education Solve the Race Problem?" *North American Review* 170, no. 523 (June 1900), p. 787.

5   The argument has been made that Social Darwinism was more at the heart of the *Plessy* case than the law. See Barton Bernstein, "Plessy v. Ferguson: Conservative Sociological Jurisprudence," *Journal of Negro History* 48, no. 3 (July 1963) and, "Case Law in Plessy v. Ferguson," *Journal of Negro History* 47, no. 3 (July 1962).

6   95 U.S. 485 (1878).

7   133 U.S. 587 (1890).

8   Sarah M. Lemmon, "Transportation Segregation in the Federal Courts Since 1865," *Journal of Negro History* 38 (1953), pp. 174, 185, and Benno C. Schmidt Jr., both quoted in Joseph R. Palmore, "The Not-So-Strange Career of Interstate Jim Crow: Race, Transportation, and the Dormant Commerce Clause, 1878–1946," *Virginia Law Review* 83, no. 8 (Nov. 1997), p. 1775. Palmore has insisted that both *DeCuir* and *Louisville et al.* were decided with technical consistency, which would indicate he believed that both decisions going against African-Americans was mere coincidence.

9   Charles A. Lofgren, *The Plessy Case: A Legal-Historical Interpretation* (New York: Oxford University Press, 1987), p. 31.

10   Quoted in Palmore, p. 1794.

11   That was the first and last time Homer Plessy would acknowledge his 12.5 percent blackness during the entire course of his case.

12   Charles A. Kent, *Memoir of Henry Billings Brown* (New York: Vail-Ballou, 1915), p. 1.

13   Ibid., p. 4.

14   Ibid., p. 11–12.

15   Ibid., p. 73.

16   Quoted in Mark Elliott, "Race, Color Blindness, and the Democratic Public: Albion W. Tourgée's Radical Principles in Plessy v. Ferguson," *Journal of Southern History* 67, no. 2 (May 2001), p. 291.

17   Ibid., p. 306.

18   Lofgren, p. 149.

19   The plaintiffs undertook a major public relations campaign, giving talks to sympathetic audiences and planting stories in newspapers favorable to their cause, the impact of which was only to rally those who already supported integration, a tiny minority of the white community.

20   White's account of his war record was never verified and substantial ambiguities about where and with whom he served were never reconciled, although no claim was ever made that he had done so less than honorably.

21   163 U.S. 542–43 (1896).

22   The Massachusetts case predated the Fourteenth Amendment, but, as Charles Lofgren has pointed out, Massachusetts had on its books laws that provided similar guarantees of equal protection of the law.

23   163 U.S. 551–52 (1896).

24   *New York Times*, May 19, 1896.

25   *Hartford Courant*, May 18, 1896, *Chicago Daily Tribune*, May 19, 1896.

26   *Boston Daily Globe*, May 20, 1896.

27   *Atlanta Constitution*, May 19, 1896.

28 347 U.S. 483 (1954). Significantly, the chief justice was writing strictly about school segregation, but the principle eventually overwhelmed any attempt to limit it to education.

29 Charles E. Wynes, "The Evolution of Jim Crow Laws in Twentieth Century Virginia," *Phylon* 28, no. 4 (4th Qtr. 1967), p. 46.

30 Earlier scholarship had indicated the same conclusion. In 1909, Gilbert Thomas Stephenson wrote that before 1896, "many of the public conveyance companies had regulations separating the races. In other words, the Jim Crow laws, when they came, did scarcely more than to legalize an existing and widespread custom." Gilbert Thomas Stephenson, "The Separation of the Races in Public Conveyances," *American Political Science Review* 3, no. 2 (May 1909), p. 189.

31 Lofgren, p. 197.

32 Kent, p. 92.

33 Ibid., p. 113.

FOURTEEN: ONE MAN, NO VOTE: *WILLIAMS V. MISSISSIPPI*

1 *Williams* is the eighth of nine voting rights cases, generally referred to as the *Strauder-Powers* decisions, in which the Court would not disallow jury selection unless an appellant could demonstrate a state law was either discriminatory on its face or as interpreted by the highest state court. The cases are, in descending order, *Kentucky v. Powers*, 201 U.S. 1 (1906); *Williams v. Mississippi*, 170 U.S. 213 (1898); *Murray v. Louisiana*, 163 U.S. 101 (1896); *Smith v. Mississippi*, 162 U.S. 592 (1896); *Gibson v. Mississippi*, 162 U.S. 565 (1896); *Bush v. Kentucky*, 107 U.S. 110 (1883); *Neal v. Delaware*, 103 U.S. 370 (1881); *Virginia v. Rives*, 100 U.S. 313 (1880); *Strauder v. West Virginia*, 100 U.S. 303 (1880).

2 170 U.S. 213 (1898).

3 Field had retired December 1, 1897, after thirty-four years on the Court. Despite encroaching senility, he had refused to resign until his tenure exceeded that of John Marshall, a display of hubris that aroused the enmity of his fellows, but since senility does not constitute a violation of "good behavior," they and anyone else who disapproved of Field's stubbornness could do nothing about it.

4 *New York Times*, Jan. 15, 1898.

5 Ibid.

6 Edward Purcell, "The Particularly Dubious Case of Hans v. Louisiana: An Essay on Law, Race, History, and Federal Courts," *North Carolina Law Review* (June 2003), p. 2010.

7 170 U.S. 213 (1898).

8 118 U.S. 373 (1886). The Court ruled that a San Francisco ordinance that prohibited laundries from being constructed of wood was simply a ruse to deny Chinese laundrymen their livelihood, and thus was in violation of the equal protection clause of the Fourteenth Amendment, even in cases where the laundry owners were not American citizens.

9 As compared to 563,000 whites. *United States Census, 1900.*

10 170 U.S. 213 (1898).

11 Which stated, "The right of citizens of the United States to vote shall not be denied or abridged by the United States or by any State on account of race, color, or previous condition of servitude."

FIFTEEN: MR. JUSTICE HOLMES CONCURS

1 The 1901 Alabama constitution also began, without irony, "All men are equally free and independent; that they are endowed by their Creator with certain inalienable rights; that among these are life, liberty and the pursuit of happiness."

2 Louis Harlan, "The Secret Life of Booker T. Washington," *Journal of Southern History* 37, no. 3 (Aug. 1971), p. 398.

3 Giles failed to seek the $2,000 in damages that was a minimum for trial in federal court, although application of monetary standards to a voting rights case was later seen as ludicrous.

4 Shiras had pledged upon his confirmation that he would serve only ten years and did so. He is distinguished as being the first justice to hire a law clerk, the future justice Louis Brandeis. Gray had suffered a stroke that left him unable to speak but, in the tradition of Ward Hunt, remained on the bench for some months afterward. He was finally persuaded to give up his seat in July 1902 and died two months later.

5 Gary Aichele, *Oliver Wendell Holmes, Jr.: Soldier, Scholar, Judge* (New York: Twayne Publishers, 1989), p. 162.

6 Ibid., 163. Although a number of scholars of late have attempted to demonstrate that Social Darwinism had no direct impact on the judgments of the Court, that Spencer's construct formed an underpinning of the racial views of Justices Brown, Holmes, and many others is undeniable. See, for example, Herbert Hovenkamp, "The Political Economy of Substantive Due Process," *Stanford Law Review* 379, no. 418 (1988); David E. Bernstein, "Roots of the 'Underclass': The Decline of Laissez-Faire Jurisprudence and the Rise of Racist Labor Legislation," *American University Law Review* 85, no. 91 (1993); or David N. Mayer, "The Myth of Laissez-Faire Constitutionalism: Liberty of Contract During the *Lochner* Era," *Hastings Constitutional Law Quarterly*, Winter 2009.

7 Aichele, p. 155.

8 *New York Times*, Aug. 13, 1902.

9 Whether Smith included the Fifteenth Amendment in his appeal because Cornelius Jones hadn't is unknown, but given the result, Jones's omission seems irrelevant. "The alleged pleading failures in *Williams* were precisely what they appeared to be: a pretext for avoiding decision. Williams lost because he did not have enough

evidence; the next claimants lost because they had too much." Gabriel J. Chin and Randy Wagner, "The Tyranny of the Minority: Jim Crow and the Counter-Majoritarian Difficulty," *Harvard Civil Rights-Civil Liberties Law Review*, Winter 2008, p. 115.

10   189 U.S. 475 (1903).

11   Day actually was more junior but did not take his seat until March 2, 1903, after arguments in the case had already been heard. His absence during arguments did not prevent Day from voting with the majority, however.

12   Chin and Wagner, p. 115. Holmes dismissed out of hand the denial of jurisdiction that both district court and circuit court judges had used to avoid ruling. "We assume further, for the purposes of decision, that [the defining statute] extends to a deprivation of rights under color of a state constitution," Holmes wrote.

13   Ibid.

14   In doing so Holmes would hardly have been committing a judicial transgression. Justices dating from John Marshall had regularly voided specific sections of a law, as Marshall did with Section 13 of the Judiciary Act of 1789 in *Marbury*, while leaving the remainder intact.

15   E. Charles Guy-Uriel, "Democracy and Distortion," *Cornell Law Review*, May 2007, p. 626.

16   Holmes's views on this issue turned out to be remarkably flexible. In his famous "clear and present danger" opinion in *Schenk v United States*, 249 U.S. 47 (1919), Holmes had no problem ruling on a political right, in this case free speech, in order to define its limits.

17   Justice Brown also dissented, but without comment.

18   Daniel P. Tokaji, "The Sordid Business of Democracy," *Ohio Northern University Law Review*, 2008, p. 344.

19   Wiecek, p. 255.

20   Morris B. Hoffman, "Reviewed Work: *Law without Values: The Life, Work and Legacy of Justice Holmes* by Albert W. Alschuler," *Stanford Law Review* 54, no. 3 (Dec. 2001), p. 612. The other biography is Aichele.

Sixteen: Movement

1   Lynching records were compiled by the Tuskegee Institute beginning in 1882 through a study of articles and other records. The material is currently in the university's archives.

2   Wells-Barnett, p. 2.

3   Litwack, p. 225. Louisiana was the only southern state to keep such detailed records, although why it would choose to advertise the disenfranchisement of black voters is unclear. Why the other states were vague as to racial voting statistics is apparent.

4 Woodward, *Strange Career*, p. 109.

5 *United States Census*, 1910, vol. 4, section 3.

6 C. Vann Woodward, *Origins*, p. 311.

7 Ibid., pp. 317–18.

8 *Statistical Abstract of the United States*, 1933, p. 239.

9 Woodward, *Origins*, p. 320.

10 Ibid.

11 Packard, p. 66.

12 *Negro Population, 1790–1915*, p. 33.

13 Ibid., p. 65.

14 Thomas Jesse Jones, "Negro Population in the United States," *Annals of the American Academy of Political and Social Science* 49 (Sept. 1913), pp. 8–9.

15 Ibid., pp. 4–5.

16 Ibid., p. 67.

17 Alferdteen Harrison, ed., *Black Exodus: The Great Migration from the American South* (Jackson, MS: University of Mississippi Press, 1991).

18 *Negro Population*, p. 70.

19 Carter G. Woodson, *A Century of Negro Migration* (Washington, D.C.: Association for the Study of Negro Life and History, 1918), p. 163.

20 Ibid., p. 164.

21 Ibid., pp. 163–64.

22 Jones, p. 4.

23 Gilbert Osofsky, *Harlem: The Making of a Ghetto* (New York: Harper and Row, 1966), p. 19.

24 Events, of course, were to play out rather differently.

25 *Chicago Defender*, Feb. 24, 1917.

26 Woodson, p. 164.

27 Emma Lou Thornbrough, "American Negro Newspapers, 1880–1914," *Business History Review* 40, no. 4 (Winter 1966), p. 476.

28 Osofsky, p. 325.

29 Ibid., p. 329.

30 Ibid., p. 326.

Epilogue: A Charade of Justice

1 See, for example, Richard Brookhiser, *Founding Father: Rediscovering George Washington* (New York: Free Press, 1996), pp. 177–78.

2 Blacks were not alone. Treatment of Asians, particularly the Chinese, was equally reprehensible, to say nothing of Native Americans.

BIBLIOGRAPHY

PUBLIC DOCUMENTS

Congressional Globe
Abraham Lincoln Papers, Library of Congress
Statistical Abstract of the United States
Statutes at Large
United States Census
United States Reports

BOOKS AND ARTICLES

Abraham, Harry J. "John Marshall Harlan: A Justice Neglected." *Virginia Law Review* 41, no. 7 (Nov. 1955).

Aichele, Gary. *Oliver Wendell Holmes, Jr.: Soldier, Scholar, Judge.* New York: Twayne Publishers, 1989.

Alschuler, Albert W. *Law Without Values: The Life, Work and Legacy of Justice Holmes.* Chicago: University of Chicago Press, 2000.

Barnes, Harry Elmer. "Two Representative Contributions of Sociology to Political Theory: The Doctrines of William Graham Sumner and Lester Frank Ward." *American Journal of Sociology* 25, no. 1 (July 1919).

"B. E. H. and J. J. K., Jr." "Federal Protection of Negro Voting Rights." *Virginia Law Review* 51, no. 6 (Oct. 1965).

Benedict, Michael Les. "Preserving Federalism: Reconstruction and the Waite Court." *Supreme Court Review* 1978 (1978).

Bernstein, Barton J. "Case Law in *Plessy V. Ferguson.*" *Journal of Negro History* 47, no. 3 (July 1962).

———. "Plessy v. Ferguson: Conservative Sociological Jurisprudence." *Journal of Negro History* 48, no. 3 (July 1963).

Bernstein, David E. "Roots of the 'Underclass': The Decline of Laissez-Faire Jurisprudence and the Rise of Racist Labor Legislation." *American University Law Review* 85, no. 91 (1993).

Bishop, David W. "Plessy v. Ferguson: A Reinterpretation." *Journal of Negro History* 62, no. 2 (Apr. 1977).

Borchard, Edwin. "The Supreme Court and Private Rights." *Yale Law Journal* 47, no. 7 (May 1938).

Bork, Robert. *The Tempting of America: The Political Seduction of the Law.* New York: Simon and Schuster, 1997.

Bowen, Francis. "Remarks on the Latest Form of the Development Theory." *Memoirs of the American Academy of Arts and Sciences,* new series 8, no. 1 (1861), pp. 97–122.

Brookhiser, Richard. *Founding Father: Rediscovering George Washington.* New York: Free Press, 1996.

"Brutus." Anti-Federalist Essays, www.constitution.org/afp/brutusoo.html.

Bryant-Jones, Mildred. "The Political Program of Thaddeus Stevens, 1865." *Phylon* 2, no. 2 (2nd Qtr. 1941).

Champagne, Anthony, and Dennis Pope. "Joseph P. Bradley: An Aspect of a Judicial Personality." *Political Psychology* 6, no. 3 (Sept. 1985).

Chin, Gabriel J., and Randy Wagner. "The Tyranny of the Minority: Jim Crow and the Counter-Majoritarian Difficulty." *Harvard Civil Rights-Civil Liberties Law Review,* Winter 2008.

Chin, Gabriel J. "The 'Voting Rights Act of 1867': The Constitutionality of Federal Regulation of Suffrage During Reconstruction," *North Carolina Law Review* (June 2004).

"Circuit Court of the United States. District of Louisiana. The United States v. Cruikshank et al." *American Law Register* (1852–91) 22, no. 10, new series 13 (Oct. 1874).

Clarke, James W. "Without Fear or Shame: Lynching, Capital Punishment and the Subculture of Violence in the American South." *British Journal of Political Science* 28, no. 2 (Apr. 1998).

"Congressional Power under the Civil War Amendments." *Duke Law Journal* 1969, no. 6 (Dec. 1969).

Cormack, Joseph M. "The Legal Tender Cases. A Drama of American Legal and Financial History." *Virginia Law Review* 16, no. 2 (Dec. 1929).

Cortner, Richard. "Plessy in Perspective: Lofgren's View." *Law and Social Inquiry* 13, no. 4 (Autumn 1988).

Corwin, Edward S. "The Supreme Court and the Fourteenth Amendment." *Michigan Law Review* 7, no. 8 (June 1909).

Currie, David P. "The Constitution in the Supreme Court: Civil War and Reconstruction, 1865–1873." *University of Chicago Law Review* 51, no. 1 (Winter 1984).

Curtis, Bruce. "William Graham Sumner and the Problem of Progress." *New England Quarterly* 51, no. 3 (Sept. 1978).

———. "William Graham Sumner 'On the Concentration of Wealth.'" *Journal of American History* 55, no. 4 (Mar. 1969).

Destler, Chester McArthur. "Entrepreneurial Leadership Among the 'Robber Barons': A Trial Balance." *Journal of Economic History* 6, Supplement: The Tasks of Economic History (May 1946).

Dethloff, Henry C., and Robert R. Jones. "Race Relations in Louisiana, 1877–98." *Louisiana History: The Journal of the Louisiana Historical Association* 9, no. 4 (Autumn 1968).

Du Bois, W. E. B. *Autobiography of W.E.B. Du Bois: A Soliloquy on Viewing My Life from the Last Decade of Its First Century*. New York: International Publishers, 1968.

———. "Reconstruction and its Benefits." *American Historical Review* 15, no. 4 (July 1910).

———. "Reconstruction, Seventy-Five Years After." *Phylon* 4, no. 3 (3rd Qtr. 1943).

Elliott, Mark. "Race, Color Blindness, and the Democratic Public: Albion W. Tourgée's Radical Principles in Plessy v. Ferguson." *Journal of Southern History* 67, no. 2 (May 2001).

Engle, Stephen D. "Mountaineer Reconstruction: Blacks in the Political Reconstruction of West Virginia." *Journal of Negro History* 78, no. 3 (Summer 1993), p. 155.

Epps, Garrett. *Democracy Reborn: The Fourteenth Amendment and the Fight for Equal Rights in Post-Civil War America*. New York: Henry Holt, 2006.

Fairman, Charles. "Mr. Justice Bradley's Appointment to the Supreme Court and the Legal Tender Cases." *Harvard Law Review* 54, no. 6 (Apr. 1941) and 54, no. 7 (May 1941).

Farrand, Max. *Records of the Federal Convention*. New Haven: Yale University Press, 1937.

Field, Henry M. *Blood Is Thicker Than Water: A Few Days Among Our Southern Brethren*. New York: George Munro, 1886.

Fireside, Harvey. *Separate and Unequal: Homer Plessy and the Supreme Court Decision That Legalized Racism*. New York: Carroll and Graf, 2004.

Foner, Eric. *Reconstruction: America's Unfinished Revolution, 1863–1877*. New York: Harper and Row, 1988.

———. "Reconstruction Revisited." *Reviews in American History* 10, no. 4, "The Promise of American History: Progress and Prospects" (Dec. 1982).

Frank, John P. "Ex Parte Milligan v. The Five Companies: Martial Law in Hawaii." *Columbia Law Review* 44, no. 5 (Sept. 1944).

Franklin, John Hope. "'Legal' Disfranchisement of the Negro." *Journal of Negro Education* 26, no. 3, "The Negro Voter in the South" (Summer 1957).

———. *Race and History: Selected Essays, 1938–1988*. Baton Rouge, LA: Louisiana State University Press, 1989.

Goff, John S. "Old Age and the Supreme Court." *American Journal of Legal History* 4, no. 2 (Apr. 1960), pp. 95–106.

———. "The Rejection of United States Supreme Court Appointments." *American Journal of Legal History* 5, no. 4 (Oct. 1961).

Graham, Howard Jay. "The 'Conspiracy Theory' of the Fourteenth Amendment." *Yale Law Journal* 47, no. 3 (Jan. 1938) and 48, no. 2 (Dec. 1938).

Guy-Uriel, E. Charles. "Democracy and Distortion." *Cornell Law Review*, May 2007.

Halbert, Sherrill. "The Suspension of the Writ of *Habeas Corpus* by President Lincoln." *American Journal of Legal History* 2, no. 2 (Apr. 1958).

Haller, John S., Jr. "The Species Problem: Nineteenth-Century Concepts of Racial Inferiority in the Origin of Man Controversy." *American Anthropologist*, new series 72, no. 6 (Dec. 1970).

Halsell, Willie D. "The Appointment of L. Q. C. Lamar to the Supreme Court." *Mississippi Valley Historical Review* 28, no. 3 (Dec. 1941).

Hamilton, Alexander, James Madison, and John Jay. *The Federalist*. New York: Heritage Press, 1945.

Hare, J. I. Clark. "The Legal Tender Decisions." *American Law Register* 19, no. 2, new series 10 (Feb. 1871).

Harlan, Louis. "The Secret Life of Booker T. Washington." *Journal of Southern History* 37, no. 3 (Aug. 1971).

Harrison, Alferdteen, ed. *Black Exodus: The Great Migration from the American South*. Jackson, MS: University of Mississippi Press, 1991.

H. M. J. "Federal Jurisdiction: The Civil Rights Removal Statute Revisited." *Duke Law Journal* 1967, no. 1 (Feb. 1967).

Hofstadter, Richard. *Social Darwinism in American Thought*. New York: George Braziller, 1959.

———. "William Graham Sumner, Social Darwinist." *New England Quarterly* 14, no. 3 (Sept. 1941).

Horan, Michael J. "Political Economy and Sociological Theory as Influences upon Judicial Policy-Making: The Civil Rights Cases of 1883." *American Journal of Legal History* 16, no. 1 (Jan. 1972).

Hovenkamp, Herbert. "The Political Economy of Substantive Due Process." *Stanford Law Review* 379, no. 418 (1988).

Jones, Thomas Jesse. "Negro Population in the United States." *Annals of the American Academy of Political and Social Science* 49 (Sept. 1913).

Jordan, Emma Coleman. "A Dream Deferred: Comparative and Practical Considerations for the Black Reparations Movement." *New York University Annual Survey of American Law 2003 Symposium: A History Lesson: Reparations for What?*

Kent, Charles A. *Memoir of Henry Billings Brown*. New York: Vail-Ballou, 1915.

Klarman, Michael J. *From Jim Crow to Civil Rights: The Supreme Court and the Struggle for Racial Equality*. New York: Oxford University Press, 2004.

Klein, Maury. *The Genesis of Industrial America, 1870–1920*. New York: Cambridge University Press, 2007.

Kousser, J. Morgan. "Response to Commentaries." *Social Science History* 24, no. 2 (Summer 2000).

——. *The Shaping of Southern Politics: Suffrage Restriction and the Establishment of the One-Party South, 1880–1910.* New Haven: Yale University Press, 1974.

Kutler, Stanley I. "Ex parte McCardle: Judicial Impotency? The Supreme Court and Reconstruction Reconsidered." *American Historical Review* 72, no. 3 (Apr. 1967).

——. *Judicial Power and Reconstruction Politics.* Chicago: University of Chicago Press, 1968.

——. "Reconstruction and the Supreme Court: The Numbers Game Reconsidered." *Journal of Southern History* 32, no. 1 (Feb. 1966).

Lackner, Joseph H. "The Foundation of St. Ann's Parish, 1866–1870: The African-American Experience in Cincinnati." *U.S. Catholic Historian* 14, no. 2, "Parishes and Peoples: Religious and Social Meanings, Part One" (Spring 1996).

Lane, Charles. *The Day Freedom Died: The Colfax Massacre, the Supreme Court, and the Betrayal of Reconstruction.* New York: Henry Holt, 2008.

Levine, Raleigh Hannah. "The (Un)Informed Electorate: Insights Into the Supreme Court's Electoral Speech Cases." *Case Western Reserve Law Review,* Winter 2003.

Levy, Leonard W. *Original Intent and the Framers' Constitution.* New York: Macmillan, 1988.

Lewis, Earl M. "The Negro Voter in Mississippi." *Journal of Negro Education* 26, no. 3, "The Negro Voter in the South" (Summer 1957.)

Lewis, Ronald L. "From Peasant to Proletarian: The Migration of Southern Blacks to the Central Appalachian Coalfields." *Journal of Southern History* 55, no. 1 (Feb. 1989).

Licht, Walter. *Industrializing America: The Nineteenth Century.* Baltimore: Johns Hopkins University Press, 1995.

Litwack, Leon F. *Been in the Storm So Long: The Aftermath of Slavery.* New York: Vintage Books, 1980.

——. *Trouble in Mind: Black Southerners in the Age of Jim Crow.* New York: Alfred A. Knopf, 1998.

Lofgren, Charles A. *The Plessy Case: A Legal-Historical Interpretation.* New York: Oxford University Press, 1987.

Lowell, Francis C. "Horace Gray." *Proceedings of the American Academy of Arts and Sciences* 39, no. 24 (June 1904).

Lynd, Staughton. "Rethinking Slavery and Reconstruction." *Journal of Negro History* 50, no. 3 (July 1965).

Mabry, William Alexander. "Disenfranchisement of the Negro in Mississippi." *Journal of Southern History* 4, no. 3 (Aug. 1938).

Mack, Kenneth W. "Law, Society, Identity, and the Making of the Jim Crow South: Travel and Segregation on Tennessee Railroads, 1875–1905." *Law and Social Inquiry* 24, no. 2 (Spring 1999).

Mayer, David N. "The Myth of Laissez-Faire Constitutionalism: Liberty of Contract During the *Lochner* Era." *Hastings Constitutional Law Quarterly*, Winter 2009.

——. "Substantive Due Process Rediscovered: The Rise and Fall of Liberty of Contract." *Mercer Law Review*, Winter 2009.

McPherson, James M. "Abolitionists and the Civil Rights Act of 1875." *Journal of American History* 52, no. 3 (Dec. 1965).

Menand, Louis. "Morton, Agassiz, and the Origins of Scientific Racism in the United States." *Journal of Blacks in Higher Education* 34 (Winter 2001–2).

Mixon, Gregory. "Henry McNeal Turner versus the Tuskegee Machine: Black Leadership in the Nineteenth Century." *Journal of Negro History* 79, no. 4 (Autumn 1994).

Morris, Roy, Jr., *Fraud of the Century. Rutherford B. Hayes, Samuel Tilden, and the Stolen Election of 1876.* New York: Simon and Schuster, 2003.

Nagle, John Copeland. "How Not to Count Votes." *Columbia Law Review* 104, no. 6 (Oct. 2004).

Nimmer, Melville B. "A Proposal for Judicial Validation of a Previously Unconstitutional Law: The Civil Rights Act of 1875." *Columbia Law Review* 65, no. 8 (Dec. 1965).

Osofsky, Gilbert. *Harlem: The Making of a Ghetto.* New York: Harper and Row, 1966.

Packard, Jerrold M. *American Nightmare: The History of Jim Crow.* New York: St. Martin's Press, 2002.

Palmore, Joseph R. "The Not-So-Strange Career of Interstate Jim Crow: Race, Transportation, and the Dormant Commerce Clause, 1878–1946." *Virginia Law Review* 83, no. 8 (Nov. 1997).

Perloff, Richard M. "The Press and Lynchings of African-Americans." *Journal of Black Studies* 30, no. 3 (Jan. 2000).

Perrow, Charles. *Organizing America: Wealth, Power and the Origins of Corporate Capitalism.* Princeton, NJ: Princeton University Press, 2002.

Peskin, Allan. "Was There a Compromise of 1877?" *Journal of American History* 60, no. 1 (June 1973).

Purcell, Edward. "The Particularly Dubious Case of Hans v. Louisiana: An Essay on Law, Race, History, and Federal Courts." *North Carolina Law Review* (June 2003).

Rabinowitz, Howard N. "More Than the Woodward Thesis: Assessing the Strange Career of Jim Crow." *Journal of American History* 75, no. 3 (Dec. 1988).

Rampersad, Arnold. "W.E.B. Du Bois as a Man of Literature." *American Literature* 51, no. 1 (Mar. 1979).

Ratner, Sidney. "Was the Supreme Court Packed by President Grant?" *Political Science Quarterly* 50, no. 3 (Sept. 1935).

Reed, Thomas B. "The Federal Control of Elections." *North American Review* 150, no. 403 (June 1890).

Rehnquist, William H. *Centennial Crisis: The Disputed Election of 1876.* New York: Alfred A. Knopf, 2004.

Rosen, Jeffrey. *The Supreme Court: The Personalities and Rivalries That Defined America.* New York: Henry Holt, 2006.

Scalia, Antonin. *A Matter of Interpretation.* Princeton, NJ: Princeton University Press, 1997.

Smith, George P. "Republican Reconstruction and Section Two of the Fourteenth Amendment." *Western Political Quarterly* 23, no. 4 (Dec. 1970).

Spackman, S. G. F. "American Federalism and the Civil Rights Act of 1875." *Journal of American Studies* 10, no. 3 (Dec. 1976).

Spencer, Herbert. "Progress: Its Law and Causes." *Westminster Review* 67 (Apr. 1857).

Stampp, Kenneth. *The Era of Reconstruction.* New York: Alfred A. Knopf, 1965.

Starr, Harris E. "William Graham Sumner: Sociologist." *Journal of Social Forces*, 3, no. 4 (May 1925).

"State Economic Substantive Due Process: A Proposed Approach." *Yale Law Journal* 88, no. 7 (June 1979).

Stephenson, Gilbert Thomas. "The Separation of the Races in Public Conveyances." *American Political Science Review* 3, no. 2 (May 1909).

"The Strange Career of 'State Action' under the Fifteenth Amendment.'" *Yale Law Journal* 74, no. 8 (July 1965), pp. 1448–61.

Sumner, William Graham. *Folkways: A Study of the Sociological Importance of Usages, Manners, Customs, Mores, and Morals.* Boston: Ginn and Company, 1907.

Thornbrough, Emma Lou. "American Negro Newspapers, 1880–1914." *Business History Review* 40, no. 4 (Winter 1966).

Tokaji, Daniel P. "The Sordid Business of Democracy." *Ohio Northern University Law Review* 2008.

van Alstyne, William W. "The Fourteenth Amendment, the 'Right' to Vote, and the Understanding of the Thirty-Ninth Congress." *Supreme Court Review* 1965 (1965).

Ward, David. *Poverty, Ethnicity, and the American City, 1840–1925: Changing Conceptions of the Slum and the Ghetto.* New York: Cambridge University Press, 1989.

Warren, Charles. *The Supreme Court and United States History.* Boston: Little, Brown, 1923.

Weaver, Valeria W. "The Failure of Civil Rights 1875–1883 and its Repercussions." *Journal of Negro History* 54, no. 4 (Oct. 1969).

Weinberg, Louise. "Holmes' Failure." *Michigan Law Review* 96, no. 3 (Dec. 1997).

Wells-Barnett, Ida B. *Lynch Law in Georgia: A Six-Weeks' Record in the Center of Southern Civilization, as Faithfully Chronicled by the "Atlanta Journal" and the "Atlanta Constitution."* Chicago: Chicago Colored Citizens, 1899.

Westin, Alan F. "John Marshall Harlan and the Constitutional Rights of Negroes: The Transformation of a Southerner." *Yale Law Journal* 66, no. 5 (Apr. 1957).

White, G. Edward. "John Marshall Harlan I: The Precursor." *American Journal of Legal History* 19, no. 1 (Jan. 1975).

Wiecek, William M. "The Emergence of Equality as a Constitutional Value: The First Century." *Chicago-Kent Law Review*, 2007.

Williams, George H. "Reminiscences of the United States Supreme Court." *Yale Law Journal* 8, no. 7 (Apr. 1899).

Wilson, Mark R. *The Business of Civil War: Military Mobilization and the State, 1861–1865*. Baltimore: Johns Hopkins University Press, 2006.

Wilson, Woodrow. "The Reconstruction of the Southern States." *Atlantic Monthly* 87, no. 519 (Jan. 1901).

Woodson, Carter G. *A Century of Negro Migration*. Washington, D.C.: Association for the Study of Negro Life and History, 1918.

Woodward, C. Vann. *The Burden of Southern History*. Baton, Rouge, LA.: Louisiana State University Press, 1968.

———. *Origins of the New South, 1877–1913*. Baton Rouge, LA.: Louisiana State University Press, 1951.

———. "The Political Legacy of Reconstruction." *Journal of Negro Education* 26, no. 3, "The Negro Voter in the South" (Summer 1957), p. 231.

———. *The Strange Career of Jim Crow*. 2nd ed. New York: Oxford University Press, 1966.

Wyatt-Brown, Bertram. "The Civil Rights Act of 1875." *Western Political Quarterly* 18, no. 4 (Dec. 1965).

Wyllie, Irvin G. "Social Darwinism and the Businessman." *Proceedings of the American Philosophical Society* 103, no. 5 (Oct. 1959).

Wynes, Charles E. "The Evolution of Jim Crow Laws in Twentieth Century Virginia." *Phylon* 28, no. 4 (4th Qtr. 1967).

INDEX

Note: page numbers followed by "n" refer to footnotes or endnotes.

A Note on the Author

Lawrence Goldstone is the author of *Dark Bargain: Slavery, Profits, and the Struggle for the Constitution* and *The Activist: John Marshall, Marbury v. Madison, and the Myth of Judicial Review*. He lives in Westport, Connecticut.